John Lowe

John Lowe

OLD STONEFACE:
THE AUTOBIOGRAPHY OF BRITAIN'S
GREATEST DARTS PLAYER

By **JOHN LOWE**
with
PATRICK CHAPLIN

JOHN BLAKE

Published by John Blake Publishing Ltd,
3, Bramber Court, 2 Bramber Road,
London W14 9PB, England

www.blake.co.uk

First published in hardback in 2005

ISBN 1 84454 179 7

British Library Cataloguing-in-Publication Data:

A catalogue record for this book is available from the British Library.

Design by www.envydesign.co.uk

Printed in Great Britain by William Clowes Ltd, Beccles, Suffolk
1 3 5 7 9 10 8 6 4 2

Papers used by John Blake Publishing Ltd are natural,
recyclable products made from wood grown in sustainable forests.
The manufacturing processes conform to the environmental
regulations of the country of origin.

Every attempt has been made to contact the relevant copyright-holders,
but some were unobtainable. We would be grateful if the appropriate
people could contact us.

DEDICATION

This book is dedicated to Peter Lippiatt, a very dear friend of mine who was taken from us on 17 November 2003.

Peter, a former coal miner from Eastwood, Nottinghamshire, joined me after his retirement in 1979, and for the next twenty years was my assistant at the numerous exhibitions and competitions we attended across the country and across the world. He would help to erect our large backdrop stage, then don his tuxedo and black tie and act as MC for the whole evening. He was very good at this, and his humour and banter with the audience made him popular everywhere we went. Once each show was over, while I signed autographs for the fans, he would change into his travelling clothes and dismantle the stage equipment. After it had all been loaded up, he would then drive me home or, if we were staying over, to our hotel.

I eventually managed to persuade Peter to play golf, and after a few years he became quite good. We spent many hours just hitting those little balls about. Peter was a very likeable man who had time for everyone and whom everyone liked and respected, including Eric Bristow, Howard Keel and Sir Norman Wisdom. He carried his autograph book everywhere with him, and I remember the day I introduced him to George Best; Peter was all fingers and thumbs as he offered his book to George for his autograph. He became even more flustered when George asked him if he wanted to make up a four at snooker!

Peter and I enjoyed many, many hours together on the road, and quite a few more in many bars around the world. He was from a hard-working background and this stood him in good stead for a career on the road. He was polite, friendly and kind, yet he could be as hard as the next person if he had to and would always hold to his opinion or view – and more than often he was right.

I was on tour in Australia when Peter's wife, Jean, rang to tell me Peter had passed away. I was very sorry that I couldn't be there to see him off on the next part of his journey, but by dedicating this book to him I can permanently record my thanks to Peter for all he did for me and for his friendship over so many years.

Foreword
by 'Old Stoneface'

Writing a biography is not difficult. That might seem a bold, perhaps even arrogant statement, but in my case it's true. Although my life has spanned sixty years, I've found little difficulty in recalling the good and the bad times, the victories and the defeats.

The problem I've found – apart from recalling exact dates of some occurrences – is trying to remember everything that would be of interest to readers of this life, however important or trivial. There is so much to tell and I didn't want you to miss a thing.

True, there are some skeletons that I would have preferred to have left in the cupboard, but I convinced myself that I would be being dishonest not only to myself but also to my fans and others who have purchased this book if I didn't open that cupboard door and invite the skeletons to step out.

Over the past few years, after a long period of disruption and unhappiness, I've finally organised and properly come to terms with my personal life. I believe that I've succeeded in putting my life into perspective and adopted an outlook that will enable me to live out my time in a contented way, happy with my lot.

Despite my continuous success as a professional dart player across four decades, I know that, if I hadn't been invited to substitute for a player in a darts match one fateful night, I would still have been successful with my chosen trade as a carpenter. (I still get tremendous pleasure out of being able to build a deck in my back yard or remodel our home.) However, as you all know, fate and coincidence dictated otherwise.

I'm in the twilight years of my darts career now. That sounds a little defeatist, but let me say that I have no intention of retiring – not just yet, at least – although I feel that chasing across the world for ranking points is beyond me now. It's not what this champion wants to do. The younger generation of aspiring players are eager to reach their individual goals, their competitive spirit just like my own of thirty years ago. Now it's their time, their place and their opportunity.

Something comedian Mickey Gunn once said describes me as I see myself today: I'm 'not as good as I was, but as good once as I always have been'. Yet I'm still the player my fellow professionals don't want to draw, the player they know will always give them a fright and a real match, and a player that, I like to think, they don't mind losing to occasionally – out of respect, perhaps, to my personal reputation as a player and as one of the men who helped to pave the way for the modern game of darts, opening the door for the opportunities they enjoy today.

I'm regularly told by thousands of people worldwide, 'John, please don't stop playing. You have another world championship in you, another major win.' Well, I've always said that time will tell me when to stop throwing those Golden Tungsten 21g darts. To those thousands, I'm pleased to say, 'Time hasn't told me yet. Time hasn't been called.' However, it *has* told me to take a different path, one that I am comfortable with, one that will enable me to share my skills with players and supporters worldwide and one that will allow me to enjoy quality time alone or with my closest friends for many more years to come. As for that 'one more championship', let's wait and see.

During the writing of this book, I learned a lot about myself. It's quite frightening, and not a little disturbing, when you read a chapter that you've written. Do you take out the things that make you look selfish, arrogant, self-pitying and uncompassionate, or do you tell it how it was at the time? Contrary to popular belief, my life hasn't been one long success story – far from it. My life has been full of ups and downs, and I've consciously or unconsciously changed direction many times, sometimes for the better, sometimes for the worse. This book pulls no punches and is as honest and as upfront as I am.

I trust that you'll enjoy the book, and thereby come to understand what the life of this particular professional dart player has been all about and why I feel it's so important to share that life with my fans and others interested in the great sport of darts.

John Lowe
Chesterfield, Derbyshire
July 2005

Acknowledgements

The writing of a biography is more than a task for one man, and without the characters I've met and the friends I've made throughout my life, my story would be a simple recollection of tournaments won and lost, and therefore, I assume, of no great interest to anyone.

While I put my success in the world of darts primarily down to my own determination, stubbornness and resolve, I couldn't have succeeded to the extent that I have without the help and assistance of people whom I could turn to in times of duress. We all need a shoulder or two to cry on now and again, people to whom we can reveal our innermost thoughts, worries, dreams and realities, and I've been fortunate to have made solid friends in my journey through this life. Sadly, my closest soulmates have departed. Peter Lippiatt and Barry Twomlow were the two people to whom I could tell all and know it was safe. They were both people who were very private, very knowledgeable and very caring.

I've made many good and lasting friends, without whom my home life and my life on the road would have been all the more difficult to bear if they hadn't have been there to provide support and friendship. Darts isn't the be all and end all of my life; I like to enjoy the simple things in life, like a pint at the local and a good chinwag with the lads and the ladies. I call myself nosey as I love to hear about other people and their happenings, bad or good.

I recently met up with an old school mate of mine, David Sheriff, whom I hadn't seen for many years until he came into the Crispin Tavern, where I drink occasionally. David has built a successful travel business but still enjoys driving his pride and joy: a luxury coach. I admire people like David, who's successful and yet whose feet are firmly on the ground. I know many similar people stationed around the world, and they have become my communication network, my way of connecting with the world we live in. There's a long list of such people, but some noteworthy contacts are Don Skane in Boston, USA, BJ Clark in Thailand, Mike Enright in San Diego, Kevin Berlyn in Australia, John Beckingham in Canada, Tom Firth in Ireland, Tony and Sue Holyoake in Calgary and many more friends around the world without whom this journey would have been so much more difficult.

And then there are my professional colleagues, those fellow gladiatorial darters who have been my adversaries and my friends, some since the very early days. I'm thinking primarily of Leighton Rees, Alan Evans, Eric Bristow and my very good friend both inside and outside the world of darts, Cliff Lazarenko.

To darts historian Patrick Chaplin, I offer my sincere thanks for his valuable input to this book and for the countless hours he's had to spend on reading and revising my endless writing. It has been a pleasure and a privilege to work with Patrick, a true professional and a very important contributor to the sport of darts and its rightful place in the archives of time.

To my children, Adrian and Karen, I say a big thank you. Thank you for just being you. Times haven't always been kind – and this book reveals that to one and all – but it can't have been easy to have been the children of someone who has been on the nation's television screens for over thirty years. You're both a credit to your mother and father, and I love you both dearly.

Finally, and most important of all, I would like to thank my wife, Karen, the one person who I adore more than anybody or anything else in life. I always remember Karen having a private conversation with my friend David Brook. When she asked him how she would cope, spending life with a celebrity, his reply to her was, 'Be yourself. Don't change. You'll be fine.' A few months later, Karen and I were married in Las Vegas. Did she change? Not at all. She adapted to the life of someone constantly in the public domain and did so because she wanted to do it, to support her husband, her friend, her lover, her soulmate: me. Thank you, Karen, for accepting me, warts and all.

The one thing that writing this book has taught me is that life is full of surprises, both good and bad. We have to accept them all, but we do have a choice: whether or not to cherish the good things in life. And, believe me, there are many of those.

Contents

Introduction

John Lowe discovered an enthusiasm for darts by chance at the age of twenty-one. The unlikely event of being asked by someone to take another's place in a darts match while the guy went to the toilet set him on a road that took him from his day job as a professional joiner to the very top of the darts ladder and becoming the Embassy world professional darts champion on no fewer than three occasions. That John was there to take over in that darts match might be called an incredible coincidence. John calls it fate.

But does it really matter what you call it? What happened on that night in 1966 was unique in the annals of sports history and heralded the beginning of an incredible darts career that has spanned four decades and even today shows no sign of abating.

Before the 1970s, darts was a game of the public house. It had been around for centuries in several different guises – including the game of 'puff and dart', where players puffed small darts through a tube at a small concentric target – but wasn't played everywhere in the United Kingdom. In the early part of the twentieth century, for instance, folk in the West Country preferred skittles and dominoes, and darts was scarcely seen, while in the 1930s the game of darts was banned in Glasgow,

Liverpool and Huddersfield and was only just catching on in Wales and Ireland.

Attempts by the brewers and others in the licensed trade to standardise the game in the 1920s prompted the spread of the game away from its main centre of London and the southeast, after which it began to take over pubs the length and breadth of the country. Darts even forced out traditional pub games that had otherwise held sway for centuries, such as quoits, which was supplanted by darts in Bolton in the late 1930s. However, the imposition of the 'London' dartboard upon those who were already playing darts on smaller boards did find some resistance, especially in Manchester, where the log-end dartboard (smaller than the London board and with different numbering and no trebles) is still used today in some areas of the city.

Until the 1950s, no national darts association had stayed the distance. Between 1920 and 1953, no fewer than four organisations had been set up to support and promote the game and all had collapsed. Then, in 1954, the National Darts Association of Great Britain (NDAGB) was founded with the assistance of *The People* newspaper. The NDAGB provided support and administered numerous local and national competitions for many years and continued to do so up until the mid-1970s, long after the newspaper had broken its connection with the Association. However, for those players who excelled at the game and wanted to try to make a living out of their chosen sport, there were few opportunities to make any money, legally, out of darts and fewer still to enable them to turn professional.

Back in the 1930s and 1940s, winners of the *News of the World* Individual Darts Championship might have subsequently found themselves promoting certain types of darts or flights – some even found their way into cabaret – but no one could make a full-time living from playing the game. Even the greats, such as Jim Pike of south London, Joe Hitchcock of north London, Bradford's Harold Barker and Cambridgeshire's 'Champion of East Anglia' George Caley, received few endorsements despite their incredible local and national success.

During the late 1930s, Harold Barker had been temporarily contracted to Gamages, a huge toy shop in London, where he demonstrated the game to children and their parents. However, this employment was short-lived as Barker, a Yorkshireman who always used to wear a scarf and flat cap when playing darts in his home county, found the south – and, especially, the collar and tie he had to wear all the time while demonstrating the art of the dart – too much to bear. He returned to Bradford, where he carried on with his exhibitions and money matches.

In 1945 Jim Pike established his own darts company with three other darts greats: Leo Newstead, Johnny Ross and Harry Head, all of whom had been members of the *News of the World* Team of Darts Champions which had raised hundreds of thousands of pounds for the Red Cross by staging exhibition matches during the Second World War.

In the early 1950s, Joe Hitchcock found fame as an exhibition player who also threw nails and performed amazing tricks with both darts and nails, and he became one of the first major sponsored players via a contract with London brewer Watneys. In addition, George Caley received some sponsorship from the Dorwin Pencil Company, manufacturers of the famous Dorwin 'True Balance' dart.

However, no level of sponsorship or competition prize money available to darts players in the first seven decades of the twentieth century came anywhere near that on offer to the new breed of darter during the last three.

John Lowe was in the right place at the right time and became one of the new breed of darts professionals during the 1970s and 1980s, when Olly Croft and his British Darts Organisation (BDO) took darts – by then a ubiquitous public-bar game – by the scruff of the neck and flung it forward at speed into the twentieth century. There can be no doubt that without the BDO there would have been no Eric Bristow, no Jocky Wilson, no Phil Taylor and no John Lowe – at least, not as professional darts players. In fact, one might argue that, without the organising zeal, enthusiasm and knowhow of Olly Croft, darts as a pastime might have disappeared altogether from British pubs. Without its profile being raised by the BDO, which in turn attracted the sponsors and, with them, television, darts would arguably have been unable to fight a sustained battle against the threat of pool or, later, video and computer games. John duly acknowledges his debt to Olly Croft.

That moment in 1966 when John stepped up to the oche in the Butchers Arms led to the creation of one of the best loved, most successful and most enduring darts players of all time. In addition to bringing pleasure to millions of darts fans across the globe, since the late 1970s John has also invested a significant amount of his own time, effort and money into raising the profile of the sport he loves and striving for justice and fair treatment for professional darts players under what at times have been extremely difficult and frustrating circumstances.

Considering John's reputation as a gentleman of darts, the quiet man, the expressionless 'Old Stoneface', the darts player who stands at the oche and gets the business done, it's difficult to imagine 'Lowey' as a rebel. However, that was exactly the epithet he was tarred with back in 1994, shortly after his third world championship success, when he and fifteen other professional darts players broke ranks with the BDO and sought refuge and a secure future with the emergent World Darts Council (WDC). At that time, John worked tirelessly behind the scenes with the likes of his great friend and adversary Eric Bristow and many others, eventually bringing about the apparent successful resolution of the 'difficulties' in the 1997 Tomlin Order.

To this day, residual difficulties remain, however, and the Professional Darts Players' Association (PDPA), which John helped to found in 1985, continues to work closely with the Professional Darts Corporation (PDC, formerly the World Darts Council), relentlessly trying to iron out the remaining creases and to provide more and more competitive opportunities for an increasing number of professional darts players.

Fame didn't come quickly to John Lowe. Although he started playing darts in his local pub at the relatively late age of twenty-one, he wouldn't become World Master until his thirty-first year. In 1977 he told journalist Deryk Brown, 'I've always been ambitious. I remember writing on a biography form for the Unicorn Championships that my ambition was "To be the best."' During his thirty years as a professional darts player, John has proved that he is this and more, and how he came to achieve his ambition is at the very heart of this book.

Back in 1979, after his first success at the Embassy World Professional Darts Championship, John was snapped up by Unicorn Products and has remained with the company ever since. (There was another company that had earlier considered sponsoring John, but they were advised that John was never going to get anywhere!) Support and loyalty are key mantras in the John Lowe moral weaponry, and this is clearly demonstrated by the fact that he stayed loyal to all of the major sponsors who have supported him over the years.

It's difficult to imagine the sheer level of demand for new professional players during the 1970s and 1980s, the rush of potential sponsors and the global search for ranking points. John Lowe was thrust into this hectic world and coped well – most of the time. The only son of a Derbyshire miner, he has achieved phenomenal success over the ensuing thirty-year-plus period and has rarely made the headlines for any other reason than his success either as a darts player, as an individual or part of a pair or team. The respect that John commands of his fans and the majority of his professional colleagues has been well earned and is a credit to his style, attitude and professionalism.

In this, his fourth book and first major work of autobiography, John looks back on his life from a completely different perspective than at any other time. Today he is settled, financially secure and extremely happily with his second wife Karen. But life still has its ups and downs, ranging from one extreme to the other, from the celebration of the marriage of his daughter, Karen, in Las Vegas in 2004 to the sad loss in the same year of his good friends Bob Murdock and Barry Twomlow and, in 2003, of his great pal Leighton Rees, a Welshman who was the first-ever Embassy World Professional Champion.

John Lowe is a fighter – a quiet, resilient fighter – who throughout his career has maintained a dignity that might have eluded other men. He is one of the most skilful, respected and honest darts players in the world today and is still up there with the best.

Patrick Chaplin
Maldon, Essex
July 2005

CHAPTER 1

From Birth to Work

It was Monday, 12 January 2004. The PDC Ladbroke.com World Darts Championship had finished a week earlier, on Sunday, 4 January. Once again, I had qualified to play – I always do – and I should have beaten Alan 'The Iceman' Warriner in the third round on New Year's Eve. After all, I was three sets up on him and the crowd was behind me. However, I lost concentration and Alan came back at me to win 4–3.

Some would point out, predictably, that Phil Taylor had won his eleventh world crown, although on this occasion he was lucky to do so. You bet. Like in my game against Warriner, Kevin Painter had Taylor dead and buried, but the magic let him down at the last moment and 'The Power' was world champion again. Meanwhile, Andy Fordham, the likeable giant from Dartford, had won the Lakeside World Championship title the previous night against an out-of-sorts Mervyn King.

I wasn't really in the mood for reflecting deeply on the outcomes of the two world darts championships – I was a little tired that morning and my brain wasn't up to full speed – so I turned on my computer and scanned through my e-mail messages. There was the usual selection of spam messages, half a dozen of which were asking if I would like to buy cheap Viagra.

(Thankfully, at my time of life, the answer is no. Say no more.) A couple were from Nigeria, asking if I would accept $25,000,000 into my bank account, apparently because I'm such a friendly guy, while another four told me how I could lose 20lb in two weeks if I didn't eat any carbohydrates after five o'clock.

I pressed the 'Delete' button and concentrated on the more serious messages. There were a few asking if I'd watched the match with Andy Fordham against Mervyn King – all the usual stuff, like 'Do you think he would beat Taylor?' and 'Will he join the PDC?' Then I opened one and just stared at it, leaning back in my chair. That single message shone out like a beacon amongst the automated dross and brought me right up to speed.

The message was from a lady in Canada who was trying to trace the ancestry of her husband, who was apparently a part of the Lowe family tree. The lady was enquiring if, by chance, I happened to be the son of Frederick Lowe, whose father was John Lowe of New Tupton. 'Yes, I am,' I said aloud.

My computer keyboard was in action immediately. I've always wanted to know more about my family and my own ancestry but had never actually had the time or opportunity to do any research. Was this my chance?

The lady and I exchanged electronic messages over the next three days. I was able to help with the missing pieces of this aspect of her research, while in return she promised to send me the whole of her Lowe file within a couple of days.

True to her word, the complete file eventually arrived at my computer. I was absolutely amazed at the amount of research this lady had conducted. My first thoughts were for my son Adrian, at that time the last of my line of the Lowes, so I forwarded the file to Adrian at his office and then settled down to reflect on my forefathers.

The extract read:

Generation no. 4
Frederick Lowe (John, George, Joseph) was born October 24, 1904, and died January 6, 1987. He married Phyllis Turner, July 17, 1937.

Children of Frederick Lowe and Phyllis Turner are Margaret Lowe, b. 1939,
John Lowe, b. July 21, 1945.

It was this exchange of emails that convinced me that I had to put the proud history of my family and my own success and achievements into a single autobiography. OK, so I've written some autobiographical books before, but they'd been selective memories and, in any event, are now at least twenty years out of date. They were also incomplete, as I'd held back on a lot of things. Besides, over recent years, my life had changed in so many ways that I knew the time had come to tell all.

Holly Hurst, my place of birth, was and remains to this day a semi-detached house on Ward Street in the village of New Tupton, Chesterfield, in Derbyshire, that most wonderful of English counties. Tupton isn't quite in the Peak District, where the Dales are plentiful, but it's only fifteen minutes' drive from the Duke of Devonshire's Chatsworth House estate. The village is split into 'New' and 'Old' parts, although I'm not quite sure why, because much of New Tupton is older than Old Tupton. When I was born, in the summer of 1945, Tupton was almost entirely a coal miners' village, with whole generations of families working down the six mines within walking distance of the village.

Perhaps surprisingly, although my father was a coal miner, his father, John George Lowe, hadn't been one. Instead, my grandfather had worked for the local council, repairing the roads. In those early days, mining work was plentiful and, unlike today, the workers went about their employment with a sense of pride and satisfaction. In order to support their large families, most put in long hours, and my father was no exception, even though there were only four of us in the family: himself; my mother, Phyllis; my sister, Margaret; and me.

Holly Hurst was a two-up/two-down semi-detached house that, in 1945, still had gas lighting and no bathroom. Being born in 1945 tends to indicate to ninety-eight out of every hundred people that you were a war baby – and yes, thankfully, I was part of the celebrations of winning the Second World War. My sister, Margaret, is six years older than me, and her entry into the world had been carefully planned by mother and father to fit the income and the size of the house, although my unplanned and unexpected arrival didn't cause any terrible problems. I was one of over 100 children born in that year in our small village alone, part of the baby boom, so I had no shortage of friends of the same age to play with.

However, my upbringing was slightly different to most in Tupton. My mother and father were deeply religious members of the Pentecostal Church. They were very open about their religion and had no problems in letting people know about their beliefs, although they weren't the kind to preach to others in the street or knock on doors, proclaiming, 'The end is nigh!' or similar. Instead, they both led by example, living good Christian lives, attending church on a regular basis and standing rock-fast by the rules of their religion – which, incidentally, meant that they couldn't spend any money on the Sabbath. And so, every Sunday, the whole family had to walk to the church – four miles away, in North Wingfield – in all kinds of weather. And I don't mean just once on a Sunday; I mean three times: holy communion in the morning, Sunday school in the afternoon and then back for the evening service after tea.

Yes, my life as part of the Lowe household was different from that of most of my pals. While they were out on the street on a Sunday, kicking a football about or riding their bikes, my big sister and I would be off to church, dressed in our Sunday best. Even as I grew up and learned to understand more about my parents' faith, I still remember enviously my friends playing on their doorstep on Sundays. I remember desperately wanting to join in, but I never did – not for many years, anyway. Sundays apart, of course, I was free to do all the things the other kids did, with one restriction: I had to be in by nightfall.

Memories of my early youth aren't hard to recall. For instance, I remember, at the age of four, the introduction of some wonderful new invention almost every month. When we eventually had electricity installed in Holly Hurst, you could at last see in every corner. Now, I'm not suggesting that my mother didn't keep a clean house, but due to the brighter illumination the old whitewash was replaced with paint or wallpaper.

I also remember when the Price family, who lived next door, purchased a television set. It had only a 9-in screen and was, of course, a black-and-white set, but to them and us it was unbelievable, a miracle of science. The Prices were so proud of being the first family in the street to have a television that they would invite everyone in to watch the news.

Then there was the old tin bath – the symbol of all miners' homes for years and years – that hung on the wall, either outside the back door or in the wash room. This was later replaced by a bathroom containing a vitreous-enamel bath, spouting hot and cold running water, and a washbasin standing proudly beside it. However, we couldn't have everything; the toilet was still outside and remained there for a few years, although the bucket we'd previously used was replaced by a proper flushing toilet.

One part of the year that I remember fondly is Christmas. Of course, this was a special time for everyone. Just like today, there were families who would provide their kids with more than others were able to, but in those days it didn't seem to matter as much. After a day or so, when their newness and some of their novelty had worn off, my friends and I would all share each other's new toys. In those days, presents would consist of one special gift (usually a game that all the family could join in with), some chocolates, sweets and, of course, an apple and orange. I would be up at five o'clock on Christmas morning to unwrap my presents. I think that, because we didn't get gifts every week like a lot of kids do today, it was a very special time, and father had to put extra hours in at work to provide us with all the trappings of the season.

I remember my fourth Christmas particularly well and often mention it at the dinner table when we have guests around. Everyone I knew that year was having a scooter for Christmas, and I'd pestered my parents to buy me one, too – a red one. Every year, about a week before Christmas, my sister and I would search the house for hidden packages. If we found any, we'd have a good feel to see if we could identify them. Usually we couldn't;

they'd be for someone else, grandad or grandmother maybe. This particular Christmas, however, when undertaking our search, I discovered that my parents hadn't made a very good job of hiding my scooter – or had they? Behind the wardrobe in their bedroom, I found a bright-red scooter. But, instead of feeling ecstatic, I was horrified. The scooter was made of WOOD!

Whenever Margaret and I found hidden Christmas gifts, we would never tell our mother or father; we would pretend we hadn't even looked and act innocent if questioned. However, on this occasion, I went straight up to my father and without any hesitation blurted out, 'I do not want the wooden scooter. It's horrible. My friends will laugh at me if I go out with that.' A few tears followed and then I ran off. Nothing was said to me for a few days and I was in a right sulk.

After about a week my mother came up to me one morning and said, 'How do you know that scooter is for you? We might be keeping it hidden for someone else down the road.' I was still in a sulk – not a nice mood at all – and replied, 'Good! That means I won't have to be seen on it.'

Christmas Day arrived and I was up at the usual time. The presents for my sister were all neatly stacked in one pile. By comparison, mine looked quite lonely – just a couple of wrapped gifts that could easily be identified as books and a game. But then I saw it: there, standing against the wall, was a scooter. Mum and Dad had tried to disguise it with wrapping paper, and I remember that, at that moment, I didn't want to take the paper off, frightened that it might be the wooden one.

Then I approached the scooter and very gently began to pull away some of the paper, which immediately revealed steel handlebars and the black rubber grips. The rest of the paper came off in seconds and there stood a red steel-framed scooter, complete with foot brake and a bell! I hugged my mother for at least five minutes. I was the happiest kid on the street.

I was allowed out at nine o'clock that morning to meet my mates and, yes, they all had identical red scooters, so we had to put tape on the handlebars so that they wouldn't get mixed up. Unfortunately, as Christmas Day that year had fallen on a Sunday,

I was allowed out for only an hour; then it was back in for breakfast before we made our long walk to church.

As time has gone by, I've thought about that Christmas more than any other. Looking back, I feel sure that, with all the other gifts they had to find, plus food on the table for the holiday weekend, my parents couldn't really have afforded the steel scooter. I reckon they bought the wooden one and purposely put it where I would find it in order to gauge my reaction. If I hadn't said anything, they would have wrapped it up. And as for their explanation that they might have been keeping it for someone else in the street – well, I knew on Christmas Day that no lad in Tupton had had a wooden scooter for Christmas. Seeing my distress, they had clearly taken the wooden one back and part-exchanged it for a steel-framed model.

Another of my most vivid memories of my childhood is that of my father sending me to Charlie Crampton's, the local barbers, to fetch a new battery for the radio. I can hear you laughing now, but it's true: our radio used to run on acid batteries, and the barber was the only man in the village who had the chargers. His shop was only two doors down from Holly Hurst, so it wasn't a hardship for me – although, with hindsight, it was probably very dangerous for a young child to be carrying an acid battery even that short distance.

We had two batteries, one that we used at home while the other was under the seat at Crampton's, where it would charge up for a couple of days. Twice a week, I would go to the barbershop, where it seemed to me that there were hundreds of batteries. They would bubble and gurgle as they charged, giving off a putrid, acrid smell. Then Ever Ready ruined Mr Crampton's trade when they introduced the dry battery, although thankfully he didn't suffer much as the battery-charging part of his business was only a sideline. His barbershop was always full of people waiting to have their hair cut, and the order of the time was invariably short back and sides. I don't think Mr Crampton's customers missed the smell of the batteries either.

One thing my father always made sure happened each year was the family holiday. He was adamant that we should all visit the seaside for one week. It would do us good, he said, and he clearly needed the break himself. I've already said this often enough but I'll continue to repeat the fact – probably for the rest of my life – that mining was very hard work. Although there was a great deal of camaraderie between the miners, the pressure of such a tough and demanding daily routine, as well as being subject to all kinds of dangers, took its toll. Many of the men would quench their doubts and fears at the local Miners' Welfare Club on Queen Victoria Road, while those like my father, who didn't drink or smoke, would save a little each week so that they could afford to take their family to the coast once a year.

Each year, therefore, my parents would take Margaret and me to either the Lincolnshire resort of Skegness, on the east coast of England, or Blackpool, Lancashire, on the west coast; the latter at the time being a major holiday destination for the working class. I preferred Blackpool, particularly for its massive funfair, but going there could prove a little costly for my father. When we visited Blackpool, we would always stay at the same guest house, The Claremont on Bloomfield Road, very close to the football ground. Indeed, I believe my father booked us into that particular guest house so that he could walk past the football ground on his way to the sea. Stanley Matthews was one of his heroes, and I think it made him feel good to know that he'd walked very close to where Stanley trained and played.

The journey to Blackpool was always exciting, as we ventured outside our village only rarely, and my father never went to London in his whole life. As we approached Blackpool, he would say, 'Whoever can spot the tower first wins a sweet.' I would sit looking through the window as soon as the train left Chesterfield station, although my sister – who, at six years older than me, wasn't so silly – would wait until we'd left Manchester before scanning the horizon for the Tower. I can't remember ever winning one sweet.

The journey to Skegness, however, was far less interesting, and I would often fall asleep on the way. Although I was nonetheless excited about going on holiday, I knew it would probably be cold, as the wind always seemed to blow in off the sea at Skegness, carrying a chill on the air, and playing on the sands for five hours in those conditions wasn't my idea of fun. Still, I liked Skegness because it was home to the famous 'Chip Alley' – a street full of fish-and-chip shops. We never stayed full-board at Skegness, ordering only breakfast and evening meal so that we could have fish and chips for lunch.

We always adhered carefully to the holiday routine, rising at seven o'clock, and then at 7:30 we would have a full English breakfast – bacon, eggs, beans, fried bread – before going off to the beach for the day. In those days, the landladies didn't like holidaymakers to be in their guest houses during the day, reasoning that you'd paid only for your bed for the night and your two daily meals, not for the use of their living accommodation during the day, so the whole family would be evicted after breakfast for the day.

I remember that we'd sit on the beach for hours. It didn't matter if the sun was out or not: this is what my father had saved for, and it was what all families did – not just us, I can assure you. The beach at Blackpool would be packed solid, deck chair to deck chair, for miles along the Golden Mile and beyond. In those days, we didn't have any money for amusement arcades or eating out; we simply stayed on the beach.

We would have a sandwich and an ice cream at dinnertime (about midday), and then we'd be back at the guest house in time for four o'clock tea. This would be a traditional cooked dinner – beef one day, pork the next, then back to the beef, then to pork, and so on. After tea we would all go for a walk for a couple of hours – mostly window shopping – and then be back at the guest house and in bed by 9:30pm. We would then repeat this routine for the next six days, and on the seventh day we'd catch the train home.

Of course, one other thing we always did on holiday was find the local church, and if no Pentecostal church could be found, we'd find the nearest Methodist one. And we would still keep the Sabbath Day holy, not spending any money on that day.

Upon our return and for the next six months, we would tell everyone about our fabulous week in Blackpool – and they were absolutely wonderful times. As a family, we enjoyed every minute of those holidays and, as children, we never complained. It was father's hard-earned money that took us there, and no matter what the weather or what the week offered us, our time away could only be good. That was the way it was meant to be.

Those early days of my childhood were very friendly ones. I didn't realise it at the time, but when I look back I remember people going into each other's homes often unannounced, just popping in for a chat. Folks returning from their allotments would hand surplus vegetables over the garden wall to their neighbours, especially those older folk who couldn't do their own gardening anymore. And as children we didn't seem to have any bullies; it simply wasn't allowed.

Almost everyone around me was of the same class – working class. There were only a few people who were of a higher social standing – for example, the village doctor, who was regarded with the utmost respect, and a few others who lived outside the normal two-up/two-down houses, who were often employers and were usually referred to with the prefix 'Mister'.

I would like to say that those times were better than today's, but that would be very difficult for me to do. Mining life brought grief to many of the families – grief that was shared by the whole community. Over the years there were many major accidents down the mines, and when such accidents occurred the whole village would come to a halt, while if there was a fatality everyone in the village would go into a state of mourning for a week or so. Constant fear was evident; no one knew which family or families would be the next to suffer, or when.

The accidents that I suffered in my youth were insignificant in comparison, exactly the same kinds of accidents experienced by thousands of other kids, brought on in the main by adolescent irresponsibility.

I fell out of a tree when I was seven years old. What was I doing up the tree? Not sure. I guess that my aim was to climb as high as I could. That was how kids entertained themselves in those days. I was about 30ft up at the time I fell and was lucky to escape with a few bruises.

A few weeks later, I ran straight into the front of the four o'clock school bus – and when you consider that we had only two buses a day through our village, you can see that this was a rare feat indeed. On that occasion I escaped with a cut to my forehead and a severe telling-off from my mother, whom the bus driver had told what had happened and who was, after all, much more frightening to her young son than any bus driver. The severe reprimand didn't seem to have had any lasting effect, however, as a year later I rode my bicycle into the same bus! That time I suffered another damaged forehead, but – even worse – my treasured racing bike had a busted front wheel.

I managed to reach my tenth year without further serious incident, but then things became slightly worse. One day, myself and Tom Price – my neighbour of the same age (it was his mum and dad who'd bought the first black-and-white television on the street) – accompanied by a couple of other friends, Roger Bayliss and John Platts, were drawn to a building site. I remember we played make-believe Olympics there with some of the steel rods the builders used to reinforce the concrete. At one point, Tom hurled one of these steel rods in my direction like a javelin from a distance of about twenty feet. It stuck into the ground about 6ft away from me and then toppled over towards me. Before I knew it, the 'javelin' had hit me on the side of the head, near my temple. The blood spurted out like water from a burst radiator, pumping about three feet or so into the air – panic stations for everyone. I remember Roger Bayliss rushed off to fetch my father while I ran to the nearest house for help, rapping on the door until it was opened by a lady, who promptly took one look at me and slammed the door in my face! I think she fainted. Luckily, her neighbour wasn't so panic-stricken and kindly bandaged my wound, tending me until Roger returned with my father.

My father had always been known for his coolness under all kinds of pressure and it has been said many times in family circles that I inherited my coolness from him. Certainly, he measured up well on that day, leaving his dinner on the table and my shaking mother clasping her hands in worry and calmly walking up the road to find me. He thanked the lady for taking me into her house and then took me off to the doctor for a stitch or two, then returned home to finish off his meat-and-potato pie, with damson jam for sauce.

Everyone thought that that was the end of the 'Olympic' incident. After all, despite the bloodshed, it was a small nick that had taken only took two stitches to repair. You couldn't even see any damage. However, a few days later I woke one morning to feel a large swelling on the side of my head where the rod had struck me. I was immediately sent to the hospital for an X-ray, which revealed that I'd fractured my skull. The doctors also found that the wound had become septic, so I had to undergo major surgery at Sheffield's Royal Infirmary, where I stayed for two weeks. My mother visited every day I was there, even though it was something of a nightmare journey for her. She would catch a bus to Chesterfield and then change to another to Sheffield, then walk the last two miles to the hospital. In all, each return trip took her three hours, and some days I was in such a bad mood I hardly spoke to her. I'm sure she was very happy when they finally said I could go home.

Thankfully, everything turned out well, but it took me almost a year to recover fully from the surgery. About twelve months later, I found out that the operation I'd undergone was really very serious indeed and that I could have quite easily have lost my life. I was young, though, so I didn't really give it much thought. To me, it was part of my normal play that just happened to go wrong. It was something that I took a long time to recover from, but I was fine.

Apart from these major and minor hiccups during my adolescence, everything was normal. However, the accident did mean that I lost almost a year of my education. This contributed to my going to a secondary modern for the second half of my education instead of attending the local grammar school at Tupton Hall.

Because of the year of missed schooling, I obtained miserable eleven-plus results. At the time it didn't bother me at all as I wasn't academically strong. I was more interested in art and sports, with cricket and football being my favourites, although most of my mates, including Roger Bayliss and John Platts, thought that I wasn't too good at the latter.

I left New Tupton Primary School with some fond memories, none more so than those of the school's headmaster at that time. Mr Roberts was a well-respected man who lived in the village and who always had a polite word for everyone – a 'Good day' or a 'How do you do?' He ran a good school that seemed full of happy children; if they weren't happy, he'd want to know why and did his best to put right anything that affected the welfare of his pupils. Yes, I liked Tupton School, but I wasn't looking forward to making the journey to Clay Cross Secondary Modern at all.

I suppose that the religious part of my upbringing affected my personality slightly. For a start, I remember that all of the parents who attended church expected their children to learn a poem or form a small choir so they could perform their renderings on Thanksgiving Day. Come the big day, I'd have always learned my poem and always looked my best, and I never complained, yet inside I hated every minute of it – standing in front of all those people, being made to do what I thought others should be doing. Of course, this makes me laugh now when I think of the many times I've picked up the microphone at the end of my exhibitions or when I've addressed the audience at the Circus Tavern, Purfleet, after a match in the World Darts Championships with absolutely no nerves. Could this be the same kid who, fifty years earlier, couldn't wait to get off that platform on Thanksgiving Day? Well, it's never too late to thank your parents, although I'm sure they didn't know what use such schooling would actually be put to!

I finished school in 1961, fifteen being the school-leaving age in those days. Only the very brightest children progressed to any form of higher education and out of our village only one qualified for this next step up the education ladder. And he did so with style.

Michael Wright was a lad who grew up with his Aunt Sally in a terraced house that backed off Ward Street. I think it would be fair to say that theirs was a poor family that had to make the pennies stretch as far as possible. Michael didn't just come top of the heap at school; he actually went on to win a place at Oxford University. I remember how pleased we all were when we found out he'd qualified for university, although we didn't know at that time which one. There wasn't any envy or jealousy; it was as though he was representing us, our village, and this has remained the case. When old pals meet years later, the conversation will eventually turn to Michael Wright, the lad from our village who had made it to Oxford.

My own life after school was never in any doubt. Like my father and most boys in New Tupton, I would be working down the mine – not quite as soon as I finished school, but there was no year out to backpack around some faraway country like many youngsters do today. The interview with the National Coal Board and the medical that followed would be conducted while we were still at school. Starting work at the mine was part of the natural process: finishing school, starting work, bringing an income into the home.

In July 1961, I was due to start at five o'clock on Monday morning at the Arkwright Colliery, where my father worked. My mother had bought me a snap tin (a container with a top and a bottom that would snap together, providing an airtight seal) for my sandwiches and a new water bottle. An old shoulder bag and a pair of knee pads had been found from somewhere, and my new shiny pit boots, although only a size eight, weighed a ton. I would be kitted out with a helmet at the pit top, where I'd also be given my checking-in token, which would hang from a board in the checking-in office, indicating to the staff exactly who was down the mine.

And so the Lowe family was about to put its next generation of miners to work. For my father, that seemed fine, but for my mother it meant one more member of the family to worry about. It certainly wasn't easy being a mother in those miners' villages, and it was little wonder that their life expectancy wasn't as high as it is today, but luckily fate was at hand.

I'm a great believer in fate and can pinpoint many times that it's played an important part in determining the road my life has taken, as it did that year.

Sunday came around and I went off to church – not my usual one, at North Wingfield, but one in Brampton, a suburb of

Chesterfield, that I'd started attending after having met up with some of its young congregation at a gospel meeting in Nottingham. Looking back on this time, I realise that there were a couple of nice girls in the group – Mary White being one of them – which made this decision quite easy for me!

One of the lads in the group, Ken, had started work as an electrician a few weeks earlier and asked me where I worked. When I had told him that I'd be starting down the mine a week on Monday he asked, 'Do you really want to do that?'

'No,' I replied. 'Not really. But what else is there?'

'Would you be interested in joining the building trade?' asked Ken. 'I suppose so,' I said.

I thought the conversation had been just that – all talk – and we left it at that. I returned home, knowing that my working life would begin at the Arkwright Colliery within a few short days.

The following Saturday there was a knock on our door. I opened the door and there stood Ken. 'I have some good news for you,' he said. 'Lowe Brothers –' a local building firm, and no relations '– need an apprentice joiner. If you're interested, the job's yours.'

I turned and looked at my mum, who was smiling. I could see in her eyes that she was hoping I'd say yes. She also knew that carpentry had been pretty much my best subject at school.

'Well? What do you think?' asked Ken.

I hesitated slightly. 'I don't know,' I mumbled. 'What have I got to do? When will I start?'

Ken replied, 'If you want the job, I said we'd go round to Bob Lowe's house tonight to have a word with him.'

I agreed to accompany him, and I swear that the smile on my mother's face grew larger.

Ken and I set off for Bob Lowe's house about six o'clock that Sunday night, en route to church. Bob lived in a nice house on Langer Lane, about four miles from our home in New Tupton, and I remember that he welcomed us warmly, his wife offering Ken and me a soft drink. Bob then asked me where I lived and a few more general questions, such as, did I like working with wood? It was a friendly conversation, and after twenty minutes I was offered the apprenticeship, which I accepted. I would start Monday – the next day.

When we left Bob Lowe's house, my mind wouldn't clear. I could see all my miner's clothes laid out at home, next to my father's. Everything had been arranged, and it was only a matter of hours before I would set off on my journey underground. Then I could see myself with a saw, cutting some wood that would form part of a roof, putting a door on or hanging a gate.

I realise now that both Ken and Bob had done their part in rescuing me from the mines. I'm convinced that Bob could probably have done without an apprentice joiner, just as I'm pretty sure that Ken made up the story about Bob having a vacancy for an apprentice. However, I think he knew what a miner's life was like and recognised that here was an opportunity to make a difference to one lad's prospects by saving him from having to work in the mines and giving him a far more healthy start to his working life.

My mother was over the moon. Her lad wasn't going to be following in the family tradition, and she was overjoyed by the fact. I'm not sure whether my father was pleased or not, but because my mother was happy, so was he. Secretly, though, I think he would have liked me to have followed in his footsteps and worked underground.

The next morning saw me waiting for the Lowe Brothers' company bus to transport me to the building site. Although I'd managed to escape starting at the mine that day, I still looked a little like a miner with my shoulder bag, snap tin and water bottle. I even had the pit boots on, as my mother warned me that building sites could be 'a little dirty'.

It was this dramatic sequence of events that first convinced me that fate played an important role in our lives – and if not fate then perhaps, as my mother believed at the time, someone guiding me from above. Maybe they're both one and the same. Whatever the cause, however, my father would be the last of the Lowe family to work down the mines.

I started seeing Diana as often as I could, and having a motorbike meant that it was no trouble for me to travel the twelve miles to her home in Brimington. It turned out that she had three brothers and two sisters, so her house was always quite full. Her father, Jack, was, like my own father, a coal miner, but unlike mine he enjoyed his pint after a hard day's work – and sometimes he'd have a few more than he ought to.

Jack was a very well-known man in his village and the surrounding area, with many friends – unfortunately sometimes for the wrong reasons. On pay day, he would call at the first pub he came across for a drink on his way home and have a bet on the horses. His original intention of staying for one hour and have a couple of pints would often turn into a long drinking spell and it would inevitably be Jack who would finish up paying for most of the drinks. Yes, friends he had aplenty, although never as many when the pot was empty.

Many a time Jack would come home with nothing left from his weekly wage packet. I was unable to comprehend how Jack could do this, as in our house my father would come home straight away and put his wages on the table. Ten per cent would be taken out for the church's tithe, my mother would be given her housekeeping, my sister and I would receive our spending money and the rest – what little there was left – would be my father's. Out of this remaining money, father would put so much aside for our annual holiday. If he could afford to, he might even have a couple of shillings left to put in the bank for a rainy day.

Yes, my father and Jack were like chalk and cheese, but both were good people in their own way. I remember that, when Jack was drunk, he would look at me and say, 'It's time we went out for a drink together.' I wouldn't say anything, and the next day he'd be the quietest man on Earth, not saying a word.

My friendship – or should I say courtship? – with Diana almost came to a sudden end one Sunday night. We'd been seeing each other for about a year at that time, and one night I picked her up on the Triton, intending to go to Oulton Park to watch the motorcycle racing. We'd gone only a few miles, however, when it started raining and then snowing. Diana hadn't brought any

CHAPTER 2

Bikes, Girls and Sudden Death

I enjoyed working at Lowe Brothers. Most of the building work was done around the Chesterfield and Clay Cross areas, while the brothers had a builders' yard and a joiners' shop at Hasland. The men who worked for them were all good guys who were, I suspect, hand-picked by Bob or his brother, Arthur, and they looked after me well.

I remember one morning, about six months after I'd started work, wondering when I would start becoming a joiner. Until that time I'd mixed concrete, laboured for the bricklayers, plasterers and plumbers, and made the tea. I'd done everything, in fact, except cut any wood or knock any nails in.

Looking back, I now understand why I was introduced to all the other trades first. I was an apprentice, after all, and Bob and Arthur were turning me into an accomplished tradesman, one who would be able to tackle almost every job needed in the house-building trade. And they were successful, for by the time I was nineteen years old I was self-employed and branching out into business for myself.

I found that I was enjoying my life as a manual worker. By that time I'd shot up in height and was nearly 6ft tall (although admittedly a little skinny), and working outdoors in the fresh air was doing me no harm at all. I'd bought a moped – a 50cc Triumph – for £25, so I could find my own way to the various sites. One gallon of petrol would last me a week, and I soon learned to take the engine to pieces and fine-tune it so I could get another 5mph out of it. Yes, I was a real boy racer. I could dash along at a breakneck 35mph!

After riding it for a year, I started to feel that the moped was a little too slow; I needed to reach my destinations faster, and that meant investing in something faster. It was at this time that my love affair with motorcycles started.

One day in 1962 I visited Eric Housley's motorcycle shop in Clay Cross. There in the window was a brand-new Royal Enfield Super Dream bike – five gears, top speed of 90mph. Without considering the repayments, the insurance or the general running costs of such a machine, I'd soon signed all of the forms and was eagerly awaiting the machine's delivery, three days later.

I'd not told my mother or father about the bike, of course; I thought I'd surprise them. Well, I did that all right. My mother almost had a heart attack when the bike arrived. She'd enjoyed a stress-free couple of years of not having to worry about me not coming home from the mines, but now here I was introducing her to a 90mph speed machine that would bring her many worrying times. 'Don't worry mum,' I said to her. 'I know how to ride,' but she must have thought that was a joke. After all, I'd gone from a moped that struggled to find a top speed of 35mph to something that would go almost three times as fast. As it turned out, she didn't have to start worrying just then, as I didn't have any money at that time to insure the bike, so it stood in our outhouse on Wingfield Road for the next month. Boy, was that hard to take!

When I did finally insure the bike and got it on the road, it became my pride and joy. I would go for 100-mile rides for no reason – that is, if I had enough money for petrol. As it happened, one of my cousins, Desmond Turner, had owned a couple of bikes, which he kept in immaculate condition, and was a very good rider himself. I'd go down to his house on Ward Street and we'd stand outside his shed until very late, just discussing bikes, and soon I knew more about one-piece engine gearboxes, twin duplex frames, extended foot rests and pressure-release valves than pretty much everyone else I knew.

I was so confident about bike riding that I'd put in to take my riding test the day I took delivery of the Royal Enfield. Of course, I hadn't realised that I'd be off the road with no insurance for a month, and when I was scheduled to take the test I'd been riding for only a couple of days. True, I'd been riding the moped for a year or more, but riding the Royal Enfield was a whole new experience. Both my father – who was just coming to terms with the fact that I was now a biker – and my cousin advised me to cancel my test, but I took no notice of either of them and instead rode the bike all day and all night over the weekend. By the following Tuesday, I had my full driver's licence.

I could not wait to get home to tell my father, who ever since I'd bought the Royal Enfield had been saying, 'That bike's too fast for you. You'll finish up in the hospital.' I told him I'd pick him up from work the next day, and he reluctantly agreed.

The next day, I met him at the pithead baths – about seven miles away from our house – at 4pm. With some reluctance, my father mounted the pillion. I wanted to make a good impression, so I eased off the throttle and kept the bike reasonably upright around the corners. We were home in about ten minutes. My father was only 5ft 4in tall and weighed 8st, and it didn't even feel like I had a passenger, except when I felt him cautiously hanging onto my coat. When we arrived home, he climbed off the bike and walked into the house. I followed a little later and found him sitting at the table, waiting in vain for his dinner, which my mother would usually put out when she heard him whistling as he came down the road. All she'd heard that day, however, was the roar of the Enfield as it approached, so when Father walked in, his dinner wasn't ready. I'd messed the ritual up big time.

As we ate, my mother asked my father what he thought of the ride. 'OK,' he admitted. 'He's not a bad driver, and we certainly made good time.'

I said, 'I'll pick you up tomorrow, then. I've a week's holiday.'

'No, no,' said Father. 'That's fine. I'll catch the bus. That way your mother will know when I'm coming home.'

That was my father's subtle way of telling me that his bike-riding days had begun and finished that day. He never once rode with me again.

My mother, on the other hand, never rode on any of my motorcycles. It wasn't that she didn't trust me; it was simply not the done thing for a lady to be seen on one. Fortunately, not all the girls were worried about this kind of thinking, and I had no shortage of pillion riders. It wasn't long before I became the talk of many of the lads.

In 1963 I exchanged the Royal Enfield for a purpose-built Triton that was a mixture of two different makes of motorcycle, the engine and gearbox being Triumph and the frame – a twin duplex, with two tubes extending down the front of the bike and joined at the bottom – being Norton. After I'd installed extended 'Cathy Tickle' extended footrests and racing handlebars, I was in racing trim. The bike had a 500cc engine and was capable of 110mph, which in those days was *fast*! To make the bike even more noticeable, I started to use vegetable oil in the engine so that, if you couldn't hear me blatting towards you, you could certainly smell the burning oil as the bike shot past you and into the distance.

Most of the lads I knew progressed from pushbikes to motorcycles, and we'd go around in packs of three or four at a time, unlike today when you're lucky if you see a motorbike every hour or so. My Triton was the biggest bike of our group, with the biggest engine, and I knew how to ride it, becoming an icon of adolescent rebellion. I'd almost stopped going to church at this time, too. My mother and father had reluctantly stopped asking me why and instead instructed me to remember all that I'd been taught: be a good person, do what's right and always respect your elders. They would then add, 'That's what Christianity is all about.' I've never forgotten those words, and to this very day I try to abide by them.

My love affair with motorcycles is a part of life I'd never want to change. The thought of controlling so much power is in itself exhilarating. I would regularly go to the major race meetings at Oulton Park, Silverstone, Brands Hatch, Oliver's Mount and many more. The big names in the world of racing at that time were Mike Hailwood, John Cooper, John Hartle, Derek Minter and John Surtees, with world champion Florian Camathias in the sidecar, on the opposite side of the bike to the others. In the years to come, these riders would be followed by the likes of Barry Sheene, Ronny Haslam and Carl Fogarty. I've met many of these professionals over the years, and they all seem to have one thing in common: they almost all come from a working-class background.

Motorcycles also introduced me to the fairer sex. On Saturday nights, all the lads would meet at the Holmegate Community Village Hall, about three miles from Tupton. We'd line the bikes up outside the hall, pay our entrance fee of four shillings (about 20p) and stand around the room, watching the girls dancing to the live band. I wasn't a dancer and to be honest I would've looked a little silly trying to jive in racing boots and leather jacket, but I did have an eye for the girls. My trouble was that I always liked those who were already taken – and the lads in those days were more possessive than they are today. Once they began dating a girl, they believed they owned them. Anyone caught just talking to their girl would be confronted with something like, 'Who are you talking to? She's with me. Carry on like this and we're going to have to go outside.'

Maybe I was born before my time, but I could see nothing wrong in talking to someone else's girl. Just because she happened to be going out with someone didn't mean she couldn't have a conversation with another guy who was just being friendly. On a couple of occasions I found myself in the minority with this kind of thinking. In fact, a couple of times my mate John Barry and I and finished up face-down on the dance floor before we even got to the invitation to go outside. Not only did we seem to pick the wrong girls but we also managed to pick the ones with the toughest guys.

In 1963 I was involved in a little fracas one Saturday night at a dance at Holmegate Village Hall. I had, once again, upset a guy, this time a real bruiser from Clay Cross named Jimmy Bray. My sin was that I had asked his girlfriend to go out with me. Well, to be honest, I did have an idea that she was with him, but I thought she had an eye for me. After he'd put me right on this, I was nursing a split lip when a very pretty, soft-spoken girl asked me if I was all right. 'Yes thanks,' I replied. 'Apart from my pride. My lip will mend.'

'You didn't do anything wrong,' the girl said.

I was surprised at first, then thought I'd better ask her if she was with anyone before my other lip was split.

'I was,' she admitted, 'but we're not together now.'

I bought her a drink and we had a long conversation, during which I learned that her name was Pam. I knew that I liked her and couldn't think why I hadn't noticed her before, as she lived only a couple of hundred yards away. I asked her if she fancied riding pillion with me to Matlock that night, after the dance – a gang of us would sometimes make the trip and meet up with other bikers from Chesterfield and nearby Belper – but Pam said she couldn't as her father had told her to be in by 10:30. I remember thinking, 'Shall I walk her home?' but the love affair with my bike was greater than my desire to hold hands with a girl, so I said, 'Goodnight,' kissed her full on the lips and rode off at a ridiculous speed towards Ashover.

That night I couldn't stop thinking about Pam, so I decided to take a ride around to her street to see if I could by chance see her. I didn't know exactly where she lived, and after a couple of hours of riding up and down near where I thought she lived, I went home.

The next Saturday night, I was at the dance quite early, and for once I was wearing shoes rather than boots. I was looking for only one person, and it didn't take long before she came into the hall. Then – big problem – she was with a guy, and they looked very friendly. I remember thinking, 'I should have worn my boots. It'll be cold on the way to Matlock tonight.' I was quite surprised, then, when Pam brought her friend over and introduced him to me. 'David,' she said, 'meet John. John, this is my cousin, who's visiting us for the weekend.'

Wow! For once I wouldn't have to get into a scrape. I was pleased to say the least and offered them both a drink. David was soon busy chatting to some other girl and I was alone with Pam.

Pam must have known I'd be inviting her to ride with me that night, as she'd asked her father if she could stay out a little later. He'd thought that she'd be going to one of her friends' houses and so said yes – eleven o'clock. Needless to say, I didn't go with the lads to Matlock that night. In fact, it was quite a time before I made that trip again.

Meeting Pam did have an effect on me. I seemed to become more mature and began thinking about other people and other things in life outside of motorcycles. I even started to frequent the church again and took Pam along with me. I guess I was trying to make a statement to others with my actions. Alas, it didn't last long; six months later, the love affair with the speed machine took over and Pam and I broke up. I remained good friends with her, but she knew she couldn't compete with the Triton or the smell of vegetable oil and sparks that flew up from the footrest as I turned the screw and cranked the bike almost horizontal, speeding around Artist Bend at Matlock. All part of growing up? I expect so. My father thought it was a speedy way to finish up in the mortuary.

People often ask, 'Can you remember where you were on such and such a date?' Actually, I have no problems remembering many famous happenings of my time. Take 22 November 1963, for instance. On that date, I'd just raced a couple of my mates from New Tupton to the Buck Inn at Holmegate. The last one there had to buy the drinks. When I arrived, well before the other two, there were about ten bikes in the car park. As I walked into the entrance of the pub, something struck me as strange, and then I realised all I could hear was the TV. I opened the door to see everyone staring at the television screen, almost transfixed. I looked at the picture for a few seconds. I didn't have to ask anyone to explain what was happening: President John F Kennedy had just been assassinated in Dallas, Texas. For the next hour, it was like Sky News today; they just played the same footage over and over again.

Another date I'll never forget was Friday, 13 April 1964 – Easter. On that day, I called for one of my mates, Tony Massey, at about 10:30 in the morning. It was a warm sunny day, perfect for biking, and so we thought we'd have a twenty-mile dash around Chatsworth Park, Bakewell, Matlock, and finish up at the Buck Inn for a Good Friday drink with the lads.

We flew up the Mile Run – a twisting road from the end of Holmegate to the top of Eastmoor – and headed across the top of Ashover, on to Beeley Moor. Then a quick left turn and we were going down Two Dales Hill, which is really very steep, with two ninety-degree hairpin bends.

As we approached the first of the two bends, a left-hander, I applied the brakes and – *ping!* – the front brake nipple sheared off. This meant that I had to rely on the back brake and the gears to slow us down. I applied the back brake, but that just caused the wheel to lock and hardly slowed us down at all. Changing down the gears did little to slow us, either. The front brake on a powerful motorcycle is all important, and we no longer had one.

It was time for a quick decision. I could negotiate the bike around the bend, but I knew that the next bend had a 20ft-high barn wall in front of it. I had to make my mind up what to do, and fast.

I decided that the best plan was to crank the bike over and hit the 2ft-high wall right in front of the first bend, hoping we'd be thrown over the wall and into the adjacent field. I hoped and prayed that there'd be no vehicles coming in the opposite direction.

My plan worked. We hit the lower wall travelling at around 25mph, but we were at an angle of about forty-five degrees to the ground. We were both thrown off the bike and into the field. I remember landing on the grass and turning to see where the bike had gone.

I then felt an almighty thud on my rib cage. It was not the bike; it was Tony. He'd been catapulted up into the air and had broken his fall by landing on me. It seemed like ages before I could breathe properly. When at last I could, and scrambled to my feet, I noticed that my helmet was no longer on my head. I had, in fact, hit a steel cow trough in the field, and the helmet had protected me from serious damage. It lay on the ground in two pieces, while the Triton was on its side about 20ft away, its front wheel still spinning.

Tony, however, was a little less lucky than me. As he flew over the wall, his arm caught a barbed-wire fence that cut him from his elbow to his wrist. Apart from that, though, we escaped serious harm.

The farmer who owned the field lived just around the corner and had witnessed the whole drama. He was standing in his farmyard as we hit the wall, saw what happened and dashed over the road towards us. He asked us if we were OK, and then his wife took Tony into the house to bandage his arm. I was in agony but said little, as I didn't want anyone to phone for an ambulance.

I looked down at my stricken motorbike. One exhaust pipe and one of the footrests had broken off. The brake lever was a little bent and the petrol tank had a dent in it. I listened in horror as the farmer asked me if he should torch it so I could claim on the insurance. 'No!' I cried. 'No.' He obviously didn't realise how much my bike meant to me. Torching it would have been like having a favourite pet put down just because it had a broken leg.

It was a strange ride to the Buck Inn that lunchtime, and probably the slowest time I've ever made. We managed to push the Triton out of the field and back onto the road and then continued our journey, oh so slowly, with only one brake, one exhaust and one foot rest. The bike sounded dreadful and I felt like my chest was going to burst, but in true bikers' spirit we cajoled that Triton to take us the ten miles to Holmegate and the pub. The first pint of John Smiths bitter didn't have time to settle in the glass as Tony celebrated his good fortune and I partook of some much-needed anaesthetic.

The next memorable event in my life was tragic and almost ended my love affair with motorcycles forever. One Sunday morning back in 1965, as usual I'd ridden down to Tupton Miners' Welfare Club to put on my tote – my selection in a weekly numbers' draw. I'd choose the same four numbers every week, and if they came out of the weekly draw I might win £20 or more. Most of the lads did this week in and week out before heading off to meet the rest of the lads at the Buck Inn.

On the previous Friday, me and Ray Spafford – a good mate of mine with whom I'd ridden motorcycles for years – went to Eric Housley's shop at Clay Cross to take delivery of Ray's new Triumph Bonneville, a beautiful 500cc machine that was the talk of the motorcycle world. We went by bus because Ray didn't want to ride the bike straight from the shop, as he was a little nervous and so had asked me to ride it back to his home for him.

By that Sunday, Ray had mastered the Bonneville and met me at the Miners' Welfare, where I was first to put my tote on. Ray was a couple of places behind me in the queue and asked me, 'What do you want to drink?'

'I'm not having one here,' I said. 'I'm off to the Buck.'

Ray replied, 'I know. That's where I meant.'

I smiled and said, 'By the time you've put your tote on, I'll be at the bar. I'll have a pint waiting for you.' And off I went. I honestly thought that Ray would catch me up. The Bonneville could really go and it had the beating of any Triton.

I set off in the usual flying fashion and in about five minutes I was at the Buck, where I ordered two pints of bitter: one for me and one for Ray. By the time I'd drunk mine, there was still no sign of Ray. I thought that he'd probably stopped to talk to someone in the Welfare.

Just then a man who knew most of us bikers walked into the pub, looked around and then came over to me and said, 'Your mate's had an accident down the road near the Woodside.' The Woodside pub was about a mile from the Buck Inn.

I was out of the door in a flash and rode down to the spot where the man had told me the accident had occurred. Ray's bike was standing at the side of the road. The tank and the exhaust were scratched, but apart from that there was no obvious damage. A policeman was sweeping fragments of glass and machine from the road. There was no one else there apart from a couple of my mates who had pulled up just after me.

I asked the policemen what had happened to Ray. Coldly, he replied, 'You can buy him a wreath.'

My mates and I were devastated. I later found out from a girl who lived near the scene of the accident that Ray had taken the bend at the corner of Coupe Lane too fast, losing control of the Bonneville and hitting a small garden wall. He'd not been wearing a helmet (they weren't compulsory in those days) and had cut his head near his temple. He'd died of asphyxia, choking on his own blood. If someone at the scene had reached him quickly enough and had turned him onto his stomach, he would have been fine.

I'd lost a close friend and was terribly shaken by the experience. I drove home that Sunday, put my motorbike in the outhouse and vowed never to ride again.

Later, Ray's mother asked me to take his bike, as she was too distraught even to think of selling it. I contacted Housley's, where Ray had originally bought it, and they agreed to buy it back.

Two weeks passed and I hadn't even bothered to look at my bike. Then, I realised that, just like Pam, even Ray's tragic death couldn't break my love affair with motorcycles – and speed. I went to the outhouse, pushed the Triton out into the street and was off down the Mile Run at 70mph, convinced that that was what Ray would have wanted.

CHAPTER 3

Marriage, Children, Sadness and Success

1966 was an epic year, not only because England won the football World Cup on 30 July that year but also because John Lowe married Diana Cuckson that very same afternoon. 'So what happened to the love affair with motorbikes?' I hear you ask. Well, the motorcycle did play its part.

I first met Diana while on a Saturday-night drinking spree in the Nelson pub on Stevenson's Place, Chesterfield, with a couple of mates. I spotted this dyed-blonde girl sitting across the room, talking to another girl. After a while I noticed that she seemed to be looking my way. I smiled and then my mates and I left for another pub close by.

In those days, just like today, Saturday-night drinking in Chesterfield was, like everywhere else, a routine. A gang of the lads, including me, would start in the Mucky Duck on St Mary's Gate and then go next door to Billy Green's, then up to the Blue Bell on Stephenson's Place, down to the Nelson a few yards away, then to the Buck across the street, and so on. If you started the route at the wrong time, you didn't meet anyone you knew, so it was important to know which pub to be in at the right time.

On this particular night, the blonde girl happened to be on the same route as us, and after visiting three pubs and downing a few pints, my courage was climbing. It looked obvious to me that she was getting ever closer to me, so I decided to make a move. I walked up to her and asked, 'Can I get you a drink?'

Her mate was quick to reply, 'You can. Two halves of bitter.'

I readily obliged and my first conversation with my future wife began.

After a while and another drink I asked the blonde – whose name, I discovered, was Diana – if I could take her out.

'I don't think so,' she replied. 'My boyfriend is in the army and he wouldn't like it.'

I thought, 'Here I go again, always chatting up someone else's girl!' I was desperately disappointed but didn't want to appear so, and so I just brushed it off. 'OK,' I said airily, and then added, 'but if you're around town next Saturday, be in the Nelson at seven o'clock and I'll buy you a drink.'

To be honest, I thought no more of that night. It wasn't until the following Saturday, when I walked into the Nelson to meet the lads, that it all came back to me. While I was at the bar, buying a drink, a fight broke out, so I moved back to the wall to avoid becoming involved. It was then that I heard this voice say, 'Fancy meeting you here.'

I turned around and there was Diana. 'Hello,' I said. 'Fancy getting out of here before we finish up hurt?' I headed for the door and, to my surprise, she followed. We crossed the road to the Rutland pub and spent the next hour chatting.

I found out that Diana was in fact Diana Cuckson and that she lived at Brimington, a village a few miles outside Chesterfield. I also discovered that she did indeed have a boyfriend in the forces. His name was Tony and they'd grown up together, almost as family friends. I sensed that I was on dangerous ground; going out with a girl whose fellow is in the army is a bit like going out with a girl whose man is in jail. Did it bother me, though? Well, yes, it did – for about two minutes.

I walked Diana to her bus and watched her disappear into the night. At that point in time, I had no idea that my long, long love affair with motorcycles was about to come to an end.

waterproofs, so it was back to Brimington. I dropped her off and then set off again for Oulton. No way was I going to miss Hailwood, Minter, Cooper and John Arkle. And after all, I'd be back by eight o'clock. I told her I'd see her in the Butchers Arms at Brimington.

When I arrived at the pub that evening, to my surprise Diana was standing at the jukebox with a guy on either side of her. Both men had their arms around her and they all seemed very friendly. I remember thinking, 'Oh, I see. She's mad with me for going on my own. This must be her way of making me jealous.' I found out from one of the guys who were playing darts that they were both ex-boyfriends, one called Tony (yes, that one, the army guy) and the other Brian.

It was a well-known fact in those days that each area of the district we lived in was almost a protected zone. People who lived in Tupton had done so all their lives. Grassmoor was only a couple of miles away, but should one of that village's inhabitants move to live in ours, people would talk about it for weeks. Brimington, it turned out, was no different, and I sensed a feeling of 'Who does this guy think he is, coming here and going out with one of our girls?' Diana milked the situation, flirting, teasing – call it what you like. I decided that something was amiss, so I donned my helmet and roared away on my bike.

I didn't hear from or see Diana for the whole of the next week. By the end of the week, I'd convinced myself that it didn't matter and made arrangements to go into town with the lads. We did the usual route of pubs, and by the time we'd reached the Nelson we were all in quite a merry frame of mind and having a great night out. I was at the bar buying the round when one of the lads said to me, 'Have you seen who's over there?'

I turned round to see Diana, her mate Brenda and Diana's boyfriend, Tony, all looking straight at me – or so I thought. They all seemed to have smug looks on their faces, as if they were mocking me, saying, 'Goodbye, loser.'

I just shrugged my shoulders and joined in with the laughter at one of my mate's jokes. As far as I was concerned, my relationship with Diana was over. Life goes on, I thought, so why make it complicated? But, of course, we always *do* make things complicated – and I did.

When Diana and her party were about to leave, I turned and said, 'Goodnight.' Tony scowled and I thought a punch might be coming my way. Diana, however, came over and whispered in my ear, 'Call me from the phone box tomorrow night at six o'clock.' With that, she rejoined the other two and left the Nelson.

In those days we didn't have a telephone at home, so any phone calls had to be made using the pay phone on the street a few yards from our home. I had no intention of ringing Diana, though; I thought that I was being used, that she was just stringing me along to make her boyfriend jealous. I was adamant that I wouldn't make that phone call. But, of course, I did.

We started going out together again that day. Tony tried very hard to win Diana back, and at one point I thought he might just succeed. I'd go down to Diana's house and he'd just be leaving, and when I'd ask Diana what he was doing there she'd say, 'Oh, he's just been to see my mother.' He was in truth friendly with the family, and I felt that they liked him a lot more than they did me. He was, after all, one of the locals, and in Brimington that counted for a lot.

At the weekends, Diana would take the bus over to Tupton. We'd spend the day together, and then at about nine o'clock I'd go with her on the bus back to Chesterfield, where she'd then catch another bus back to Brimington.

In those early days we enjoyed a couple of holidays together, one time spending a week in my Aunty Kathleen's caravan at Skegness. That was an experience; it rained for the whole week. The caravan was quite old and the water found its way in through the roof, right above the bed. I finished up getting out of bed in the middle of the night and fixing a plastic bag over the hole. By the time I'd plugged the leak, I was soaked. Still, we were young and it was those kind of things that we talked about when we got home.

The relationship was going great, and on one Sunday night in February 1966 I asked Diana if she thought we should get married. That was it – no going down on one knee – just a simple question over a pint in the Blue Bell at Wingfield, three miles from where we lived. Her answer was just as simple: 'I suppose we should.'

And so it was that, on 30 July 1966, at Brimington Parish Church, I married Diana Cuckson. We were both twenty-one years old at the time. It was a memorable day, and not just because of the wedding. After the church service, I sat in the kitchen at the Cucksons' home in Oxford Close and watched England win the football World Cup. It made my special day even more so. Everyone was in good spirits, and the double celebration gave Jack a good excuse to get pissed. Amazingly, even my mother and father took a drink that day, explaining that it was only right and quite acceptable to toast the bride and groom. However, they weren't too pleased with Diana's family, especially Jack, who they thought was interested in only one thing. Looking back, I think they were right.

After all the celebrations were over, we left for our honeymoon in London, taking with us the £60 I'd borrowed from my father's weekly savings. It was every penny he'd owned at the time, although of course I promised to pay him back as soon as I could, and when a Lowe makes a promise, you can guarantee it's their bond. We stayed at the Sussex Gardens Hotel, in Sussex Square.

1966 was not only memorable for England winning the World Cup and my marriage to Diana but also for the fact that it was the year I became seriously interested in darts. Fate struck again when I was asked to take someone's throw in a friendly darts match at The Butchers Arms at Brimington.

I was in the pub, drinking, chatting and watching four guys throwing darts when one of them decided he wanted to go to the toilet midway through his doubles match. He turned round to see who was in the room. His eyes fell upon me – presumably because I happened to be the closest - and he handed me his darts, asked me to take his turn and then disappeared into the gents.

Who the guy was I have no idea, but I thank him from the bottom of my heart for the life he literally handed to me. All I remember was that when he returned from responding to the call of nature he saw I was enjoying myself so much he let me carry on playing. Shortly afterwards he left the pub leaving me playing with his darts. I kept those darts for many years. I visited the Butchers Arms regularly to see if I could maybe bump into the owner. I remember the darts were made of brass and they had feather flights but sadly I lost them somewhere. Maybe I gave them away when I changed to tungsten darts in the early 1970's. I could not honestly say. Thinking back now it would have been nice to still have that very first set of darts; the darts which set me on the road to success in the sport, including three Embassy World titles in three separate decades.

One thing I do know is that, if I had not been asked by that unknown dart player to take his throw I would not be writing this story. Or just maybe fate might have intervened at some other time. Who knows? Whatever, that was the beginning of a 40-year attraction, engagement, maybe, some might argue, a *marriage* to the sport of darts. Did darts play such a role in my early married life that I was married to both Diana and to darts?

Unfortunately though, life with Diana was strained from the off. In those days, many newlyweds stayed with their parents while they saved up to rent or buy a place of their own, and Diana and I were no different, living with my parents at Tupton. In our case, however, there was an instant clash – a matter of 'Whose house is it anyway?' – between Diana and my mother and father, who had their own way of doing things. The pots had to be washed after every meal, the cushions straightened after rising from the settee, the bed made as soon as you got out of it in the morning. It was a way of life to my parents. They had little and what they had was precious. Meanwhile, I was working seven days a week on the M1 motorway, shuttering bridges, culverts and the like, trying to save enough money to put a deposit down on a house of our own. This, however, didn't help relationships at home, and as a result Diana was pretty miserable.

Thus, after two years of hard work, it was with great relief that I was finally able to say to Diana, 'We can afford to buy one of the new bungalows on Woodside.' What I meant, of course, was that we could afford the deposit on one of the houses being built behind the Woodside pub, close to where Ray Spafford had been killed on his motorcycle. The bungalow cost £3,200 and the deposit was just £600, which in 1968 was a great deal of money. We applied for a mortgage and were very excited at the prospect of owning our own home. As soon as the contract was signed, I set about negotiating with the builder to do most of the work myself, and I ended up doing all the joinery on the bungalow to save money. This meant that I was working from eight 'til five on the building site and then five 'til midnight on our home, seven days a week. Still, I was young, and long hours and hard work never did worry me. We eventually moved into our new home in July 1969.

The day we moved must have been the best day of Diana's life – well, her married life, anyway. She'd finally freed herself of the in-laws. She had her own kitchen and everything was pristine. We were very happy for a year or so. Although we did struggle a little to pay the mortgage and the household bills, we managed to go out on a regular basis – probably five nights a week! I was playing darts by then and was in three leagues, plus competitions. We were both working, so our money was pooled and relevant expenses, such as housekeeping, rates and heating, were all taken out before we knew how much we had to spend on enjoyment.

At that time, Diana was working for Trebor Mints in Chesterfield and we would regularly meet with her workmates there at weekends. In order to give each other some space, we agreed that it would be OK for each of us to go out one night each week – Friday – without the other. On those nights, Diana would go out on the town with the girls while I'd either play darts at Clay Cross or go up to Matlock with the lads. The arrangement was a kind of stress relief, a chance to get out of each other's hair for a while. As such, it worked well, and it helped us to maintain a good relationship – for a while, at least.

One Friday night in 1970, we each went our separate ways – mine to the dartboard at the Parkhouse Hotel, Diana's to Chesterfield for a night out with her girlfriend Brenda Royal. I arrived home about 10:45pm and, as one of the lads in the pub had given me a rabbit, I decided to cook some rabbit stew for us both, so we could have some supper together when Diana got home after taking the eleven o'clock bus.

The bus came and went. I thought, 'She must have missed it. That's OK. She'll catch a taxi.' An hour passed – then two, then three. I went to bed and fell asleep. When I awoke, at about 6:30am, there was still no Diana. I did not know what to think. Maybe she'd got drunk and decided to stay with her mate, or perhaps she'd gone to her mum's house. I reassured myself that everything would be fine and that she'd be home soon.

At two o'clock on Saturday afternoon, Diana finally walked into the house. 'What happened?' I asked. 'Where have you been?'

Diana replied, 'I stayed with Brenda. We were out a little late.'

I was reassured. It was just what I'd thought. I thought, 'No problem' – and then it occurred to me that Diana had never stayed out before.

Imagine my amazement, then, when it seemed like the next minute Diana was packing a case and telling me that she was going to stay with her friend for a few days, that she needed a break. It didn't take me long to realise that her friend was another man. She'd not been out with her girlfriends on Friday nights; she'd been seeing someone else.

We didn't argue. I pretended it didn't matter. We didn't have any kids, so no harm had been done to anyone. Of course, that was clearly a lie; I was hurting terribly and would never forget it.

Diana stayed away for five days. I did miss her, to be honest, but worse, I felt let down. I'd had no idea that anything had been wrong with our marriage, but I was naïve. I admit now that I'd been so wrapped up in my darts that I hadn't noticed my wife was becoming bored. Sitting in a pub night after night, watching your partner throw darts all night long, isn't a recipe for a happy marriage. Maybe Diana should have told me that it was getting her down instead of pretending that everything was OK, but equally I guess I should have noticed that something was wrong. At that time, however, darts was becoming a major force in my life, and perhaps, unnoticed by me, the love of the game was destroying my marriage. I felt bitter towards the guy who had stolen my wife, whoever he was, but most of all I felt sorry for my parents. I knew that the news of Diana's affair would hurt them terribly, so I never told them about it.

I never once tried to make contact with Diana or go knocking on the guy's door, but as it happened, I didn't need to; Diana came home under her own steam about a week later. I never discovered the real reason why she came back. Maybe our new home was a key factor. Maybe the grass on the other side wasn't as green as she'd hoped. Or maybe she really did care for me.

In that time she was away, I tried to think of what I'd do if Diana did come home. Looking back, it was quite funny when she did. She just walked in and unpacked her things, and we got on with life as if nothing had ever happened. Perhaps it was better that way.

Inside, I blamed Diana's girlfriend Brenda Royal for the fling. I'd never got on with Brenda and I thought it was her way of getting at me, not so much to break up the marriage but to rock the boat. Well, Brenda, the boat had been well and truly rocked. The seeds had been sown and it was only a matter of months or years before that act of deception would be the excuse for my own infidelity.

Perhaps surprisingly, family life in the Lowe household soon settled back into a routine. I tried to cut down on my darting activities. Instead of playing every night of the week, I'd play on just six! I was improving all the time, though. At that time I was in the best team in the area (many would say the best team in Derbyshire), which made it difficult for me to take a night off. Almost without exception we reached the finals of every competition we entered, and those matches would have to be fitted in between local league nights. Despite my best efforts, it wasn't long – probably a couple of months – before I was playing seven nights a week once again.

For some reason – perhaps it was an unspoken desire to preserve our marriage – Diana and I decided to try to have children, and when, in 1972, Diana told me she was pregnant, I was delighted, although unsure how we were going to manage the mortgage and all the outgoings when she had to finish work. I suppose I knew deep down that I'd have to cut down on my darts, perhaps to just a couple of nights a week.

Sadly, the decision was taken out of my hands when, three months into the pregnancy, Diana had a miscarriage. It was a traumatic time for both of us and, understandably, it was a few months before our life was back to any semblance of proper order.

When normal life did resume, we decided to try again for a baby. It did not take long before Diana was pregnant again, and this time everything went just fine. On 14 April 1973, our son, Adrian, was born and the continuation of the Lowe family tree was assured.

As all new parents know, having a baby changes your life considerably, and I was no exception. I was now the only one working and had to put in many hours of overtime in order to pay the bills. Then, in 1970, we decided to sell our first home in Coupe Lane and purchase a semi-detached house in Clay Cross, a much cheaper place to live. Ironically, the couple who sold us the house were divorcing and had to take a quick sale. I paid only £4,000 for the house, and the overheads were also considerably smaller, although the place was in need of a bit of work. Being a carpenter, of course, I could do everything myself, and it gave me a chance to put my training in the building trade into practice. It only took a few months to get the house in good shape and increase its value by £10,000.

Living in Clay Cross also meant that I was now nearer the pub where I was playing my darts. The Prince of Wales' landlord, John Sutton, was a keen supporter of the game and looked after the darts team very well, and it was his pub that I represented in my first World Masters Championship in London, back in 1976, when I became champion after beating Welshman Phil Obbard three–nil in the final.

We had a good team at the Prince of Wales, probably not as good as the Parkhouse Hotel's team, who we used to play with, but splitting from them and going to another pub made the league far more interesting and gave most of the teams in the league a chance of being successful. Previously, it would have been a foregone conclusion that the Parkhouse team would make a clean sweep of all events.

The arrival of Adrian meant that Diana and I didn't go out together very often, maybe just once at the weekend. I was still playing darts almost every night, so Diana would be at home on her own – not the perfect recipe for a happy marriage. We would row almost constantly, mainly over the amount of time I'd spend playing darts in the pub. She was absolutely right about one thing, though: while I was playing darts every night for hours on end, I wasn't out womanising. Despite having a young child, darts was the first and last thing on my mind. It had become my obsession. Life became a fixed cycle of work in the daytime, darts at night, darts on Saturday afternoons, darts at Sunday lunchtime, darts, darts and more darts.

Then, in early 1975, we had another surprise: Diana was pregnant again. The stork revisited the Lowe household on 9 February and brought us a daughter, Karen.

Karen's birth was very unusual. Diana went into labour at home. I rang the doctor, who in turn rang the ambulance. The doctor arrived at our house in time, but the ambulance didn't. Karen was delivered in our lounge, with two-year-old Adrian watching. The doctor said after the birth that Adrian was probably the youngest person to witness the birth of a baby, or at least the youngest at any birth he'd attended.

The arrival of Karen didn't change our way of life – or, to put it more correctly, it didn't change mine. The darts continued to take precedence over everything and everyone, and now that she had two children to look after, Diana was getting out even less often. In those days, babysitters willing to take care of two kids were difficult to find. One was OK, but two? No thanks.

Eventually, Diana and I came to an agreement whereby she would go out on Wednesday nights while I'd stay home and look after the kids – and so she joined the Prince of Wales' ladies' darts team. I guess she was thinking, 'If you can't beat 'em, join 'em.' I hung a dartboard over the fireplace in my lounge, temporarily replacing a picture we'd hung there, and on those Wednesday nights while I was looking after the kids I'd practise for four hours. It seemed to be the perfect arrangement – for me, anyway: Diana enjoyed her night out and I enjoyed my night in. Anyway, there was no league darts on Wednesdays.

I played darts with the Prince of Wales team for a few years, and then in 1978 I began to play with the team at the Willow Tree at Pilsley, a small village about two miles from Clay Cross. The pub's landlord, Jack Brewin, was another keen supporter of darts and would regularly accompany me to matches.

At this time I'd become intent on winning the most prestigious darts event in the world, the *News of the World* Individual Darts Championship, and decided to play my league darts from the distance stipulated in that competition: 8ft. This meant that I was giving away up to 12in to my opponents, who were throwing from shorter distances. I lost a few matches, but that didn't worry me. If I was going to win 'the big one', I had to play from the *News of the World* throwing distance.

A good friend of mine, Barry Twomlow, who lived a few miles away in Staveley, had won the *News of the World* title in 1969 while playing for the Red Lion in Chesterfield, a pub run by former heavyweight boxing champion Peter Bates. Barry, too, had the theory that the best way to win the competition was to practise playing from the 8ft mark. This knowledge had been passed on to him by Tommy Reddington – a Derbyshire man, from Alfreton – who had won the event twice: once in 1954/55, while playing out of the New Inn, Stonebroom, and again in 1959/60, while playing out of the George Hotel, Alfreton.

My dream almost came true in the 1976/77 competition, although I lost in the semi-final at Alexandra Palace to Mick Norris, who then went on to win. Three years later, in 1979/80, I reached the semi-finals again, this time losing out to Stefan Lord from Sweden, who, like Mick, went on to win the competition. But then, in 1981, it was my turn to go one better and reach my first *News of the World* final. This time I made no mistake and won the greatest darts event in the world at Wembley Arena, beating the 1977 winner, Mick Norris, two–nil. I was over the moon. I'd already taken the World Masters, the British Open and the British Pentathlon titles, and winning the *News of the World* Cup completed my set of major events in world darts.

Everyone celebrated at the Willow Tree in great style. A friend of mine, Geoff Smith, filled the Cup to the brim, and it held fifty-four pints! It was party time, but needless to say Diana was at home looking after the kids. I stayed at the Willow Tree until late and naturally had to leave my car, so I ended up sharing a taxi home with the barmaid, Penny Priest. I remember quite well the kiss she planted firmly on my lips when we reached her house. It was a kiss that was to change my life.

I was at last on my way, in darting terms; a full-time professional. I was ranked the world's number one darts player and I had a great lifestyle, a nice car and money in the bank. It was soon time to move house again, so I bought a new house called – appropriately enough – Lakeside that was being built next to a large pond called the Lido at Wingerworth, a very nice village about two miles out of New Tupton. We moved in 1981 after selling the house in Clay Cross for £42,000, making a nice profit in the process. This also meant that I needed a mortgage of only £16,000 for Lakeside. I was on the ladder and success at darts had opened up a whole new life for us.

Meanwhile, my private life was in turmoil. That goodnight kiss from Penny Priest had led to a few dates together, and we became lovers. I knew that cheating on my wife was wrong, but I kept reminding myself that I was only doing what Diana had done to me when we were first married. Selfish? Perhaps. At the time, though, I was thinking, 'If Diana can do it, so can I.'

The sad thing is that I was really fond of Penny, and I knew she felt the same way about me. Despite my increasing fame, she never asked anything of me. OK, it wasn't the greatest relationship – such arrangements rarely are – and we could meet up only now and again. She deserved a lot better. Penny was a very attractive girl and knew we'd be going nowhere, so she started dating a local lad – I presumed in an attempt to break away from me. It didn't work, however, and we still met quite a few times over the next two years.

Looking back at that time and the situation, I suppose I was hoping it would all come out in the open, as this would have forced me to make a choice, Diana or Penny, and yet, strangely, everyone who knew about my relationship with Penny kept quiet. However, it was inevitable that the affair would eventually end. Penny wanted a life of her own. Then she met another guy and settled down with him. Me? I just carried on playing darts.

Playing darts on a full-time professional basis meant that I didn't get to spend a lot of time at home. I'd be away from home for days on end. And, yes, there were plenty of girls. You probably won't believe me when I say that I talked to them at the many exhibitions I attended, signing their autographs and anything else they requested, but that that was where it ended. After that it was off to the hotel – just my driver, Peter Lippiatt, and me – and bed.

Diana was in fact very supportive of my travelling, and indeed with the fees I was paid for playing exhibitions we were better off, financially, than we'd ever been. In the building trade I'd take on a supply-and-fix job and sometimes have to wait months before I received payment, while sometimes I wouldn't be paid at all.

There were awkward times, though, like those occasions when the phone would ring, Diana would pick up and there'd be no one there. Even if it was a wrong number, Diana would suspect it was a girl I'd met on the road. Not surprisingly, this caused some friction between us, but overall the rewards cancelled out any disappointment or concerns.

The Lowe family had been at Lakeside for only four years when I spotted a house for sale just around the corner, literally a few hundred yards away, on Hayfield Close. The property had half an acre of land – all landscaped – and was built of Derbyshire stone, with five bedrooms, a snooker room and a large garage. It was at the top of the range and the asking price was £110,000 or nearest bid. I knew we could get a good price for our Lakeside property and so instructed my insurance agent to put in a bid of £100,000 for the new place. We later met the owners' asking price and I paid a deposit of £10,000 to secure the purchase.

I was elated at our new home, although Diana was a little intimidated by its size. She was worried that it was too large and that we might not be able to afford it, remembering when we'd had to sell our first house because the mortgage repayments were too high. Adrian and Karen, on the other hand, loved it, as they both had big bedrooms and plenty of garden to play in.

The house had everything and was built very well. I had a new kitchen fitted, installed a snooker table and became 'John Lowe the darts player who lives in the big house at the end of Hayfield Close'. I enjoyed having a nice house, always having believed that bricks and mortar were the best investment anyone could have. We'd needed to borrow only £22,000 so the repayments were quite acceptable. I guess we had everything we could wish for. The only thing missing was the good husband/wife relationship.

Despite the new house, I was miserable, and my friends would tell me so. I was the darts player who never blinked – 'Old Stoneface', as I came to be called. I was also the darts player who never smiled, and it soon became obvious to everyone that things weren't good at home.

Diana and I never discussed the problems between us. We'd sometimes argue late at night, usually after a drink, and then the next morning Diana would pretend that nothing had happened and revert to being what she thought was normal. The kids, of course, knew better; they'd hear the arguments but never said anything. I'm sure we were all miserable.

And then the world changed.

CHAPTER 4

Perfect Darts, Perfect Kids, Imperfect Marriage

In 1984, I spent some time away in Norwich, doing a few exhibitions for a friend of mine, John Carmichael. John was heavily involved with darts in the Norwich area and owned a trophy shop. Almost everyone in the darts world knew him; at 6ft 4in with white hair, John wasn't the kind of person you could forget easily. While I was in Norwich, I was staying with another friend, Eddie Harvey, who owned a hotel, the Marlborough, on Stacy Road and was a longtime friend of John's, having gone to school with him. Indeed, they were almost inseparable.

On this trip, my aim was to warm up for the MFI World Matchplay that was taking place the following weekend in Slough. Eddie and John were known by almost everyone in Norwich and we would be out until all hours, mainly socialising. On this particular trip, however, my intention was to be sociable but in bed by twelve midnight.

Everything went to plan – except for the last night of the visit. On that night we were invited to the opening of a new bar/disco on the outskirts of Norwich. Time went out of the window and we arrived back at Eddie's at 3am, at which point I was a little worse for wear.

The next morning, I drove to Slough. With such an evening

behind me and having done so little preparation, I didn't think I stood much chance in the competition, but I couldn't have been more wrong. Lo and behold, the next day, 13 October 1984, when playing against the 1983 Embassy World Professional champion, Keith Deller, I played a perfect game, scoring 501 with nine darts. Although it was recorded and transmitted a little later in the day, my nine-darter was the very first perfect game ever scored on television. (At this point, I have to say, shame on Sky TV and their commentators when they claimed that Phil Taylor's nine-dart game some eighteen years later was history in the making, in effect perpetrating one of the biggest darts myths ever told. They chose to bypass the record books, instead bestowing their own, inaccurate accolade on Phil, possibly in an attempt to boost ratings.)

I received £102,000 for those two minutes of arrow-throwing. Now *that* was history in the making, and at the time of writing it's still the largest amount of money ever won by a darts player. To add to my winnings, I actually went on to win the championship itself, a victory that earned me another £12,000, plus I collected a bonus of another £1,000 for achieving the highest checkout in the contest – 161 – to make a grand total of £115,000.

After such a fabulous pay day, one might have imagined that life at home would improve. In fact, things did improve a little, but I still felt miserable – and trapped. I had a wife, two great kids, a big house and the best car money could buy, but the main ingredient – happiness – was missing. Even so, that perfect nine-dart 501 game is such an important part of my life and my darting career that there's an entire chapter of this book devoted to the event, describing the importance and magnitude of the win and its impact on my life and those around me.

During this time I would take all the bookings on offer, and there were plenty. I would travel all over the world, attending every open darts event I could. I very much doubt that I was home for more than four months of the year. I could handle that quite well, but when I'd return home for only a couple of days at a time, the arguments would begin.

Diana was now going out more. The kids were growing up fast and they became used to the fact that their father worked away most of the time. They had many friends who would come over to the house, and they could usually be found in the snooker room. Diana would go out on Wednesdays and Sundays to Clay Cross to meet with her friend Dot, and on every occasion she'd come back the worse for drink. I didn't approve of this, and I told her so, but it made little difference; she thought it was acceptable behaviour. I'd tell her, 'You're just like your father,' and she'd reply, 'I know.' I'd then stay up until the small hours, watching TV until I knew she was asleep.

Not surprisingly, things became worse between us. We argued about everything and nothing, mostly after the drink had flowed. The kids hated it and made it clear that they couldn't wait to leave home, and when they were eventually old enough to look after themselves it meant a new lease of life for Diana. Whenever I was at home, she expected us to go out every night. She'd have her coat on, ready and waiting. It was like, 'You've been out all over the country, now it's my turn.' She refused to drive at any time, having only one thing in mind when we went out together: drink.

Despite our stormy marriage, Adrian had done really well at school, passing all his exams with flying colours. After qualifying in 1990, he went off to Coventry University, where he studied Applied Mathematics and Nuclear Science on a three-year sandwich course, taking one year out to work at Sellafield nuclear power station. I remember all the accommodation on campus had been taken, so I took him to look at some rented digs. We visited quite a few houses around the Stoke area of Coventry, all of which were owned by Asian people and, to be honest, none of which were anything like his home at Hayfield Close (although, of course, if they had been, the rent would have been unaffordable). We eventually found a three-bedroom house in Stoke that was suitable, with the downstairs lounge serving as a fourth bedroom. The landlord and I agreed on a weekly rent of £30.

Two weeks later, just before the start of the new term, I drove Adrian and his possessions to Coventry to start his new life.

When we arrived at his accommodation, we were met by the three other lads who would be his housemates. They all had their mothers and fathers with them, and I was very conscious of the fact that Adrian was there with just his father. The mothers were busy filling the cupboards with food, everything from bananas to gravy granules, whereas Adrian hadn't let us pack anything other than the bare essentials. 'Just give me some money and I'll sort out what I need when I settle in,' he'd said, ever the sensible one.

I left him with his new housemates and travelled home. Diana made a few comments about how she worried about Adrian leaving home and wondered if he'd be all right at Coventry. 'Yes,' I agreed. 'I'm sure he'll be fine.' I remember thinking that, if she'd been that concerned, why hadn't she come with us to make sure he'd be all right?

I returned to Coventry – again on my own – two days later, the first day of term. That night everyone met in the uni bar – and what a revelation that was! There were over 1,000 students in one room, packed twenty deep at the bar, and Becks and Guinness was being served at £1 per pint. What lucky people! I spent an hour or so chatting to Adrian's mates and a couple of others who recognised me from TV, and then it was time for me to leave. As I left, about a hundred students began chanting, 'One hundred and eighty! One hundred and eighty!'

As I left Adrian that night, I knew he'd be fine – and in fact I was somewhat jealous of my son. I would have loved to have been able to follow the road he was taking, but it was no good wishing now. If father had only made more money; if I hadn't fallen out of that tree ... But I'd climbed my own ladder and made my own way, taking the opportunities as they presented themselves. At least my career as a professional darts player was lucrative enough for us to send Adrian to university and give him a good start in life.

I often returned to the university and would take Adrian and his mates out whenever I could. If I was playing an exhibition in the area, I would arrange for them to be allowed into the venue and leave them a drinks tab behind the bar. Afterwards we'd all go off to an Indian restaurant and have a good meal.

I remember one of those nights as if it was only yesterday. Adrian and three of his mates had come to a darts exhibition at a large Miners' Welfare Club in Nuneaton, near Coventry, for the Federation Brewery. I'd arranged for the usual bar tab, but this time my son and his mates almost drank the place dry.

After the exhibition, we all piled into my car and went to a nearby Indian restaurant on Stoke Road, where – as usual – I let them order whatever they wanted. When the starters came, the table was overflowing with poppadoms and relish by the boatload. Every last broken piece of poppadom was devoured. Next came every kind of curry one could think of, with dishes of rice and naan bread, Bombay potatoes and onion bhajis, filling every available space on the table. Ten minutes later, though, the table was empty! I remember my driver, Peter, turning to me and saying, 'I think they've eaten the salt and pepper pot, too.'

When it was time to pay the bill, the owner of the restaurant came over to deliver it to me personally. 'Thank you so much, Mr John Lowe, for using my restaurant,' he said. 'Please – you are welcome to come again.' I'll bet. My son and his mates had gone through £175 of food and drink, all in under an hour.

When we dropped Adrian and his mates off at their house, every one of them thanked me for the meal and Peter for seeing them home safely. I remember that the conversation on the way home hadn't been so much about how much they had eaten or drank but just nice, polite conversation between a group of teenage friends. Their behaviour that night was a great sign for that generation.

Adrian did very well at university, not running into too many problems with the workload, and I think he quite enjoyed the experience. He'd occasionally come home for the weekend, mainly to see his girlfriend Karen, and I'd ask him if he had any problems and how he was managing on his weekly allowance of £70. 'No problem,' he'd say. 'In fact, I've learned how to live on under £20 a week.' It turned out that there was a Chinese guy living with them, and Adrian's mates would ask him to make them rice in his special cooking pot. I guess rice goes with everything.

One weekend Adrian told me that they were having problems with their house's landlord. They wanted a leak fixed in the bathroom, which also needed decorating, so he asked me what I'd do about it if I was in his position. I advised him, 'Give him the option. Either he does the work or you do it and take the cost out of the rent.' They did just that.

A couple of weeks later, Adrian rang and asked me if I fancied a night out in Coventry. I thought the lads were maybe getting hungry, so I said yes and went down on my own on the Friday night. When I arrived, there were six guys at the house, all playing darts. (Yes, earlier I'd fixed them up with a Unicorn dartboard and a couple of sets of tungsten darts.) So I went upstairs to the small spare room in which they'd installed the dartboard – and when I entered the room, I couldn't believe my eyes. Every space on the dartboard wall had a flattened beer tin fastened to it. They'd bought all the brands of lager and bitter they could find, and over the course of a year they'd managed to fill every space!

However, I got an even bigger shock when I went to the bathroom. As I'd suggested to Adrian, they'd reached an agreement with the landlord that they'd decorate the room and deduct the cost from the rent. They'd kept their part of the bargain, having decorated the whole bathroom with black and white symmetrical squares. Even the bath, toilet, sink, cistern – the lot – were decorated in that way. It was truly a work of art.

'What does the landlord think of this?' I asked.

'Not a lot,' replied Adrian. 'He just murmured something like, "Thank you very please."'

When I drove home that night, I was again thinking, 'Look at what I missed out on.' If only I could have been a Michael Wright.

I hear you say, 'That's a little hard on yourself John. After all, you've been successful in your own right, in your own field.' Yes, that's true, but – and it's a big but – I knew that I would have enjoyed university. I liked what I saw: students who had never previously met bonding together, carving out new friendships and learning to cope with the help of others. I don't class myself as a failure because I didn't go to university; I just envy those who did go down that road, and I know I'd have enjoyed the experience immensely.

Adrian graduated from Coventry University in 1994 with a First-Class BSc (Hons) in Applied Mathematics. The graduation ceremony, held in Coventry Cathedral, was one of the proudest events of my life. Diana, Peter Lippiatt and I sat in the pews, waited for what seemed like an eternity as every student's name was called out, after which they'd walk up and receive their degree. At last it was Adrian's turn. With all 6ft 3in of him dressed in a gown and mortar board, he walked tall and upright and looked the Dean straight in the eye as he was handed his degree. I knew he was proud of his achievement; I certainly was, and his mother had a tear or two. It was a very special occasion for us.

After the ceremony, we had just enough time to have our photographs taken and congratulate Adrian, and then we left him with his fellow graduates, as Peter had to drive me to Birmingham Airport, where I was departing for Denmark to compete in the Danish Open. He would then drive Diana back to Chesterfield. It was back to the big house for her and back to the dartboard for me.

As Adrian was about to leave university, my daughter, Karen, was leaving home to start her own university education, after having won a place on a course in Surface Pattern Design at Staffordshire University, Stoke on Trent. This time, when we went to look over Karen's future accommodation, Diana came along too. Was this a case of a mother looking after her daughter or the salving of a guilty conscience, after not visiting Adrian once during the three years he'd been at Coventry University? I would sincerely like to think it was the former.

Karen took to uni life instantly, quickly making friends – and a couple of enemies. That was never hard for Karen, who always wanted to be the boss and would always tell it like she saw it. Not always a good idea, but that's Karen. Her course, unlike Adrian's, was quite expensive, and I had to provide almost all of the equipment she would use. Fortunately a friend of mine, Stephen Gillott, who was managing director of Carlsberg Brewery, had a daughter doing the same course and had found an art supplier through his business and promised to introduce me to them. This made life a lot easier and a lot less expensive than it might otherwise have been.

Diana and I would visit Karen frequently, largely because Karen wasn't too keen to come home at weekends. She valued the time with her new-found friends and they'd party quite a lot. I also think that the atmosphere between Diana and me didn't encourage Karen to return home. There was, however, another factor. Karen had made a lot of friends at university, and weekends in the Student's Union bar, with Guinness at the very reasonable price of £1 per pint, was a star attraction. I was amazed when I visited the uni club to see the girls drinking Guinness. Every one of them had a pint in front of them. I guess that was the generation that rid us of the assumption, 'A pint for the man and a half for the lady.'

Karen graduated at Trentham Gardens with a degree in Surface Pattern Design in 1996. When she came home, it was never the same; it was as if she'd found her own freedom, her own space. She valued it so much that she came up to me one day after being home for a few weeks and told me, 'Dad, I have to get out of here and find my own place.' I understood. I felt a lot like that myself.

As a family, we took regular holidays, many of them abroad. Disneyland, Florida, was a big favourite, while Spain was another. We'd start each holiday in good spirits, but inevitably the arguments between Diana and me would begin after the first week. We'd fight all day, and then there were long silences during which the kids would pass messages between us. And when we eventually arrived back home, we'd act as if nothing had happened, telling one and all what a great time we'd had.

I remember one holiday very well. How could I forget it? It was 1993 and we'd booked to go to Florida with our friends Joe and Carol Mooney. Joe was a director of the pub chain Temperate 92, who'd bought the Unicorn pub in Chesterfield. We'd hired a beautiful house in Kissimmee, but we almost didn't make it there.

As we boarded the aeroplane, we were told that the in-flight drinks were free. Not a good idea. Diana asked for a brandy almost every time the stewardess came down the aisle, and in less than a couple of hours she was the worse for wear. For the last two hours of the flight, she unceasingly hurled abuse at me. I was embarrassed to say the least. Most of the passengers knew me, but all I could do was apologise. That flight was the longest I've ever taken.

When we finally arrived at our holiday home, Diana went straight to bed. No unpacking – nothing. The next morning, she got up and carried on as if nothing had happened. I always wonder what Joe and Carol must have thought about that; they must have been expecting a dreadful time. I wasn't going to let that happen, though, so I just went along with it to keep the peace and, more than anything, to make our friends feel comfortable.

Believe it or not, the holiday turned out to be great. I love Disneyworld, so it was laughter all day, but then it was backs to each other all night.

We survived as a married couple for another year, and even booked to go back to Florida on our own. Things hadn't improved any, but I was used to life as I knew it. I pretended to myself that everyone else's lives were just the same, that I'd made my bed and just had to lie on it. Our second trip to Florida would perhaps give us a chance to save our marriage. I was more than willing to give it a go.

Unfortunately, just like the previous year, Diana succumbed to the dreaded drink. Again she hit the freebies on the plane on the way out, and by the time we'd reached the baggage claim at the airport she was drunk and up on her high horse. This time, however, it wasn't me she was abusive to, but a security man who'd come over to tell her to put her cigarette out. The poor guy! She laid into him like he was some sort of criminal. Even the threat of taking her away to the local police station did no good.

I was unsure what to do. Eventually, I managed to grab her cigarette and yank it out of her mouth – at which point she fell over her suitcase. I grabbed her by the arm and literally dragged her out of the terminal and into a taxi. Within minutes she'd fallen asleep on the back seat.

Would you believe it? The next day, Diana woke and behaved as if nothing had happened, not even mentioning the incident at the airport. For me, that was the last straw. I didn't think I could take anymore. I was at the point where any love I might have had for my wife had gone. I now disliked Diana intensely and utterly.

We had stumbled through life, adding year after year onto our marriage – twenty years, twenty-five years, on and on. During those years, Diana had told me many times that she'd be leaving me when the kids had gone. I would always reply, 'Good.' I was so miserable, but I simply didn't have the guts to do anything about it.

Admittedly, I'd had the odd fling. In 1995 I'd met a girl from Canada named Andrea Sorrenston. We'd met at the Canadian Open Darts Championship and had hit it off instantly, then arranged to meet at the next tournament, in Las Vegas, and then again at the Boston Open. We'd go out to dinner together and talk for hours, and eventually we became something more than just good friends. So it came as rather a shock when I received a telephone call one night at home from Andrea, who was ringing to tell me that she'd decided to get married to one of her old boyfriends. Admittedly we'd not seen each other for quite some time, and Andrea had decided – just like Penny had – that she wanted a life of her own, including kids. I, of course, was taken – married – and she couldn't see me leaving my big house and all the trappings of success and heading off to Canada.

But my life rolled on after Andrea had left it. By this time, Diana and I had stopped having sexual relations completely. This wasn't something I was proud of, and little did I know at the time that Diana was telling everyone that it was all my fault.

Back in 1992, I'd joined with some friends and bought a local pub, which we refurbished and reopened as the Unicorn. The pub was given a great boost when I won my third world championship the following year. When I'd come back from Lakeside with the Embassy World Professional Darts

Championship trophy, Diana and I had headed for the Anchor on Factory Street to celebrate. (We couldn't use the Unicorn as it was still undergoing refurbishment.) The drinks flowed good style, with everyone joining in. That night I met Paul 'Raga' Rawsen and his wife, Karen. I remember thinking at the time how good Karen looked and how lucky he was to have a nice wife like that. Despite the celebrations, I suppose I was feeling sorry for myself.

Anyway, it was only a matter of a few weeks before I found out that Karen was a good darts player, unlike her husband who loved the game to bits but was unable to improve his game. They both joined the Unicorn darts team and we became friends.

I noticed over the next year or two that the relationship between Paul and Karen was stormy, to say the least. One of the customers confirmed that it was and told me that things became quite violent behind closed doors. I took little notice at that time. After all, it was none of my business. All I was interested in was filling the pub and the till.

The Unicorn was a good pub with a good atmosphere, and we enjoyed some great nights there. I was still Diana's husband to everyone, and no one seemed to be aware that our marriage was a complete sham. Every night I wasn't working, we'd go to the Unicorn, where Diana would sit with her friend Sheila Cannon and I would play darts with the lads. We'd eventually go home at about eleven o'clock, and when we'd get back Diana would go to bed and I'd watch the TV until I fell asleep, sometimes waking at three or four in the morning, freezing cold.

The directors of the company set up to run the Unicorn were all from different walks of life. They all held good jobs and the pub was only a pastime for them – a pastime that turned into a nightmare.

We'd problems with staff from the start, with money going missing. When the member of staff responsible repaid the money, we kept her on. But then, in 1997, the same person was caught again with her fingers in the till. Again she repaid in full, but by then the pub was on a downhill slide.

Along with fellow director David Brook, I decided that action had to be taken, so I proposed to each of the five other directors that I'd buy all of his shares for £1. After a few discussions, they decided to sell, recognising a good offer when one was presented. I was, after all, taking on a debt of over £30,000. It took me a whole year to turn the Unicorn around into a profit-making business and I lost a few friends in the process. Even so, now that the company had only two directors – myself and David – things were much easier to control. The downside was the amount of time I was putting into the business. Instead of being out earning money by playing in exhibitions, I was in the Unicorn entertaining visitors. (The full story of the Unicorn 'experience' is described elsewhere in this book.)

In 1997 something happened that would change my life forever. The Rawsens had an almighty fight. Although it had been behind closed doors, it resulted in Karen going to the hospital and later to the police station. A restraining order was served on her husband, Paul, and Karen decided to file for divorce on the grounds of physical abuse.

I'd become good friends with Karen, while I still often talked and played darts with Paul. One day I asked her out for a meal. She agreed and we became close – so close, in fact, that I knew I'd fallen in love with her.

This was the beginning of the end of my marriage to Diana. Karen and I tried to keep our dates secret, even though Karen had no need to, as she was technically on her way to becoming single. However, she thought it was better that no one knew about us until we were both absolutely certain that we wanted our relationship to continue. Not for the first time Karen's soon-to-be-ex-husband Paul was regretting his actions and tried his best to get back with her.

People began to talk. They noticed that Karen and I would often stand together at the bar, doing the Saturday crossword, and that we'd often play darts together. I suppose it was obvious that something was going on. To say that I was worried at this time would be untrue, however, although I couldn't go anywhere without being noticed as I had a truck with 'LCL Pils' advertising all over it and kept my jaguar at home in the garage.

Karen and I would meet on Saturday afternoons and go for a ride into the Derbyshire villages, such as Youlegrave, where the George Hotel was one of our hostelries. I'd played an exhibition there back in 1972 and my photograph was still on the wall, complete with flares and long hair! We had many a laugh at the George, and we still do when we go back there.

Back at the Unicorn, Diana's friend Sheila Cannon was becoming more interested in what Karen and I were doing. At one stage she even asked Karen if anything was going on between us – as if Karen would tell her! (Sheila was known as 'the Derbyshire Times', and for good reason.) Diana, Sheila and Paul would all stand together at the Unicorn bar, making plans and trying to dig up the dirt.

I couldn't work out why Paul was bothered, as he had another girlfriend by that time – and not one, in fact, but two or three. If he was trying to get back together with Karen, he was going about it in a rather funny way.

Then lots of silly things began to happen. I received an envelope in the mail containing two white feathers, which I presumed was supposed to imply I was a coward. I questioned a few people who I thought might have sent them but, not surprisingly, all denied having anything to do with it.

Then one night in the Unicorn, Paul followed me into the toilet. I knew what was about to happen. He asked me what I was doing with his wife and if I was taking him for a fool. No, I said; I was not taking him for a fool, and whatever it was I was doing, it was nothing to do with him. I told him he was making it quite clear that he didn't want to have anything to do with Karen, so why the questions?

His reaction was as I expected. First, he gave me a load of verbal abuse and then a fist came my way. To this day, I'm not sure if it connected, although I'm told that it did by a friend of mine, Neil Marsden, who'd realised that something was amiss and came into the toilet to investigate. He grabbed Paul and told him to calm down before the police were called. I went back to the bar.

But was that the end of the matter? Oh, no. I found myself explaining to Paul that I was seeing his wife, who I presumed was soon to be his ex-wife. I told him that I didn't consider that I was doing anything wrong – well, other than the fact that I was still living at home with Diana. To my amazement, he shook my hand and asked me to look after Karen. Then, the very next moment, Paul was asking Karen if she'd visit him when I was away! We all knew what that meant.

A few months later, Karen divorced Paul on the grounds of her husband's unreasonable (ie violent) behaviour.

Then everything came to a head one Friday morning in October 1997. That day I arrived at the Unicorn at about 12:30 and there, outside the door, was a cameraman and another man with a notebook in his hand. I only had to take a look at the camera to know he was a professional.

'Hello John,' said one of the men. 'We're from *The Sun*. We understand you're having a relationship with a divorcèe from your darts team.'

The full story of this part of my life is recorded elsewhere in this book. Suffice to say here that I asked the guys from *The Sun* to tell me what they'd been told and by whom.

I agreed to co-operate, however, and the *Sun* reporter told me that Paul had called them and informed them that I'd broken up his marriage, and that the newspaper had paid Paul £400 for the story.

I then gave them my side of the story, about me and Karen and about the restraining order placed on Paul that prevented him from going anywhere near Karen. I agreed to have my photograph taken, just as long as they included the Unicorn's sign in the shot. Well, I thought, if I was going to appear in the national daily comic, I might as well promote the pub at the same time.

When I arrived home a few hours later, the press had visited my house to interview Diana. She didn't seem too upset when I got back, and she didn't have a go at me. I think she'd known what was coming. The reporters had also interviewed Karen.

The story was out the next day, a half-page slot under the headline – in typical *Sun* style – 'SLING YER ARROWS: WIFE DUMPS DARTS ACE LOWE OVER AFFAIR WITH DIVORCÉE IN PUB TEAM', then going on to relate, 'Bitter wife Diana, John's partner for thirty-two years, has filed for divorce.' Apparently, Diana had said to the reporters, 'Paul wants revenge on John and I don't blame him.'

In fact, I was quite relieved to read *The Sun*'s comments, which read, 'Door-to-door pop salesman Paul, 37, was dumped by 40-year-old Karen after he was twice convicted of assault.' I thought, 'Nice one. At least they told everyone about that.'

To be honest, there wasn't anything in the article that was really bad. It was as if no one had had anything to say. It was really just a story about a well-known celebrity whose marriage had hit rock bottom, who had met someone else and who had left two people moaning and complaining and passing the blame when really it was their own fault that this scenario had occurred.

I felt sorry for my kids, though, who I hadn't told about the affair. Adrian seemed to accept it readily enough – I suppose he'd seen it coming – while Karen went straight into 'must protect my mother' mode.

I was just relieved that it was finally all out in the open. Nobody could do or say anything about us any more. I was down the solicitors' the next day, instructing them to settle the divorce amicably and as quickly as possible – although I'd soon find out that was easier said than done.

Anyone who has been through a divorce will understand it when I say, 'Ouch!' Many will say, 'What a waste of money' – money that could quite easily have been split between the two people going through with the divorce instead of going into the solicitors' account.

I had no trouble with sharing the family assets with Diana, insisting that the house should be sold and all proceeds split equally. I didn't argue about who should keep the contents of the house, either, agreeing to let Diana have ninety-five per cent of the proceeds – everything she'd asked for, really. All I wanted was a couple of things that I considered personal to me, plus a couple of incidentals.

After the family home at Hayfield Close had been sold, which happened very quickly, I went out house-hunting and inside two weeks had found a house that suited me just fine, a four-bedroom detached property with a double garage and a large kitchen (important, as my hobby is cooking). I knew it needed quite a lot of work doing to it, but I'd already been through that with the house at Clay Cross, so I didn't think it would be a problem – indeed, more of a joy – to put the house in exactly the shape I wanted.

Diana, it turned out, had also been doing some house-hunting, and had found a bungalow at Tupton. I found the fact that she intended to move to my birthplace ironic, thinking that it was surprising that she didn't jump at the chance to move closer to her mother at Brimington. I never did find out why she made that decision.

As divorces tend to go, ours was pretty messy. It became obvious to me that Diana's friends, and one in particular, had been telling her to get every penny she could from me. Again, I found that strange, as I was instructing my solicitor to be fair and share everything, and her solicitor was demanding exactly the same. That, to me, sounds like an agreement. I couldn't imagine what was causing the hold-up.

Letters were exchanged and demands were made, and then – lo and behold – I was informed that my bank account would be frozen. I needed money to proceed with my house purchase, but Diana's solicitors saw this as a movement of funds – half of which, they claimed, belonged to Diana. I agreed to pay Diana a considerable sum, even though my solicitor told me that it was in excess of the amount he was sure a court would award her, while Diana's solicitors had no problem advising her that the offer was good and fair. They agreed instantly, and things then began to race ahead.

At that time, I stopped doing exhibitions and went only to the competitions after my solicitor advised me that I'd be silly to keep working, only to have half of all I earned taken away from me. In a way, that suited me fine as I was working on my new home and had meanwhile moved in with Karen at her home in Boythorpe.

You'd think that all the trouble and stress of divorce, buying and selling houses, trying to sort out legal requirements and the like would have taken its toll, but for me it was exactly the opposite. It was as though a great weight had been removed from my back. At last I could think straight and I could see a light at the end of the long dark tunnel that I'd been trudging through for far too long. I believed that everything was going to be just fine from then on.

In December 1998, Karen and I moved into our new house. I'd refurbished everything inside, installing a new bathroom and kitchen and decorating throughout. It was perfect for us. Karen was very happy and I was like a little kid with a new toy.

While I'd been doing up the house, I gave my son the task of filing the weekly account sheets for the Unicorn. What Adrian's summary revealed shocked and dismayed me: there was a shortfall in the banking of £800. I couldn't believe it. 'Not again!' I thought. I confronted the member of staff with the findings and full repayment was promised. I doubted that very much, but I had to hope. In the meantime – some may call me mad – I left that member of staff in charge of the Unicorn but tore up her contract.

CHAPTER 5

Cloud Nine

1999 was an epic year for me, the year in which I asked Karen to marry me, even going down on one knee in the Unicorn, and she accepted. I asked her if she'd like to get married in Las Vegas and she thought that was a great idea, so I started making arrangements through my good friends Bob and Marcki Murdock, who lived in Las Vegas and who I'd known since the Queen Mary days and the North American Open at Long Beach. The wedding would take place on 12 August at the Mandalay Bay Hotel and Casino, one of the very best hotels in Vegas. (Many of the world championship boxing matches are held there.) Marcki Murdock arranged everything, keeping in touch by email. This way, we even chose the wine for the dinner and the restaurant we'd be eating in – all without picking up a telephone.

You might think that, after being married for thirty-two years, I'd have liked a break before committing myself to another long-term relationship, but I didn't think that way. Although many of my friends advised me to wait, 12 August couldn't come soon enough for me. I wanted so much to put my life on a happy track, and I knew that Karen was the one who could make that happen. I made a promise to her that I wouldn't go to any darts events or exhibitions without her, unless of course she was ill or special circumstances arose. The arrangement worked like a dream, and we soon became an inseparable pair.

Before we could set off to Las Vegas, however, there was another wedding to attend. My son Adrian and his longtime girlfriend Karen Smith – yes, another Karen – were to be married on 28 May. I was really pleased for them both. They'd been going out with each other since their Tupton Hall school days. Karen is a lovely girl, sensible and intelligent, and of course I can't speak highly enough about my son. I respect him for who he is and how he treats others.

Naturally, Adrian and Karen's wedding had its difficulties, coming so soon after my divorce from Diana in February 1999. Adrian asked if I minded if they didn't invite my wife to be, considering all that had happened over the last year. Karen understood and, to be honest, she hadn't thought it would have been right for her to turn up on my arm, anyway.

I told Adrian and Karen, my daughter, that I'd meet them at the church on the day of his wedding, and then after the service I'd go to the reception and the dinner, stay for an hour or two and then leave. I knew only too well that, once the drink started to flow, Diana would more than likely have a few words to say to me.

On the day of the wedding, I was a little surprised when I walked up the path to Wingfield Church to see Diana's friend Sheila Cannon sitting on a seat a few yards away from the church, and then, when I approached, she stood up and greeted me like a long-lost uncle. 'Wow,' I thought, 'Things might not be so bad after all.'

Wrong! When I walked around the corner, my daughter was with her boyfriend, Karl, and her mother. They all looked very smart; Diana always liked to dress the part. I walked across and said hello. Two replied; one didn't (no prizes for guessing which one). And that set the pattern for the rest of the day.

All the way through the church service, as the photographs were taken, the guests were welcomed and the dinner was served, Diana was conspicuous by her glares and the sustained silence she radiated. It didn't matter to me, but I thought it wasn't fair on Adrian and Karen, whose day it was meant to be. And it really was a lovely day; the sun was shining and Karen's mother and father had arranged a really special wedding for their daughter. I was also nicely surprised when Diana's mother and family all spoke to me and shook my hand when they came in, hoping that this meant they didn't have any malice towards me.

I remember saying goodbye to the newlyweds and thanking the bride's parents, but sadly I didn't get a chance to say goodbye to my own daughter. She'd been at her mother's side, playing a support role. At that time, she hadn't made her mind up about my new relationship.

When I got home that night, Karen was waiting for me and wanted to know all about the wedding. I smiled, knowing at last that I had someone who really cared about me. I opened a bottle of champagne and we toasted the bride and groom.

Soon it was August and Karen and I were on our way to Vegas. We arrived on Wednesday 9, three days before the big day, as we needed time to arrange for a wedding licence and to take care of any last-minute arrangements. Marcki had done a fantastic job and everything was in place. The next day, when we went downtown to Clark County Offices to pick up the licence, I was amazed to see so many couples waiting in line. Some even had their wedding outfits on, ready to get to the church as soon as their licence was granted!

Saturday morning came and we were both a little nervous. We'd arranged to meet Marcki and Bob Murdock at about 1:30pm in the lounge bar of the Riviera Casino, where a couple of vodkas were the order of the day. We were joined there by Don Skane, my longtime mate from Boston and a great guy, while Keith and Kim Deller and Mike and Michelle Enright – more of our friends – from San Diego were to meet us at the chapel at the Mandalay Bay Hotel, which had arranged for a white stretch limo to pick us up at the Riviera and take us to the chapel.

When the car arrived, it was just like it is in the movies, except no heads turn anymore when a 30ft limo pulls up outside a hotel in Vegas; people don't even look to see who's getting in. Still, that didn't matter. Karen and I felt special, and I could tell that, for all the years Bob and Marcki have lived in Vegas, they still like that feeling of being made special.

The car drove away from the Riviera almost silently. It was impossible to hear the engine. We only had a few minutes' travel ahead of us, though, so the large bar and the crystal glasses in the rear of the car remained in the cabinet.

We arrived at the Mandalay Bay and one of the doormen opened the door of the limo and welcomed us to the Bay on the Strip. And then, when we walked into the waiting area of the chapel, a pleasant surprise was waiting for us: about ten of my friends from the Royal Hawaiian Darting Club were there, waiting to go into the chapel to help us celebrate our marriage. The group included Chuck Jelinsky and his wife, Carole, and David Mellor, the club's secretary. It was a great surprise, although I must be honest and say that, at the time, I was worried that I hadn't invited them all to dinner.

We did not have to wait long before it was our turn. The wedding wasn't the register-office-type affair we have in the UK, nor the stereotypical ceremony in a little white chapel on the Strip with Elvis presiding – although I'm not knocking either of those type of weddings, having enjoyed being at both. For our wedding, Marcki had booked a lady minister from Vegas, a personal friend of theirs, to conduct the ceremony. I felt that this was going to be something special and I wasn't disappointed.

Bob and Marcki would be standing with us, taking the positions that in the UK would be reserved for the best man and matron of honour. Soon everyone took their places and the wedding music began to play. The distance from the door of the chapel to the dais, where the minister would perform the service, was only 100ft or so, but I enjoyed every second of that short walk. I was a very proud man, with a beautiful lady on my arm, although I could tell from the way Karen was holding my arm that she was feeling a little nervous.

When we reached the minister, Bob and Marcki came up to join us. The minister then began the service – a service that was quite personal. She spoke for fifteen minutes or so about the virtues of marriage, and then she went on to tell me that if I ever let Karen down in any way she would come looking for me!

Then it was time for the vows, which we both said loud and clear, looking straight into each other's eyes. I heard a little sniffle to my right, and only later when watching the video did I find out who it was: Marcki Murdock, a guy from Chicago who'd made his home in Las Vegas; Murdock, who'd worked the casinos, becoming pit boss and then finally earning enough to buy his own place, the Happy Valley Inn. There he was, with a handkerchief to his eyes, wiping tears away from under those dark shades of his. It was a moment I'll treasure for ever.

When the minister eventually pronounced us man and wife, the audience all applauded in true American let's-make-some-noise fashion. There were big smiles on everybody's faces. They were all really pleased that the man they'd known for over thirty years was at last truly happy.

Then the lady who ran the chapel asked me if everything had gone to plan. I said yes, but told her that I was a little disappointed as I'd asked for the wedding to be videoed and yet hadn't seen a camera anywhere. She then very politely pointed out that, in today's age of modern technology, the cameras don't have to be seen, and then pointed out some tiny boxes in each corner of the room that I'd thought were infrared security devices. They were cameras, of course, and had captured the wedding from every conceivable angle. What's more the video was already finished, having been edited and set to music, and was in the next room, waiting for collection. Well, let's be honest, this *was* Las Vegas; if you can't get that kind of service there, where can you?

We spent the next forty minutes being snapped by a professional photographer in various places around the chapel, and then it was time to say thank you to the staff and leave for a celebration drink. At this point, I must say to anyone thinking about marrying in Las Vegas, it's a great experience and it's one of the finest locations you could choose. The Mandalay Bay service, complete with video, a bottle of fine champagne, flowers for the bride and groom, and a limo from the hotel and downtown to collect the wedding licence cost me just £600.

When we returned to the Mandalay Bay, we made our way to the sumptuous lounge area of the casino, where I quickly did a head count and ordered a bottle of champagne for everyone in the party. We had only an hour to drink and talk to old friends, and then it was off to dinner at the Oriole, Charlie Parker's famous restaurant, which was also at the casino. I'd invited only close friends to the dinner, as I wanted it to be a special, intimate occasion shared with friends that could all be united around one table. We weren't disappointed.

Our guests for the dinner were Bob and Marcki Murdock, Keith and Kim Deller, Mike and Michelle Enright and Don Skane, and each guest chose his or her own food from the menu, although the wine had been pre-ordered some six months earlier – and we were about to find out why.

Inside the Oriole is a wine tower, thought to be the only one of its kind in the world. It's made of glass and rises some 70ft into the air. Each bottle of wine is kept in a temperature-controlled area designed to suit its flavour. The wines at the bottom of the tower are priced at around $45 per bottle, but the higher you go, the dearer they are, the ones at the very top fetching $2,500 per bottle! Needless to say, we didn't go very far up the tower, but then again we weren't too near the bottom. To retrieve your wine from the tower, girls dressed in black one-piece jumpsuits, looking a little like the man in the TV advert for Black Magic chocolates, go up on ropes, take out the wine and abseil back down again.

The restaurant doesn't have many tables – probably a dozen in the area where we were seated – but they're well spaced out, and you're aware when you're sat at your table that it's your own special party gathered together. Our table was right next to the double glass doors, which were propped open, letting in the balmy ninety-degree air. Outside on the patio area there was a small wall, about 3ft high, behind which was a pond on which six large pink swans were swimming in pairs. It was hard to believe we were in Vegas, the city of lights. We were far from the constant clashing of slot machines. Here it was quiet. No machines, just good friends and a fine meal. Perfect.

The dinner lasted for four hours. There was no need to rush. We had no less than six waiters serving us with food and wine. I sat Murdock at the end of the table, as I knew he'd like that, and anyway he looked like he belonged there, taking his place as the Boss – or should I say pussycat? As ours was a small party, everyone had a chance to express his or her thoughts on the day, and it wasn't until it was my turn to give my thanks that the best-kept secret of the day come out. I remember thanking all our friends for making the day special, and then I produced an envelope from which I took out a card. I handed the card to Bob Murdock and wished him a happy birthday. Pretty soon the sniffle was back, although this time I think we all suffered from it.

Karen and I stayed in Vegas for the next week. I took part in the North American Open, managing to reach the final with my playing partner, Keith Deller, although we later lost to Reg Harding and Shayne Burgess. I wasn't so fortunate in the singles game; I think the wedding celebrations might have caught up with me there!

After the tournament, we were off to Hawaii for our honeymoon. We'd booked into the Beachcomber Hotel, just off Waikiki Beach, arguably the most famous beach in the world, and we had a fantastic time there. Hawaii is a place that grows on you. You don't really know you're going to miss it until you've left, and then you can't wait to revisit it again sometime in the future.

Waikiki itself is an incredible place, as anyone who's been there will tell you. You sit there on the beach with thousands of others, the big surf rolling in only a few yards away, while behind you are rows of beach bars and hotels, and when you're too hot and need a cool drink you just step back a few yards and sit on the deck of some bar and try the local Mai Tai, a colourful vodka-based drink soaked with many wonderful Hawaiian mixers. Looking out to sea, you can see hundreds of people, all waiting for the surf to rise. Then it's up on the surfboard and everyone races in towards the beach.

Just down the road is Honolulu, the capital of Hawaii and a town that everyone should visit, if only to take the boat ride – as we did – out to the sunken warships still there from the Japanese attack on Pearl Harbor in 1941. It's a truly moving experience.

We finished our trip over the big pond with three more days back in Las Vegas and then it was home to start married life.

The next few months after our return were dramatic. The missing funds from the Unicorn had been repaid, so David Brook and I decided it was time to leave the pub business before we were burned again. Owning a pub is a very hands-on business, and the temptation to give free drinks to friends, borrow a few pounds out of the till or maybe take a bottle of spirits with the intention of bringing one back in its place can be hard to resist, and I was relieved when we'd sold the business. Once again, I could concentrate on my darts.

By April 2000, the Unicorn was history. I made a promise not to visit, as it was only fair to let the new management have a chance to bury the ghost. I did keep out for a while, but old habits die hard and we'd call in every now and again, although that was mainly to see my old mate Satchmo. 'Satch', as we call him, is a Jamaican who runs his own garage, repairing cars old and new, and he's also a great singer. I take him with me to some of my local exhibitions, where I play the darts and he entertains the crowds afterwards. We usually celebrate our birthdays on the same day, although the actual dates are a couple of months apart. Whenever we hooked up, ten minutes would turn into two hours and we'd have a great time.

One thing that was a little hard to bear was that Karen's ex-husband, Paul, would also use the pub, and occasionally the previous managers would be in, too, so the pub didn't have the best of atmospheres. But, of course, that works both ways, and eventually Karen and I chose to stay away entirely.

CHAPTER 6

No Blame, No Regrets, Moving On

They say time is a great healer. Well, that all depends on what needs healing.

It's now 2005. I've been divorced for over six years and Karen has been for slightly longer. My children have accepted that my divorce from their mother was inevitable, and I'm sure they know by now that it didn't just happen because I met Karen. My marriage to Diana had broken down irrevocably before I'd met her, and it would have been only a matter of time before one of us left or, even worse, something terrible had happened.

It was probably a shock for Diana that I chose to leave first, taking the first step to giving us both new lives. I don't lay the blame with anyone; Diana and I were equally to blame. I know that the change in my work pattern didn't help matters. From being a daytime worker, almost overnight I became a world traveller – and I travelled on my own. That's not a good recipe for trust for either party. The mind begins to wander. When someone is 3,000 miles away, the saying 'out of sight, out of mind' rings very true.

Diana did a great job bringing up my children while I travelled the world, playing darts and generally having a good time, and I'll always be grateful to her for that. I've tried to forget the bad times and get on with my new life with Karen. At the time of writing, Diana has a new boyfriend who by all accounts is a decent bloke, and I'm told that they're happy together and share the same interests in life.

Meanwhile, on the other side of the equation, Karen's ex-husband, Paul, seems to be getting on with his life, too. He never struck me as being someone who wanted a lot out of life; as long as he had a few pounds in his pocket, a drink with his mates, a girl at his side and the odd fight now and again, he was happy, which just shows how different we all are. Paul and Karen didn't have any children of their own; her son, Jason, was from an earlier relationship.

And then it was marriage time once again. My daughter Karen had decided that a trial period of seven years is long enough and that it was time she married her boyfriend. Many years ago she was a bridesmaid at the wedding of the daughter of one of my friends. It was a grand affair with a marquee accommodating 200 people, a pig roast and a bottle of wine for every guest. It had cost an arm and a leg, but the bride was the only daughter of the family, and that was the norm – if you could afford it. Sadly, the marriage did not last two years. I remember saying to Karen, 'If you decide to get married, take a good look at that relationship. Let me take you to Las Vegas to get married and have a great honeymoon. I'll give you a cheque for what the wedding would have cost over here.'

I never thought for one moment that she'd take me up on my offer. Well, she did, and in June 2004 Karen married Karl Heaton at the MGM Grand Hotel in Las Vegas. Following in dad's footsteps? Probably not. Just common sense. Because they'd lived together for so long, many people thought that they were married already, so what did they need a toaster for?

I know what you're thinking: like father, like daughter? Well, in this instance, yes. At 5pm on 26 June 2004, my daughter, Karen, entered the Forever Grand Wedding Chapel. She was about to become Mrs Karen Heaton.

A lot of planning had gone into making this day a very special one. I'd booked the chapel some eight months prior to the wedding, while a room in the Grand Tower with views of the Las Vegas Strip and its casinos had also been secured with the help of my very good friend Marcki Murdock. Dinner, meanwhile, had been booked at the steakhouse at Circus Circus, an award-winning restaurant and, indeed, one of the finest in Vegas. It's also situated at the opposite end of the Strip to the MGM, making it perfectly placed for the bride and groom to enjoy a ride down the Strip in a gleaming white limousine.

Although the planning of the wedding had been meticulous, I was understandably a little apprehensive that things wouldn't run smoothly, although as it turned out I'd had no need to concern myself. One thing at which the Americans excel is service; you ask and they provide, and in a courteous manner that many countries should heed and adopt.

The wedding party was small and manageable, comprising fourteen in total: the bride and groom, my wife and myself, Cliff Lazarenko, Don and Barbara Skane, Ian and Audrey Logan (at whose daughter's wedding Karen had been bridesmaid), Marcki Murdock, Andrew Gosling (the best man), David Brook and Kaarn, his Thai girlfriend, plus Jay Tomlinson, my good friend and editor of *Bull's Eye News*, who was covering the wedding for his magazine. Karl's mum and dad were unable to be with us for medical reasons, but they more than made up for their absences by holding a reception for the bride and groom upon their return home to Lancashire, serving up an entire pig roast! However, Diana, my ex-wife, refused to come to Las Vegas for her own personal reasons (none of which, I have to admit, I found valid), nor did she make it to the reception back in the UK that Karl's parents organised.

I'd planned the whole Las Vegas experience down to the last detail: meeting the party as they arrived at the airport, checking them into their hotel suite, having a bottle of champagne and a vase of flowers delivered to their room on arrival, and then off to Clark County Court to obtain the wedding licence. Of course, I'd had a similar experience five years earlier, when I'd married Karen, and it's fascinating. There's usually a line of around fifty people, all waiting to go into the office that issues the wedding certificates. Some are dressed in full wedding attire with large limousines waiting outside to whisk them away to the little white chapel or some other exotic place to be married, while others have arrived in whatever they dressed in that morning: torn jeans, shorts, even fancy dress. Many of the latter obtain their licence and then get married straight away on the steps outside the courthouse.

On 25 June, the day before the wedding, I took Karl, Karen and Andrew (nicknamed 'Goose') into the Golden Nugget, which is almost next door to the courthouse and one of Las Vegas' oldest casinos, to show them the world's largest solid gold nugget. I was glad I did; they remarked, 'The casino should cash it in and spend the money refurbishing.' They were quick to realise that downtown Las Vegas has been left behind as the Strip has moved into the twenty-first century. The MGM Grand, Mirage, Balagio and Monte Carlo casinos are so modern and impressive that older establishments like the Golden Nugget, Banions and the Four Queens have been left looking tired and outdated. I felt pleased; my friends had entered Vegas at the top end, and now they were witnessing the not so good. Personally, I always feel a sense of history and nostalgia when I visit downtown Vegas, as that's where it all began. I imagine Frank Sinatra and Dean Martin sitting at the blackjack table, with the rest of the Rat Pack looking on. I wonder if they really did that sort of thing.

That evening, we all met up for a drink in the MGM's cocktail bar, intending to let everyone mix and get to know each other, then call it a night around midnight. Intentions are one thing, however; Cliff Lazarenko is another.

Midnight came and most of the party had left for bed. Those that were left – me, my wife, my daughter, Karl, Goose, Cliff, David Brook, Roger Wilkinsen (producer of Sky Sports) and Don Skane – were in good spirits. The drinks were flowing and Cliff was in party mood. Then the girls decided that it should be Karl's last night of freedom and retreated to bed at about 1:30am. I promised to follow shortly.

At 5:30 in the morning, it was decided that we should drink a toast to all the good people we'd lost during the year. We started with a large Absolut vodka on the rocks with a twist of lime, Bob Murdock's favourite tipple, and then we had a large scotch in remembrance of Barry Twomlow, the man who taught the world to play darts. A large brandy followed for Peter Lippiatt, my driver and MC for over twenty years.

By now we were on a roll and decided that it was about time we had a drink to all our friends, the ones who had departed and the ones who remained. It was champagne time!

I finally decided to retire at 6:30am, leaving Cliff and David Brook deep in a discussion about which drink they'd order next. I remember smiling to myself as I entered the elevator and thinking, 'I don't have too many close friends, but the ones I do have are the best.'

I was up bright and early on Saturday 26 June, my daughter's big day. I still had some last-minute preparations to make – booking a limo, getting my suit pressed and getting a deal on the champagne. For obvious reasons I didn't want to pay the early-morning price of $116 a bottle, so I needed to enlist the help of someone who could make decisions – in this case, the casino drinks manager. (One good thing about Vegas is that, if you need to see someone about ordering drinks, you don't have to wait until opening time; the bars never close.) By nine o'clock that morning, I'd ordered eighteen bottles of champagne at $45 a bottle. This was going to be a good day!

My wife had arranged to be with my daughter and escort her to the beauty salon for her last-minute facial, after which they'd meet us at the chapel. Meanwhile, I arranged to meet with everyone in the casino's cocktail bar, just a few minutes' walk from the chapel, at 4:30pm, an hour before the wedding was scheduled to take place.

When we met up at the bar, everyone was looking great. We had a couple of drinks there and then made out way to the Forever Grand Wedding Chapel. I went into the brides' dressing room and, let me tell you, I was amazed. My daughter looked absolutely stunning. I know all dads will say the same on their daughters' wedding day, and rightly so, but this was different. I was witnessing an amazing transformation. The Karen I knew and visited in Longridge, Preston, usually wore a pair of jeans and a nice top, but here, before my very eyes, was this elegant lady, dressed for the most important day of her life. To say I felt proud would be the biggest understatement of all time. I had to turn away for a brief moment, pretending I had something in my eye, but I don't think I was fooling anyone.

The wedding service was wonderful. I walked my daughter into the chapel, stopped halfway down the aisle and the minister then asked, 'Who will give this lady to be wed?'

'I do', I replied.

Karl then walked up the aisle from the front of the chapel, shook my hand, took hold of Karen's arm and escorted her to the front of the chapel. I took my seat alongside my mate Cliff Lazarenko while my wife stood next to my daughter and Goose stood with Karl.

The ceremony itself was a solemn occasion and yet cordial. The minister impressed on the couple the importance of their vows and the true meaning of the rings they were about to exchange. Karl was in good form, making sure everyone in the chapel heard every word he spoke. The only hitch came when the minister asked him to place the ring on Karen's finger. He let go a little early and the ring fell on the floor. Everyone laughed, including the minister, and of course the moment was captured for ever on DVD, as well as being webcast live. (Well, what else would you expect? This was Las Vegas!)

When the service was over, the bride and groom moved into the studio next door to have their photographs taken by Jay Tomlinson, who was busy capturing every moment for *Bull's Eye News* and everyone was congratulating everyone else. I breathed a sigh of relief, glad that everything had gone according to plan – in truth, probably better than planned.

Soon it was time to get everyone together for the drinks reception before we made our way to dinner. The champagne corks popped for the next hour and the cameras never stopped flashing. I'd bought twenty disposable cameras with me from England and now handed them out to the guests and asked them to click away, anywhere and at any time. This way, I reasoned, we were sure to finish up with some great informal shots of the bride and groom and their guests. I wasn't disappointed.

After the reception it was time to make the journey down the Strip to Circus Circus, and as we left the building the biggest white stretch limo I'd ever seen was parked, waiting for us, outside the main entrance to the MGM. The smiles on Karen and Karl's faces said it all.

I'll never forget that twenty-minute drive down the Las Vegas Strip. I knew the windows were tinted and that no one could see in, but I still imagined that they were looking at all of us, the happiest people in town.

I'd eaten at the Circus Circus steakhouse many times over the previous twenty-five years, and the dinner we had there that day was, as always, superb. Bob and Marcki always insisted that we had dinner there at least once every time we came over, and I was pleasantly surprised when the maître d' welcomed me with the words 'Hello, Mr Lowe. It's nice to welcome you back. Thank you for allowing us to serve you on such a wonderful occasion.' I was left thinking, 'Can this day get any better?'

The manager of Circus Circus had laid out seating for fourteen people in the centre of the room. The other diners were seated around us, which made for a great atmosphere, and everyone seemed to join in with the party spirit. As I asked the guests to order from the menu, I knew in advance from many years of eating at the Circus that no one would be disappointed.

As we waited for our starters, the newlyweds opened the many cards they'd received, while I asked Goose, the best man, to read them out. Normally that wouldn't have been a problem, but with all the other diners within earshot he asked if he could pass.

'No problem,' I said. 'I know just the man for the job.'

Turning to my left I handed the cards to Cliff Lazarenko, who was only too pleased to take centre stage, and in his own inimitable way he proceeded to read them out to one and all. He did stutter a little when he opened one card, however, that read, 'Good wishes and good luck' and was from Robbie Williams. Yes, *the* Robbie Williams had taken the time to send Karen a card!

Actually, I know Robbie's father very well and he told me that Robbie was in Los Angeles at that time, looking to buy a house, and I'd contacted him and told him that, if he had the time to join us for dinner, he'd be most welcome. He did the next best thing and sent a lovely card.

Dinner at the Circus is never rushed. We sat down at eight o'clock and, before we knew it, after the speeches had been made, and the chefs and all the staff had all been thanked for making the night truly memorable, it was midnight and time to make our way back to the MGM and finish the day off with a nightcap.

When we returned to MGM's cocktail lounge, the bar manager approached me. 'Mr Lowe,' he said, 'would you like me to bring the remainder of your champagne for your guests?'

'I certainly would,' I replied, and soon the champagne was flowing again. We all sat around, reminiscing about Karen and Karl's day – a day that I think will be talked about for many a year by the people who were present for it. And talking of which, as we were sat there, who should walk into the bar but Steve Davis? The snooker champion duly obliged us by having his photograph taken with the newlyweds.

There was no set time for the day to end; the end came when the last drop of champagne left the last remaining bottle. One o'clock? Two o'clock? Who knows? The bride and groom had left us long ago, while others had also said their goodnights and gone to bed. Of those left, my wife was sat on my right with Cliff, David Brook, Don Skane and Barbara opposite. Cliff held out his hand and gave me a firm handshake. 'Well done, mate,' he said. 'It was a great day. One I'm truly proud to have been a part of.' A few tears rolled down his face. I knew then that it was time to leave before we were all crying.

A few days later, on 1 July, we escorted Mr and Mrs Heaton to the airport and said our goodbyes. It was now time to turn my attention to darts and the Desert Classic. Sadly, though, the happy feelings we had did not last long. On Saturday, 3 July we received a telephone call to say that my wife Karen's mother had passed away. She'd been ill for some time, but her death still came as a shock. I immediately rang the airline and changed our tickets. We flew home the next day.

But for every sad day there seems to be, eventually, a compensating day of joy and that day came on 18 May 2005 when the Lowe family line was assured for another generation by the birth of my beautiful grandson James, a son to Adrian and Karen.

When the birth is over and when any fears about health have been allayed and you see the miracle that is life before you there is nothing but happiness and joy. It took me such a long time to come to terms with what the birth of James meant to the Lowe family. I was overwhelmed and so, so happy.

Back in September 2004, Adrian and his wife Karen came round to see Karen and me to tell us that they were expecting a baby. Apart from the hugs and kisses of congratulation a few glasses of bubbly were drunk in celebration and with a wish for a trouble-free pregnancy. In fact, the next nine months simply flew by and then on that Wednesday in May when Karen finally gave birth to a healthy baby boy I felt an immense sense of pride. I was a granddad for the first time and I loved it!

A number of people have told me in the past that they felt older the day they became grandparents. Well, in my case, it was quite the reverse. I felt several years younger. It was a feeling I cannot put into words, but one I know many thousands of you have experienced. The joy of grandparenthood seems unrelenting!

While I wished Adrian and Karen a healthy child, I could not help but have a few selfish moments hoping that the baby would be a boy. To be honest, I was almost praying for a boy – not just for myself you understand but for my father and his father before him. Tradition is something we British are associated with, that and a respect for traditional family values. In my view, tradition can be no better demonstrated than carrying on the family name. However, tradition aside, if the baby had been a girl, I am absolutely sure that I would love her just the same as I do James.

And talking of tradition, one tradition that I could not ignore was wetting of the baby's head. James is a few months old now but I am still wetting his head, but at the same time remembering many friends who have left this life and wishing that they had stayed that little while longer to see the 'Old Stoneface' crack with smiles at the arrival of baby James.

Cheers to one and all!

That is my family story – so far.

Now on with the darts!

CHAPTER 7

My Quest to be Best
The Embassy Years

Only one thing can make you the best in most sports; to be world champion. You could be the number-one ranked player in the world, but that wouldn't make you the best in the public's eyes or those of your peers. Everyone has a place in their chosen sport, and not all can make it to the very top. Those who do are the true champions – the world champions.

My quest to be the best started at a club called the Heart of the Midlands in Nottingham in 1978, at the very first Embassy World Professional Darts Championship. There were only thirteen players in that inaugural event and – would you believe it? – only three were Englishmen: Alan Glazier, Eric Bristow and me. Then there were two from the USA (Conrad Daniels and Nicky Virachkul), two from Sweden (Stefan Lord and Kenth Ohlsson), two from Wales (Alan Evans and Leighton Rees) and two from Scotland (Bobby Semple and Rab Smith), while the remaining two (Tim Brown and Barry Atkinson) were from Australia. A truly representative world field? Not really. The truth was that thirty-two top professional darts players couldn't be found in the UK, so the field was made up with players from other countries.

All the players were nervous at the start of this big event. This was new to everyone – the BDO (British Darts Organisation, the organisers), the sponsors (Imperial Tobacco) and the players. BBC Television had never covered a seven-day darts tournament before and they were just as apprehensive as everyone else.

My first opponent was Scotland's Bobby Semple. The match was the best of eleven legs, and I needed very little time to get into the groove, beating Bobby by six legs to one. But it wasn't an easy victory – not on your life! – but I did enjoy my new-found fame as a TV sportsman.

Things stayed the same in the last eight with another six–one win, this time over Tim Brown of Australia.

The semi-final, however, was much harder and was the best of fifteen legs. I was up against a seasoned professional, Sweden's Stefan Lord, who I beat by eight legs to four – a good result considering the quality of my opponent.

In the other semi-final, Leighton Rees was playing the 'Happy Thai', Nicky Virachkul, after having beaten his friend and playing partner Alan Evans in the quarter-final quite easily. He didn't have it all his own way with Nicky, though, and almost lost the match, but he came out the winner by eight legs to seven. I thought I could see a crack in Leighton's play, though; his average had dropped from thirty-one per dart to twenty-six per dart, and I thought I'd probably beat him on that form.

Unfortunately, that turned out to be wishful thinking as Leighton proved he was back at his brilliant best for the 21-leg final, beating me to win the first Embassy World Professional Darts Championship by eleven legs to seven. When I left the tournament, though, I wasn't that disappointed; I knew I'd be back and one day would lift the trophy in my quest to be the best.

In 1979 the Embassy World Championship moved to a new venue at Jollees nightclub, Stoke-on-Trent, which was a far bigger place than the Heart of the Midlands and had a real theatre atmosphere. The BDO had also changed the format of the tournament from legs to sets. I could not wait to get started and had been practising hard. The number of competitors had been increased to twenty-four, with sixteen players playing in the first round and then the top eight (including myself) coming into the event in the second round. At that point I'd play the winner of the match between Doug McCarthy and Charlie Ellix. I had great respect for both players, but I thought Charlie would beat Doug and I knew I'd have to play at my very best to beat him.

First surprise of the event: Doug beat Charlie by two sets to one. I felt a little happier with this result!

When the first round had been completed, it was my turn to take the stage. I played really well and was never troubled by the competition, attaining the highest average of the first round (thirty per dart) and beating Doug two sets to nil.

Jocky Wilson made his entrance to big time darts in this second Embassy, and he was my top quarter-final opponent. I knew he was a good player and could be controversial, but I also knew that, if I played my game, he was going to find it difficult. As it turned out, I beat Jocky three–one in a game that was better than the score line suggested. And so I was in the semi-final for the second year in a row.

Leighton Rees, the defending champion, was going nicely and had dropped only one set, while Eric Bristow – many people's favourite to win – was dumped out of the event by Wales's Alan Evans, three sets to one. I played Dover's Tony Brown in the semi-final in a very tight match, sneaking a three–two win, while in the other semi-final the Welsh boys, Evans and Rees, battled it out. Then Leighton came through, and it turned out that the final would be a repeat of the previous year.

I was travelling home after each round to Chesterfield but when it came time to play the semi-final, I needed to be free from all distractions and so decided to stay at the event hotel. On Saturday, 9 February 1979 I was up early, had breakfast and walked to Jollees, all the time quietly thinking that it might be the biggest day of my darts career. When I arrived at the venue at about eleven o'clock, the cleaners were still in the building, so I went into the small band room backstage to practise. I helped myself to a vodka and orange juice and began pounding the treble twenty.

It was quite a while before Leighton appeared. When he did turn up, he looked over to me and said, 'Having an orange, John?'

'Yes, Leighton,' I replied. 'You know me. Not really a drinking man.'

'That's not what the cleaner just told me,' he said, and with that he went out of the room and over to the official practice area to sharpen up. First blood to Leighton.

The match was nothing like the pre-match wind-up the media had built up. It was great for me, but very disappointing for Leighton. I went off like a rocket and before the audience had settled down I was three–nil up, at which point we took a break, to return for the evening session at 7pm. That second session, I was still on form and won the match five sets to nil before some of the spectators had the chance to take their seats! I was the new world champion. My quest had been realised. I was the best.

In darts, you can't rest on your laurels. Think you've made it? No. You have to prove it all over again. Nothing short of winning the same title twice convinces anyone that you weren't just lucky. I knew I had to go back to Jollees the next year and prove that I was a worthy winner. And so in 1980 it was a case of 'Long live the king; the king is dead' for John Lowe when I was outplayed and well beaten (two–nil), being dumped out in the first round by my good friend Cliff Lazarenko.

1981 was a little better. I was playing well at that time and knew I'd take some beating. However, during the quarter-finals I caused a bit of controversy in the quarter finals in my game against Welshman Ceri Morgan because for some reason I kept leaving the centre bull (fifty points). I didn't do this intentionally; it just happened. Not once did I go eighteen, double sixteen or ten, double top; I just went dead centre and finished on the cork no fewer than seven times. The commentator for the match, Tony Green, said that I was out of order and that I was, for want of better words, 'taking the piss', and a lot of players agreed with him. I just thought, 'Sod the lot of you.' All parts of the dartboard are there to be hit. The bull is double twenty-five, and should the chance to hit it come my way, then bingo!

So it was that I found myself in the final for the third time. This time I was up against the 'Crafty Cockney', Eric Bristow. It was a good final and one I feel I should have won, but sadly it wasn't to be. Eric claimed the first of his five Embassy titles by beating me five sets to three.

It was a similar story in 1982, when once again, after seven days of hard play, I made the final, this time up against Scotland's wee Jocky Wilson. Once again I finished runner-up, and once again the score line read five–three. The defending champion, Eric Bristow, had done what I'd done after winning in 1979, although in Eric's case he'd gone out in the first round to Irish player Steve Brennan.

The next year, 1983, was a great one for darts. It was the year of the underdog – the underdog in question being Keith Deller. Keith came to the finals via the difficult route, through the qualifiers, and played quite brilliantly all week, averaging around twenty-nine points per dart in every match. On the way to becoming champion he knocked out Nicky Virachkul, Les Capewell, defending champion Jocky Wilson and – oh yes – me. Then, in a great final, he beat Eric Bristow after Eric declined the chance to finish on the bull's eye and keep the match alive. Keith then calmly took up his position at the oche and threw sixty with his first dart, fifty-four on a treble eighteen with his second and double twelve with his third for a 138 out-shot. Game, set and match! The 'Milky Bar Kid' was the new Embassy world champion.

The following year, things were very much different for me. In 1984 I was on top form, having played some fantastic darts in exhibitions and promotions for my sponsors, Unicorn, and I went into the first round firing on all cylinders. During that year's tournament I achieved the best average at any Embassy to date, beating Tony Brown by two sets to nil with an average of thirty-three points per dart. I carried on in this vein in the second round, beating John Joe O'Shea, a great Irish player, by four sets to nil. Welshman Ceri Morgan was next in my sights, and it was another whitewash, this time five–nil. I arrived for the Friday night semi-final very confident of reaching the final and my second title win.

I'd been up most of Thursday night with an irritating cough, and by the time I'd reached the venue I was sweating and didn't feel good at all. 'Just my luck,' I thought. 'I've played brilliantly all week, and now I feel rotten.'

I asked Peter, my driver, to fetch me some strong tablets. He came back with some paracetamol. I downed four tablets and, without thinking, asked for a large port and brandy.

By the time the caller announced the start of the semi-final, I was feeling a little better. I took the stage and instantly felt the 100-degree heat burning down on me. I knew there and then that it wouldn't be my night. I tried – by God, did I try! – but it was no good. Sweat was pouring off me. The tablets and the port and brandies – yes, I'd had a few – were fighting each other inside my body. I thought I was going to die.

I remember the MC calling, 'Game, set and the match to Eric Bristow,' and thinking, 'Thank God – it's over,' and then I left the stage and went back to the band room, where Peter was waiting.

'Are you OK?' he asked.

'Yes,' I replied. 'I'll be fine in a few minutes.'

Then Olly Croft came rushing into the room to see if I was all right and asked if I needed a doctor.

Eric Bristow was very kind in his TV interview. He said, 'That was not the John Lowe I know playing up there tonight.' I went home that night saddened by the fact that I'd played so well all week but then, at the last moment, I'd been pole-axed by a virus. Eric went on to win the Embassy, beating Dave Whitcombe by seven sets to one in the final.

On 5 January 1985, I made my annual pilgrimage to the hallowed Jollees, along with the rest of the world's professional darting fraternity. Another Embassy was upon us, and before I knew it I was in the quarter-final. This time my opponent was the 1983 world champion Keith Deller. What a fantastic match that was! I upped the Embassy average record to thirty-four per dart and between us we scored twenty-five ton-eighties. Keith eventually lost, chalking up an average of thirty-two per dart, and I found myself up against Cliff Lazarenko in the semi. On that occasion Cliff was enjoying the best darts of his career, and it was a tough match. I finally won by five sets to three, but the scoreline flattered me.

I was once again in the Embassy final, and no surprises who

my opponent was. Yes, once again, it was Eric 'the Crafty Cockney' Bristow. This time, unlike the previous year's semi-final, when I was very ill, I didn't match Eric's quality of finishing. He was deadly on those doubles and lifted the trophy again after beating me six sets to one.

The following year, the Embassy moved venue again, this time to Lakeside Country Club at Frimley Green, Surrey; turnout at the tournament had become so large that Jollees was no longer big enough to accommodate the many hundreds of spectators. It was a great move, as the new venue was one of the finest cabaret spots in the country, and it also suited darter Bob Anderson as it was the home ground of Surrey County dart team, who he played for.

I sensed it was going to be Bob's week, and he almost proved me right. The 'Limestone Cowboy', as he'd come to be known because of his bright rhinestone cowboy shirts and the fact that he was from Swindon, progressed to the quarters, where he found he was playing yours truly. In one of the best matches of the week, Bob beat me by four sets to three, then had some bad double misses in the semi-final which saw him go out to Dave Whitcombe.

Dave was then up against Eric Bristow in the final, and by his own admission he 'failed to turn up' – not literally, of course, but that day his skills didn't travel with him to the oche. It was an easy victory for Eric, who won six sets to nil.

The following year, 1987, I thought my game was better than anyone else's in the world. I was playing really well and feared no one, and I couldn't wait for the Embassy to come around, although I was a little concerned that I might go off the boil at the wrong time, especially as I'd spent all Christmas throwing thousands of darts. Then, early in the new year, my case was packed and I was off to Lakeside at the crack of dawn on 10 January.

At that year's tournament I was the number two seed and Eric was number one. I thought I had the toughest section of the draw, but my first game was a stroll, and I beat Bobby George by three sets to nil. Then my second-round clash against Dave Lee from London was a high scoring game, and once again I topped the thirty-three-per-dart average while beating Dave by three sets to one. Then it was time to take on my mate 'Big Cliff' Lazarenko, and in that match I was able to raise my game and came out the winner by four sets to nil.

After beating Cliff, I was up against Jocky Wilson in the semi-final. Jocky played well, averaging 30.95 per dart, but it was to no avail; I was in top form and I put Jocky away by five sets to nil.

The final was the one I'd been waiting and hoping for: a rematch with the Crafty Cockney, the match all darts fans wanted to see. In fact, this was the tenth year in succession that either Eric or I had been in the final, and I was up for this match like no other. Thankfully, it was a great game, and it also brought me my second Embassy World Championship title when I beat Eric by six sets to four. It had been a long time coming, but now I had proved myself a worthy champion.

On 17 January 1988, I made my entrance from the player's room at Lakeside to take the stage in front of a packed audience of around 1,500 people cheering and shouting my name. I was the defending champion, and once again I was in the final. My opponent on this occasion was Bob Anderson, after I'd disposed of Eric Bristow in the semi-final, believing that I'd finally laid his ghost to rest.

This final was also one of the greatest ever Embassy finals. Mine and Bob's averages were almost identical. However, I missed a few doubles and Bob didn't, and he became the 1988 Embassy World Professional Darts Champion by six sets to four.

Then, at the 1989 tournament, I wished I hadn't presumed that the ghost of Eric had been banished and that he wouldn't beat me again. How wrong could I have been? I was having a great championship right up until the semi-final. It was then when I faced the Crafty One, and again Eric put on a great display and sent me back to the dressing room after a five–one bruising.

That year, Jocky Wilson had clawed his way to the final, his matches against Alan Warriner and Mike Gregory both going down to the wire. However, Jocky put all that behind him when he stepped onto that stage for the final against Eric Bristow and threw some great darts. At one stage he was beating Eric by a country mile, but then he fumbled a little and watched as Eric won four sets in a row. Jocky was lurching, snatching his darts, and things were looked pretty bad. But then, out of the blue, he returned to form and won the tenth set to claim his second Embassy world crown.

The next year's tournament was a rather quick one, by my standards, as I was at Lakeside for only three days before I was packing my bags and going back to Wingerworth. I was well below my usual form that year, and the World Championship isn't the place to be struggling, as Scotsman Ronnie Sharp proved when he put me out of my misery by three sets to two. That year Phil Taylor from Stoke-on-Trent made his mark on the championship when he went up against Eric Bristow, his mentor, in the final. The Crafty Cockney couldn't match Taylor's power and lost by six sets to one. The master had been beaten by his apprentice.

The next year, my form, although good in the international and world open competitions, wasn't up to the pressure of the world championships, and once again I was packing my bags after only a couple of days at Lakeside. This championship, like the one of the previous year, was the signal of a new champion arriving on the scene, Dennis Priestley, who stamped his mark on the championship and his name on the trophy after beating an out-of-form Bristow by six sets to nil.

In 1992, however, I was hoping for better things. I'd prepared well and was feeling confident. All I needed was a couple of wins under my belt, and then I'd know that I could challenge for the title. So it was that I beat Oyvind Aasland from Norway three–nil in the first round and followed that by beating American Paul Lim in the second, achieving an identical score line. The quarter-finals, however, were a tight affair and I only just managed to beat Graham Miller by four sets to three, after which I was up against Phil Taylor, who had named himself 'the Crafty Potter'. I had a good match but missed doubles cost me dearly and I was out by five sets to four. That year's final, between Taylor and

Mike Gregory, was one of the greatest darts matches of all time, going all the way down to the wire, though Phil finally edged it six sets to five to claim his second Embassy title.

The year was 1993, and it was a year of turmoil, when discontent reigned supreme at Lakeside. The Embassy received more publicity arising from the players' actions than they did from the championship itself. The Players' Association (or 'Union', as some would have it) decided that they'd had enough of seeing their sport disappear from television screens and wanted a say in the running of the game. Meetings with the BDO had failed, so more drastic action was needed, so the players mandated the newly founded World Darts Council (WDC) to represent them at all future world championships and darts events worldwide. The cat was out of the bag and the shit had hit the fan.

Through all of this, the players kept on turning out the magic, and at that year's tournament no fewer than eleven players averaged over thirty per dart in the first round. However, things behind the scenes got worse and BDO officials stopped speaking to the breakaway players. Their attitude was one of 'If you don't behave, we'll take our board down.' I carried on pursuing my usual routine, only practising down the pub, away from the venue, whenever possible.

That year, my second-round opponent was Dutchman Raymond van Barneveld, who was something of a national hero in the Netherlands, and our match was filmed for Dutch TV. However, the TV crew didn't get what they were looking for; their champion was beaten by three sets to two.

In the next round, the quarter-finals, I had a brief scare in my match against Kevin Spiolek but that was about it; the rest was a walk in the park. Then I put out Bobby George – bad back and all – in the semi-final. (Two weeks later, I received a wonderful picture from a lady from Essex that showed Bobby leaping four feet in the air, having just won a leg. The message on the back of the photograph read, 'Good exercise for a bad back.')

The final against Alan Warriner was a rather one-sided affair. It would be the understatement of the decade if I said that Alan was nervous; as he stepped up onto the stage, he could hardly hold his darts and his hands were sweating like mad. It was his first big-time final, and I knew he would learn from it. That day, 9 January 1993, I won my third Embassy title – each one in a different decade – which I guess is testimony to the stubbornness of this Derbyshire lad.

I enjoyed the winners' banquet put on by Embassy that night, using it as a soapbox from which to launch a breakaway group of darts players. There were plenty of red faces to match their coats in the BDO camp when I announced that I'd be represented by the World Darts Council from then on. I could almost hear Olly saying to his BDO colleague Sam Hawkins, 'We'll see about that!' And then my victory night was completed when Peter Dyke of World Promotions said I could keep the Embassy trophy for winning the title in three different decades. I didn't know it at that time, but that was to be the last Embassy championship I'd ever play in.

AVERAGE PER DART		
YEAR	ERIC BRISTOW	JOHN LOWE
1978	24.9	28.77
1979	24.73	29.13
1980	27.99	28.81
1981	29.7	28.34
1982	25	28.74
1983	30.42	30.23
1984	31.52	30.07
1985	31.05	30.46
1986	31.03	29.84
1987	30.42	31.33
1988	29.49	30
1989	29.97	30.25
1990	30.45	29
1991	29.88	29.63
1992	28.67	30.38
1993	28.68	29.16

Many people say that the Embassy championship belonged to John Lowe and Eric Bristow, and I happen to agree with them. Indeed, the facts prove it to be so. Many say Eric played better than me over the sixteen years we competed while others say that I played the better darts and was unlucky not to have won the event more times. This can easily be decided by reading the statistics below, which I've included so that everyone can make up their own minds:

Eric's average per dart over the 16 years: 28.99
John's average per dart over the 16 years: 29.63

FINALS
Eric 10   John 8

CHAMPION
Eric 5   John 3

BEST AVERAGE PER DART YEAR
Eric 1984 with 31.52   John 1987 with 31.33.

Of course, I suppose most people will judge who's best purely by the number of victories they achieved, in which case it's five–three to Eric.

Actually, there's another interesting statistic that I believe indicates the hold Eric and I had over the Embassy World Professional Darts Championship. For the first fourteen Embassies, either Eric or I or both of us appeared in the final. It makes you wonder what might have happened if I hadn't been asked to play that match years ago while the guy went to the toilet or Eric's dad hadn't got him interested in the game as a lad.

Without me around, I think Eric would have done what Taylor did in the 1990s and has continued to do in the new millennium – clean up. Without Eric around, I believe I would have won all eight of the Embassy finals I appeared in, and more.

CHAPTER 8

The Champions and The Greats

My autobiography spans sixty years and darts has played an important part during that time – thirty-nine years so far. Which means that – yes – I was twenty-one before I started playing the sport.

From 1972 onwards, I met and played against the best darts players of the time. Once I'd climbed the ranking ladder to the very top, though, the roles were reversed; it was the next generation of players who were competing against me, and that's the way it still is today. Whenever and wherever I play, my opponents – not surprisingly, perhaps – seem happy if they beat me, knocking me out of a tournament and taking the top scalp. They then usually lose in the next round. That, I guess, is respect.

I write this chapter with the greatest of respect for all of the champions of the sport, and there are many worldwide. However, not many of those champions could easily fit the description of 'champion of darts and a gentleman of life'; that's an accolade that can only be bestowed on the few. Leighton Rees and Barry Twomlow immediately spring to mind, both pioneers and gentlemen, setting proper examples for the subsequent generations of the sport of darts to follow. No biography of mine would be complete without due respect being paid to these two great friends and to some of the other true greats of the sport, and in this chapter I've listed a few such players, from the early 1940s through to the present day, that I believe deserve especial mention.

There are many stories about darts that take place in the early 1900s. Those that have any bearing on the sport have been well documented, especially the one about King George VI and Queen Elizabeth, the Queen Mother, playing a match in Slough in December 1937. Then the circle turned and in 1984 I achieved a perfect nine-dart game there. It was an honour to have followed a king and queen to the oche at Slough, even if it was forty-seven years later and at a different venue.

The names of the legends of the 1930s, '40s and '50s live on today, such as those of Jim Pike, captain of the *News of the World* team of dart champions during World War Two and beyond; Leo Newstead, a member of both the *News of the World* Team and the St Dunstan Four, a team established in 1945 to raise funds for the war-blinded; John Ross, a man who dedicated his entire life to the sport; and Joe Hitchcock, a sensational exhibition player and captain of the St Dunstan Four. All of these were champions in their own right, and I salute them all and pay tribute to their special contribution to the history of the sport of darts.

Of these greats, the only ones I ever met were John Ross, then in his capacity as the secretary of the National Darts Association of Great Britain, and the late, great Joe Hitchcock. John worked tirelessly for darts all his life. He first discovered the game in an amusement arcade in Poplar, east London, when he was fifteen and became hooked from that moment. His organisational flair was undisputed, and he contributed greatly to the success of the *News of the World* Championship and other major events, such as the NODOR Fours.

I met Joe when he came to the second Embassy World Professional Darts Championships at Stoke-on-Trent. Although he was a master of darts, he never won the *News of the World* title, for the simple reason that he never entered it. He's quoted as saying, 'I didn't enter because I was told too many players would drop out if I did.' Good one, Joe.

In the days of these champions, darts was a collar-and-tie

game, although it was played, like today, in the many bars and pubs around the country. The dartboard would usually be fixed over or near a coal fire, with a dim light shining above. When the wind blew, the smoke would come down the chimney and the dartboard would be obscured, and the players would have to wait until it had cleared before taking their next throw.

Joe Hitchcock would play his exhibitions for the Watneys Brewery dressed in a tuxedo and bow tie, and would perform amazing tricks with nails and darts, knocking bottle-tops off of people's ears and matchsticks off their tongues. It was said that he would drink a bottle of rum every night during an exhibition, and when questioned about this he'd ask for three small glasses to be placed on the bar. He would then ask for three pieces of raw meat to be placed in each glass, and when that was done he'd pour whisky into one glass, brandy into the second and rum into the third. He'd leave the glasses at the bar all night, and at the end of his show he'd ask the audience to view the glasses. The meat in the whisky and brandy glasses would be shrivelled, but the meat in the rum glass would be as new. That, he explained, was why he drank rum. Another good one, Joe.

When I won the second Embassy World Professional Darts Championship, against Leighton Rees in Stoke-on-Trent in 1979, after I'd been presented with the trophy by Ray Reardon, then world snooker champion, I went backstage into the band room to have a quiet little celebration with a couple of friends. Then Joe Hitchcock, dicky bow and all, walked into the room. He held out his hand, shook mine and said, 'John, you're a great player.' I thanked him for his kind words, and I'll take them with me forever. Joe Hitchcock was truly one of the greats.

The next era of darts had many champions. The three Tommys – Reddington, Barrett and Gibbons – all won the *News of the World* Individual Darts Championship twice and were the dominant names from 1952 through to 1965. During that time, of course, and probably up until the late 1970s, the *News of the World* Championship was the supreme championship, the one everyone wanted to win.

Then along came another Tommy, the flamboyant Irishman Tommy O'Regan. Tommy was a chip off the Joe Hitchcock block, a natural player, except that he probably drank a little more than Joe. He was a money player and always had plenty of people who would back him. Tommy won the National Darts Association of Great Britain Individual event for three consecutive years, from 1970 to 1972, and ironically went on to become the first and only Irishman to captain the England dart team.

Back in 1975, after I'd been knocked out of the Unicorn World Pairs in London, Tommy was also out, and he invited me down to the Norfolk Arms in Fulham High Road with him and Cliff 'Ticker' Inglis. Little did I know that they had the intention of relieving me of my money! We played on a wooden dartboard for five hours, and I left that day with £500 of their money. Despite that, we became good friends from that day on.

Then, in 1993, I remember walking into the Sahara Hotel, Las Vegas, and seeing a big guy with a cigar in his mouth standing by the bar. He beckoned me over and shook my hand. 'Paul Hong,' he said. 'You must be the famous John Lowe.'

'Yes' I replied. 'I've heard a lot about you, Mr Hong, from Barry Twomlow.'

'Yeah,' said Paul. 'Barry is one of the good guys.' Then he added, 'I hear you play for money?'

'That's right.'

'Well,' Paul went on, 'I have a guy who'll take you on for $1,000 today. Fancy giving him a game?'

To be honest, I was a little wary at this point. I'd never met Paul before that time, and I had no idea who he was talking about, so I asked, 'Who is the player?'

At that point I felt a tap on my shoulder. I turned round and there, with a great big smile on his face, stood Tommy O' Regan. It had all been a wind-up. We drank and talked about old times for the next two hours. Tommy, it seemed, had moved to America, and during the latter part of his life had played and worked in Di's Den in Chicago. I always thought Chicago somehow suited Tommy, an Irish, almost mischievous rogue in the rogue capital of the world. Tommy was a champion, and he was also one of the greats.

In fact, a whole bunch of top players emerged in the O'Regan era. In 1973, in England, Yorkshire Television (YTV) was producing a programme titled *The Indoor League* that covered many indoor pastimes, including darts. It had been devised during a discussion in March 1972 between Donald Baverstock (then a programme director with YTV), director Peter Jones and a youngish darts and shove ha'penny enthusiast named Sid Waddell, and was presented by the famous England cricketer Freddie Trueman.

The Indoor League was the first ever weekly programme to feature darts and ran for a number of years. Its introduction brought players like Harry Heenan, from Scotland; Charlie Ellix, from London; Tony Brown, from Dover; and David 'Rocky' Jones from Wales to our screens.

The programme even featured a ladies' championship which helped raise the profile of the ladies' game on TV. Notable women dart players included Brenda Simpson, from my home town of Chesterfield; Loveday King, from Cornwall; Jean Dickinson, from Stockport; Sandra Gibb, from Wales; and Greta Hallgren, from Sweden, who all became quite famous through the exposure of ladies' darts being shown on television.

The Indoor League was also responsible for my own introduction to television viewers, and I was amazed by the number of people who stopped me in the street to say, 'Well done,' 'Keep it up' and 'We always watch you on the telly, John.' And that was from just one appearance!

The Indoor League also introduced two very famous dart players to the public: Leighton Rees and Alan Evans – the dynamic Welsh duo. For many years, Rees's name was never mentioned without the name Evans, and vice versa. The two were inseparable, also; wherever one went, the other would be there too. A darts organiser from Bristol named Eddie Norman recognised the potential in this great partnership and in 1974 advertised them in *Darts World* magazine as 'the world number one and world number two darts players'. Looking back that time, I don't think anyone could argue with that assessment. There wasn't an official world ranking table back then, but if there had been I'm sure Eddie Norman would have been proven right. Of course, which of them was number one is another matter.

Leighton won *The Indoor League* on two occasions, beating Alan Evans in 1974 and Charlie Ellix in 1976, so judging by these results I'd have to put Leighton at the top of the world rankings. He was on top form when he won the contest in 1976, and when he reached the final of the *News of the World* Championship at Alexandra Palace later that year there wasn't a bookie in sight who didn't have him as the favourite to win.

On the day of the *News of the World* Championship final, Leighton's opponent was Billy Lennard from Lancashire. As it happened, there was an unfortunate delay before the match when, just after the semi-final, the television company covering the event decided to go out live with the grand final, so the two players had to wait for an extra forty-five minutes while the crew set up their gear. Leighton sat on the edge of the stage for most of this time, and the long wait affected him much more than it did Billy, causing him to lose his third attempt to lift the title. Billy played darts for England the next day and won the Man of the Match award, before going on to become probably the finest darts player Lancashire has ever produced.

Leighton was so disappointed at losing in the final of the *News of the World* Championship. He knew that it this was the one everyone wanted to win. Sadly, he never achieved his aim of winning that tournament, but after failing to win it in 1976 he didn't have to wait long before he was back on the television, contesting another final: the inaugural Embassy World Professional Darts Championship, held in Nottingham in 1978. In the final, I was his opponent, and he beat me by eleven legs to seven, but I had no complaints. I was playing great darts, but I was fairly and squarely beaten by the better player – well, on that day, at least; the result was reversed the following year.

However, this wasn't the end for Leighton. He was a legend in the Welsh valleys and at that time probably the best-known professional darts player in the world. He'd pack out the venues he played in and was always in demand for exhibitions. I regard

Leighton not just as one of the best players of all time but a personal friend. Many was the time after a home international match, or an England v Wales match, that the pair of us sat at the bar until the late hours. And no, we didn't always talk about darts; we spoke of family, friends – the things good friends discuss. Such was his fame that in his home town a street was named after him: Leighton Rees Close.

Sadly, Leighton died on Sunday, 8 June 2003, aged 63. The *Times* obituary for Leighton described him as 'the first world professional darts champion who helped popularise the game on television' and one of players who 'ushered the game into [its] new era', while the pages of *Darts World* were crammed with tributes from friends and admirers the world over. It was my pleasure to have known Leighton, a true champion of sport, a gentleman of life and one of the greats.

In 2002 I had the privilege of interviewing Leighton for my website. It was the last interview that he would undertake. In view of the long-lasting friendship that existed between us and the high regard in which he was held across the entire international darting community, I think it's wholly appropriate that that friendly, frank, humorous and final interview be included in this book in memory of a truly great player, so I've included the full text in Appendix 1.

Of course, I can't mention Rees without mentioning Alan Evans. The arguments in Wales concerning which of these two players was the best will continue for many years. In terms of championship wins, Leighton might just edge it, but in terms of sheer darting brilliance, Alan might be ahead. One thing I can say is that I think that Alan was the best ton-eighty player of his generation. Like Leighton in 1976, he was runner-up in the *News of the World* Championship in 1972 and was then beaten two years in a row in *The Indoor League*, first by Tommy O'Regan in 1973 and then by Leighton in 1974.

At this time, Alan was playing money matches all over the country. His favourite game was the best of five rounds of 3001. Yes, that's right – 3001. He would call it a 'chaser', and that's usually what his opponents were doing: chasing.

I remember one very memorable challenge match at Manchester's Belle Vue Hotel when Alan was up against Nobby Clarke, a flamboyant Lancashire player. Before they began the match, which was the best of three, Alan took the microphone and announced that he wanted everyone in the audience to put one 10p piece each into the jars that were being passed around the room for every ton-eighty he scored in the match, with all proceeds going to a local charity. He then announced that, if he didn't score twelve maximums, he'd put £50 of his own money into the fund. Then, just to get one over on Nobby, he pulled £50 out of his pocket and put it into one of the jars, saying, 'I may just as well do it now to get the fund started. I'll be able to afford it after I beat this guy!' By the time the first two legs of the match had been completed, Alan had hit the twelve maximums promised. For someone barely 5ft tall, he was a master of the treble-twenty bed.

In 1975 Alan's game seemed to go up a notch and he won the World Masters and the British Open within a month of each other. At this time he was in hot demand for exhibitions worldwide and was the first professional to conduct an extensive tour of the USA. But Alan had problems too, suffering with ill health and constantly seeking medical attention. He also had a fiery temper. On one occasion, on leaving the Michael Sobell Centre in London after the Elkadart London Classic, one of a group of players on the upper floor of the venue shouted down, 'Oi, Alan! Bighead!' Before I knew it, Alan had bounded up the stairs and hit the guy full on. He then turned and calmly walked back down the stairs, leaving four or five guys fighting like mad, not knowing who'd thrown the punch. I did. It was the little guy from the valleys.

Like Leighton, Alan and I became good friends, speaking to each other on the phone quite often, and I feel that he contributed to my fame in the darting world. Back in 1976, I'd won the British Pentathlon in July and I'd qualified for the 1976 World Masters in London. I was making good headway in the competition, going through the field with relative ease until I reached the top sixteen, where I'd meet Alan, the defending champion and favourite to take the title again. There were busloads of supporters following him from Wales in the audience, but they were disappointed that day as I beat Alan in a tight match. He congratulated me and told me to go on and win the title for Wales, which I think was one of the greatest compliments I've ever been paid. I adopted his supporters for the rest of the tournament; the only time they didn't shout for me was when I played Welshman Phil Obbard in the final.

The exhibitions that Alan played at were always packed to the rafters. If he didn't entertain on the dartboard, he'd do so on the microphone. I attended one exhibition he played in Newcastle, where he acknowledged me on the mic by saying, 'I see John Lowe's in the room tonight. This is the second time I've seen him today. I passed him on the motorway. He was doing a ton. I was doing one hundred and eighty.'

Alan's career was stopped in its tracks, however, when he was banned from playing for a year in 1979 after an incident at an international match, after which he never fully recovered his tournament potential. He then signed a contract with Carlsberg and committed himself to the exhibition circuit. It's worth mentioning at this point that, while Evans and Rees were undoubtedly the best-known pair in darts, they only ever won one major title together: the Danish Open Pairs in 1978.

I once called in to visit Alan at his father's pub, the Ferndown in the Rhondda, and we had a good old chat. Then his father came over and joined in the conversation. At just after 10:30 that night, one of the lads in the pub came over to Alan's father and asked him if they could stay in the pub to wait for the bus as it was bucketing it down with rain outside. 'No, you can't,' said Alan's father. 'Ten-thirty is closing time and I want to shut up.'

I was a little taken back and thought he was joking, but I soon found out he wasn't when he ushered the lads out into the rain. 'They're just a load of trouble,' he said. 'They come in my pub, drink this terrible beer and then want to stay when we're shut.'

I found out later that Mr Evans Sr was a non-drinker and didn't particularly like those who did drink, which I thought was a rather strange attitude for a landlord to have. His son, though, the darling of the valleys, was and always will be known as one of the greats. During the late 1970s, darts was becoming one of the most popular sports – maybe even *the* most popular sport – in the UK, and there were a lot of new faces taking up the game. When I won my first World Masters title, back in 1976, I wasn't aware who the markers were on the stage, but after the final dart had been thrown and I'd beaten Phil Obbard – who, it turned out, had been one of them – a tall guy wearing dark glasses turned to me and shook my hand. 'Well done,' he said in a Cockney accent. 'You don't know me, do you?'

'No' I replied.

'Well, you will soon,' he said. 'Eric Bristow's the name.'

That was some introduction! True to his word, though, I soon became aware of who he was. This brash Cockney seventeen-year-old from Stoke Newington burst on to the darts scene and spread across it like an embarrassing rash. He was everywhere with his big head, big nose, big mouth and a darts game that could back up his bragging to the full.

Instead of saying this at the end of my account of Eric, I'll say it now: if it hadn't been for Eric Bristow I firmly believe that it would be me instead of Phil Taylor who held the record of world titles. I'd just reached the top of my game when Eric made his entrance, and for the next decade and more we battled it out for the top honours in every event across the world. Many things have been said about Eric, probably best by Tony Brown, the best dart player to ever come out of Kent, who once turned to Eric's father, George, and said, 'You know, if you'd taken him to church like any other good father instead of the pub, we'd all be better off.' George, it turned out, had played darts with his son since Eric was only eleven years old.

Eric played for London in the Inter-Counties League when he was seventeen and for England at the age of eighteen, and it would be easier to write down the events he *hasn't* won than to annotate his many wins. In 1981, I paired up with him to play the British Open Pairs, which we won – and continued to win for the next three years, at which point we decided to stop playing in pairs and instead leave the record as it stood, unbeaten. We also played the World Cup pairs together and won no fewer than six times in the next seven championships.

Eric almost made the World Masters his own, winning the title on five occasions and then going on to win the Embassy World Professional Darts Championship – also five times. I only have to look at my own name on every trophy I've won to see Eric's, which appears at least once on almost every major darts award, and I suppose I should regard that as a tribute to us both. Only three Embassy trophies have ever been given away permanently to the champion: one to Eric for his three consecutive wins, one to me for winning in three decades, and one to Dutchman Raymond van Barneveld.

Eric and I exchanged the captaincy of England and both held the position for several years, between us sharing almost all the prize money for a number of years and becoming very successful. In 1984, Eric told me at the Flowers Dartsathlon in Bristol that his manager, Dick Allix, thought I was no longer as good as Eric and that he should stop sharing with me, so we shook hands and went our separate ways. A few weeks later, I scored my perfect nine-dart 501 and picked up the winner's cheque for that, as well as one for £1,000 for the highest out-shot – a total of £115,000. Still, Eric was one of the first to congratulate me.

Eric's career as one of the finest players ever to throw darts almost came to an end in the late 1980s, when he developed a condition known as 'dartitis' – an inability to release darts. His action became tearful to watch, and many considered that he would ultimately have to quit the sport. He battled on in an embarrassing way, however, losing to players he'd have beaten easily before the dartitis struck. He still didn't give up, though, and ten years later Eric is throwing good darts once again. Although he no longer competes in the big events, he travels the world, playing exhibition matches to packed audiences. We do a 'Darts Legends' tour together, where we play members of the audience and then play a head-to-head match against each other. It's just like the old days, neither of us giving an inch.

I played him in one such match in Stockport in 2003. I was leading five legs to two and was struggling to find the double. Then I hear this Cockney voice behind me shouting, 'Come on!

Stop fucking about. Get the job done. I know what you're trying to do.' Believe me, I *was* trying – as ever – to beat him.

Eric now works for BSkyB as a darts pundit, doing the introductions and assessments of the matches. He can still ruffle some feathers and has retained that sharp tongue of his. During the 2004 World Championship, Phil Taylor was dropping names at every chance he could in the interview box, prompting Eric to say, 'Everyone at Sky has made an appointment to see the doctor tomorrow. They all have bad backs, picking up the names Taylor keeps dropping.'

The Crafty Cockney has been part of the sport for over thirty years. During that time I've been friends with him, I've fallen out with him and I've celebrated on more than one occasion with him. Indeed, my own darting career wouldn't have been the same without him. Eric Bristow, MBE, is simply one of the greats.

The next entry on my list of greats will come as no surprise to anyone – except perhaps to the player himself. He's won two world titles, but he didn't win a list of other major events. However, to deny him his rightful place as one of the great players of his time would be an injustice. I'm referring, of course, to the one and only John Thomas Wilson, better known to dart players and spectators around the world simply as Jocky.

Unlike Eric Bristow, who appeared on the darts scene in a blaze of confident swagger, Scotsman Jocky more or less just appeared. The first time I met him was at the 1975 British Open in London. It was the day of the top sixty-four, and Jocky had made it through. His name was called out a few times but he didn't come to the desk. Then someone beside me pointed him out, sitting on the floor. I could hardly see his face because his hair was so long. There was a Marks & Spencer carrier bag by his side containing six cans of beer. Jocky just sat there with an open can in his hand, oblivious to the world. The last time I saw him, in 1994, he still had a can in his hand.

Jocky won his first World Darts Championship in 1982. He played great darts all that week and beat me in the final by five sets to three. Seven years later, he was back at the top of his game, reaching another Embassy final, this time beating Eric Bristow six sets to four and attaining an impressive average of 31.44 per dart.

Jocky didn't have the best style in the sport and would very often seem to lunge with his last dart. Many are the times I've heard people say, 'His game's not pretty to watch, but the results he gets are spectacular.' He was without doubt one of the most gifted players who ever threw darts.

Jocky, however, had a terrible conflict of personality. One minute he could be the nicest man on Earth and the next extremely offensive, to say the least. I've lost count of the number of times he'd come up to me and said, 'Sorry about last night.' I would always reply, 'Why? What did you do?' and he'd say, 'Oh. So it wasn't you, then?' He would then proceed to apologise to everyone he'd been with the previous night, until he found out if he'd upset anyone.

Jocky was Scotland's most famous darts player and represented his country at many World Cups. At one such championship, in Nelson, New Zealand, we met in the final of the singles game, and before the game began he said to me, 'Now don't take me wrong, John, but for the next half an hour or so, I don't like you.' Good one, Jocky! He lost. We shook hands and went off to the bar for a drink.

As I mentioned earlier, I can't put down a long list of major wins for Jocky, although I suppose that winning the Embassy World Championship twice should be enough, as one Embassy is worth more than 100 of the others. It's my belief that his temperament stood in the way of his becoming a multi-titled champion. One example of this occurred in 1984 during an event sponsored by Dry Blackthorn Cider in Oldham, where Jocky's opponent was a player named Terry Downs.

Terry was the slowest darts player who'd ever taken part at any of our events, taking almost two minutes to throw three darts. He was so slow in his match with Jocky that Jocky asked someone in the audience to pass him a chair onto the stage so that he could sit down between throws. Needless to say, Jocky was becoming more and more frustrated, and he began to lose the match (although Terry's six maximum ton-eighty's didn't help). When the final double was scored and Terry was declared the winner, Jocky stormed off the stage to the player's room, where he threw abuse at anyone in sight for the next twenty minutes. Then, in walked Terry. He went straight up to Jocky and apologised for his slow play. Then he planted a big kiss on Jocky's cheek.

'What the fuck are you doing?' demanded Jocky. 'You've just beaten me, and now you're trying to give me AIDS!'

I'll remember that night for many years. It finished with Jocky hurling a TV at the wardrobe in his hotel room. Maybe he should have been a rock star instead of a darts player.

However, despite all his failings and insecurities, Jocky will always be remembered by those both in and out of the game, if for no other reason than the fact that a BBC researcher once put his picture up on the big screen in one episode of *Top of the Pops* while Dexys Midnight Runners were performing 'Jackie Wilson Said'. I'm sure more people laughed with Jocky than laughed at him. He now lives back in Kirkcaldy, his home town in Scotland, having retired from the sport in 1994, and has rarely been seen by anyone since. Many think he should have continued playing, although I personally think he was right to quit while he still had his health; Jocky endured his fair share of trials and tribulations, and I wish him and his wife a happy and healthy retirement. He was certainly good enough to test the finest and is, without doubt, one of the greats.

Before I bring things up to date with my selection of truly great players, I'd feel bad if I didn't mention some of the other big names of our sport – all Embassy champions and, indeed, champions in their own right – including Bob Anderson, Dennis Priestley, Keith Deller, John Part, Steve Beaton and Ritchie Burnett. There are also many others, like Alan Glazier, who might not have won the biggest title of all but still deserve a place in the darts hall of fame for their determination and resolve and dedication to the sport.

One player I can't miss out from this chapter is Raymond van Barneveld, or 'Barney' as he's known to his many followers. I would have put him in my list of greats, but only one thing

A family affair.

Above: I am pictured here with my mother Phyllis, sister Margaret and father Frederick.

Below left: Jack and Sydney, my grandparents.

Below right: Taking a dip in the icy cold sea!

Proudly holding the News of the World Champions Trophy after winning the competition.

rophy time again!

bove: Gary Newborn presents me with the Grand Masters Trophy at Butlins.

elow: My first world championship success when I won the Embassy Cup.

Above: In 1979, David Coleman interviewed Leighton Rees and I about our darts caree

Below: With golf being another love of mine I was keen to meet a world number one, Nick Faldo, when we were presented with sponsored cars.

Above: My son Adrian and my daughter Karen – my pride and joy.

Below: I was so proud the day Margaret Thatcher presented me with a gold star. Other recipients include Sebastian Coe.

Taken on the day I met my all-time hero – Muhammed Ali. My son gets up close to the greatest sportsman of all.

bove: Here I am with my England team. I was very proud to be chosen as the captain.

elow: I played for John Prescott's charity RNLI at the Houses of Parliament.

Jetting off to another match!

prevented me from doing so: he won his three Embassy world titles while playing against lesser players. By the time Barney achieved his success, all the big guns had left the BDO and were playing on Sky TV with the WDC. I know that many will scoff at this and say that I can't prove he wouldn't have won at least one world championship if the rebels had remained, but it's nevertheless difficult to see how he would have stood up to some of the other names on the list.

Barney knew that he was the best of those that were left. He was handed a world crown on a plate. He has managed to win three Embassys, equalling my own tally, and he really should have won more. Nevertheless, he's done wonders for the sport of darts in Holland, where thousands now play. His website has a huge following, and I believe he did the right thing in staying with the Embassy and the BDO. His pockets are probably full to overflowing, but the question will always haunt him: would he have won a world championship while competing against the likes of Taylor, Warriner, Priestley, Lowe and co? I think he might have sneaked one, but three? Not a chance.

In the farcical head-to-head match against Phil Taylor at the Wembley Conference Centre in 1999, where the pair played for one hour on ITV. It appeared that Barney was so humiliated that he didn't even acknowledge his own orange supporters. Then, when ITV agreed to host a rematch in 2004, Barney and his management turned down the offer, which was reputed to have been for £100,000. I wonder why? Taylor is quoted as saying that he thought Barney was running scared. I agree. Barney is a champion, but a great? I don't think so.

Finally, my list of great players would not be complete without one player, 'The Power' himself: Mr Philip Taylor. Phil has dominated the sport for the last decade and more, just as Eric Bristow and I did for ten years before him, and he has done so by playing quite brilliant darts. Winning twelve world championships, playing against the very best players in the world, is something special.

I remember when Phil joined the travelling professional circuit, way back in the 1980s, when Eric Bristow gave him the chance to compete by paying his way. The first time I met him at a tournament was at the Canadian Open, back when he was nicknamed 'the Crafty Potter'. No, this was nothing to do with snooker; Phil is from Stoke-on-Trent, the centre of an area in England known as the Potteries.

How well I remember that first encounter. Phil was playing with Eric in a four-man team who were up against my team of Bob Anderson, Cliff Lazarenko, Ritchie Gardner and myself. I wasn't on very good terms with Eric at that time, and in fact we hardly spoke to each other at all. It was noticeable that Phil was a great admirer of Eric, however, and it seemed he copied him away from the board as much as he tried to copy his on-board antics. After the match, which we won convincingly, I shook Phil's hand and told him, 'Don't grow up like Bristow.' I did not mean Bristow the darts player; I meant the Eric Bristow of that time. He just smiled and swaggered away, Bristow fashion.

It was only a few years before Phil made it to the very top, winning his first Embassy crown in 1990 and his last in 1992. In that second victory, he was very fortunate to get past me in the semi-final, scraping through by five sets to four, averaging 30.49 to my 29.66. On that occasion he played Mike Gregory in the final, which turned out to be one of the best ever finals and one that Phil won again by a short margin: six sets to five, with an average of 32.53.

In 1993, Phil was expected to retain his title, and was indeed the bookies' favourite, but he didn't count on Kevin Spiolek, who produced one of his better weeks of darts and dumped the champion out by three sets to one. That was the last year we'd take part in the Embassy, and that year the championship belonged to me.

Phil soon bounced back, though, and after his six–one defeat in the 1994 World Championship by Dennis Priestley he started on the best run of World Championship wins ever, winning no fewer than nine in a row. Poor old Dennis Priestley; if Taylor hadn't hit such a winning streak, he would have undoubtedly been the outstanding player of the decade. As it was, he was relegated to the runner-up spot on no fewer than four occasions by Phil.

Phil's haul of titles in a thirteen-year span include twelve World Championships, six World Matchplay titles and five Grand Prix wins. In fact, his list of world titles isn't that great for a player of his class, but there's a good reason for that: he just didn't enter many of them. Phil's goal was always to emulate his friend Eric Bristow by winning the *News of the World*, and when the tournament was resurrected in 1997 Phil's dream came true. He won the title in true championship style, although it's true that the throw had been reduced from 8ft to 7ft 9in.

In the early years of his success, Phil used to say to me that he maybe wished he'd stayed with the BDO, reasoning that he'd won four PDC world titles and still no one knew him. In his view, Eric and I were far better known because we'd won our championships on terrestrial TV. He was right, of course, and it took several more years before Phil became known to the general UK public.

Phil didn't just become a great player overnight, though. Without doubt, he practises more than any other player I've ever met, except maybe one: the John Lowe of the 1970s. Phil is where he is today through sheer dedication to darts. People today often ask, 'Is he the best ever?', and indeed his name is certainly dominant in the record books, but would he have won as many titles in the Bristow–Lowe era of the 1980s? That I can't say, but I do know he did Mr Barneveld a big favour by leaving the fold of the BDO.

The legend of Phil 'The Power' Taylor became immortalised when he achieved a perfect nine-dart game in the World Matchplay Championship at the Winter Gardens, Blackpool, in 2002, when he picked up a cool £100,000 cheque and went on to win the championship.

However, Phil's career hasn't been all roses. In early 2001 he appeared on the front pages of the tabloid press under the headline 'DIRTY OLD MAN: WORLD CHAMPION DART PLAYER IN SEX OFFENCE CHARGE', and more of the same followed. It appeared that Phil had been charged with committing sexual offences in Scotland against two girls he'd offered to drive home in 1999. Phil didn't even tell his wife until the case had been heard in court, and in his autobiography he admits that those were dark days, a time when he even contemplated suicide. He was fined £2,000 by the Scottish Court and at one stage seemed determined to appeal, but later he wisely decided to let the matter drop.

And then there was more bad news for Phil in 2002. When Phil, my wife and I were flying home from Saskatoon, Canada, Phil was very quiet during the connecting flight to Toronto. When the plane landed and we stood up, I asked Phil if he was feeling all right.

'Not really,' he said glumly. 'I was told this morning the powers-that-be at the Palace have withdrawn my MBE.' It turned out that the events in Scotland had caught up with him.

I said I was sorry to hear that, and I really did mean it. I honestly thought I might receive one myself at some point, if not at the end of my darting career, and I have grave doubts now that anyone in darting circles will ever receive one.

Many a man wouldn't have come through such a turbulent time. To even think of winning world championships after such a public humiliation would be more than most could stand. But Phil threw himself into his darts and practised for hour after hour. His ultimate goal was to achieve positive press, and he later did just that by going on to win another Professional Darts Corporation World Championship title, another World Matchplay and another Grand Prix.

Phil is now financially secure – and so he should be; in other sports, anyone winning so many world championships would be worth millions more. In his phenomenal career, Phil has done remarkable things for darts, putting the sport right up there with the best of them. If the man at the top succeeds, of course, the men lower down the division also reap the rewards, and over the last five years prize funds have increased dramatically and players' potential earnings have almost doubled.

Success breeds contempt, however, and many players resent Phil's earning capacity and the constant media attention directed towards him. Me? I say, 'Thank you, Phil ìThe Powerî Taylor. The cake is a big one and there are many pieces. I'm quite happy to pick up some of those pieces.'

Phil Taylor, 'the Crafty Potter' from Stoke-on-Trent, is truly one of the greats, but is he the greatest? Only time will tell.

CHAPTER 9

The Greatest of All Sportsmen

Without darts and without being a world professional darts champion, I would never have had the opportunity of meeting a man regarded by many, including myself and millions of people across the globe, as the greatest sportsman of all time. OK, if people were asked today in general conversation right now in the UK who is the most famous and well-known sportsperson in the world, many would say rugby World Cup hero Jonny Wilkinson or the superstar footballer David Beckham, but I'm talking about the greatest of all time. Think again – take a little time to reflect – and before long I believe only one name will come to mind – or, possibly, two: Cassius Clay and Muhammad Ali. In my opinion, he is simply the greatest living sportsperson of this or any other generation.

My love of boxing goes back to when I was four years old, back when my father would listen to boxing commentaries, especially the world title fights, on the radio. (Like hundreds of other families in the late 1940s/early 1950s, we didn't have a television set.) From that early age, I joined him around the radio whenever a fight was on and grew to love the sport. Because there was no visual image, listening to the radio spurred my imagination to such a degree that I hung on to every word the commentator said, not daring to miss a single one. The experienced commentators described every move, and it seemed I could feel every blow. I became part of the audience, watching the fight at the ringside. Dempsey, Marciano, Cockel and Woodcock – great fighters of their time – came alive inside my head and in our living room. 'Audio fighters' is probably the best term I can use to describe them; fighters who became better and even more real when the commentator was on form.

With the introduction of television, of course, boxing became something other than a noble art. With the new physical dimension came the showmanship, the PR and also the money – shedloads of cash for the participants and their trainers and entourages. It also brought a new appreciation of the sport to my father and me. When we watched the fights on our first television, which my father bought in 1953, it was like they were taking place right there in our living room. (I imagine the younger people of today can't imagine life without a television but, believe me, to witness that visual miracle for the first time stays in your mind for ever.)

Although I was never a fighter in a physical sense, I did have my moments in the playground, but that's all they were: moments – a push and a shove here and there, a lot of rolling about. Watching boxing on TV took its toll on me, though, and I'd be drained after twelve rounds. I was *there*, in the ring with the fighters, exchanging blows and feeling the impact of every punch. I still feel that way today; whenever I watch a top fight, whether it be held in Las Vegas or Bethnal Town Hall, I'm in there, heart and soul.

When Cassius Clay first came on the boxing scene, it was like a new beginning for the sport. This brash young fighter from Louisville, Kentucky, dared to say that he could and would put Sonny Liston down and out. (That was, of course, after he'd taken care of Floyd Patterson.) He was quite unbelievable. My father used to say to me, 'This guy is getting into a load of trouble. His mouth will probably get him killed. There are a lot of dangerous people in boxing who don't like people interfering with the way they control the sport.'

I realised later, when I was older, that the 'dangerous people' my father was talking about were the Mafia. For whatever reasons, they didn't interfere with the career of the young Cassius, although a young pugilist named David Jones nearly did. Before their fight, Cassius avowed, 'If he beats me, I'll crawl across the ring and kiss his feet.'

I watched the match, which Cassius won, I know not how. Maybe the forces my father had told me about recognised the new kid on the block and didn't intend his progress to be damaged by a mere journeyman.

I followed the progress of Cassius Clay for the whole of his amazing career. He became my sporting hero, bar none, and I often thought what it would be like if I ever met 'the Greatest'. What would I say to him? Would I be able to say anything? I filed those thoughts away in the section of my brain reserved for daydreams.

Then, one Friday in October 1981, I received a phone call from a lady at BBC Radio inviting me to come down to London to appear on a Sunday show titled *Studio B15*. The idea was that I'd play darts with a Welsh lad who played well in practice but suffered from nerves when match day arrived. I was about to say yes when I realised that that Sunday I was due to play in an inter-county match for Derbyshire, who were playing at home in Matlock, so I politely refused the offer. (To be honest, I thought it was a bit of an inconvenience to travel all the way to London for a radio show, so it did not bother me very much.)

Within a couple of minutes, the lady called me back and asked me what appeared at the time to be a most unusual question. 'If there was a possibility that your all-time sporting hero would appear on the same show as you,' she said, 'would you be interested then?'

I paused and then challenged her to tell me who it was. When she replied, 'Muhammad Ali,' I froze. I was so amazed to hear his name that I couldn't speak. I was in a state of shock. Once I'd recovered, though, I accepted the lady's offer.

The show was scheduled to be broadcast at midday on Sunday, and the lady asked me to bring a dartboard and darts and – most importantly – not to tell anyone that Ali would be on the show. She also asked me to get there in plenty of time.

Even though I was under orders not to mention that Ali would be on the show, I just had to tell someone, and that Saturday night I went out with my wife, Diana (to whom I was still married at the time), and some friends and 'broadcast' the news to one and all. Curiously, though, no one believed me. 'Why would Ali want to be on a radio show?' they asked. 'He's a TV man.'

I began to think that they might be right. Why, indeed, would he appear on radio? Was this just a ploy to get me to appear with the Welsh lad? Surely the BBC didn't work that way. Numerous doubts began to form in my mind, but ultimately they made little difference. One thing was for sure: I wasn't going to stay at home and risk finding out later that I'd missed the chance of a lifetime, the chance of meeting my all-time hero face to face. I'd never forgive myself.

Again completely contrary to the request from the lady at the BBC, I rang my good friend Geoff Smith, a very good darts player with whom I practised regularly. We both played for the Park House Hotel darts team at Danesmoor, where we once won fifteen tournaments in a row, including the NODOR Fours. I knew that Geoff, too, was a massive Ali fan, so I told him about the phone call from the BBC and asked if he fancied making the trip down to London.

'Pick me up at eight,' he said immediately, and I remember thinking, 'At last! Someone believes me.'

In addition, my son, Adrian, decided that he wanted to come down with us. He couldn't understand what all the fuss was about at the time – but then, he was only eight years old.

We picked up Geoff at eight o'clock on the morning the show was to be broadcast and made a very nervous journey to London. When we arrived at the BBC studios, there was an excitement in the air that I'd never felt before and haven't since. It seemed like the entire staff of the BBC had come in to work. There were cleaners, DJs, commissionaires, just about everybody who worked there, doing nothing but just standing there.

We were eventually met by the show's producer, a young black girl, who seemed really nervous. Obviously, this was no ordinary man arriving at the BBC that day. Ali was truly an icon, and I was actually going to meet him and speak with him – or would I?

The producer ushered us into a small room in which the show would be recorded. The room was fitted with a glass wall, on the other side of which were the recording equipment and the people who worked the machines. Adrian and Geoff were asked to sit in the control room while the show was being recorded.

First, though, we had to wait for Ali, who was doing an interview with some children in another studio. He'd just finished shooting the film *Tobacco Road* and the children were critiquing it. The producer turned to me and said, 'We don't know how he'll handle the kids if they rubbish him and the film. He may just walk off without doing your part of the show.'

At that point, I remember thinking, 'Great. So near and yet so far.'

'By the way,' I asked the producer, 'what is my part of the show?' I'd suddenly realised that this hadn't been explained to me. In my excitement at the prospect of meeting Ali, I'd forgotten to ask about the details. What were they expecting of me?

'You'll be discussing how to overcome nerves,' said the producer.

Surprisingly, just a few minutes before going on air, I heard myself asking her, 'Why me?'

She turned and said, 'Because no one thinks you have any.'

I must point out now that over the years I've built up a reputation of being at ease on the oche. Even on the World Championship stage, I never appeared fazed. That's why I've earned the nickname 'Old Stoneface'. My facial expressions seem to display a sense of inner calm, and my darting action is the same – only my throwing arm and hand move, while the rest of my body stays rock solid.

Does that mean I don't get nerves, though? Well, on facing a dartboard maybe that's the case, but right then and there in the studio, believe me, I was very nervous. How could I be any other way? Around me, all the BBC people were panicking: 'Will he do the show? What will he think of the programme? Will he be nice?' and so on. To be honest, although I was very nervous indeed, I wasn't as frantic as the production crew, especially the producer.

Then I was brought back to reality when the producer said to me, 'Right, John. You settle down in the studio and your kids can watch the show through the glass partition.' I had to smile. Kids? I know Adrian was only eight, but Geoff was older than me! Foolishly, I told Geoff about it afterwards, and he's never let me forget it. He now calls me 'Dad'.

I looked around the studio. It was nothing like what I had expected. There was a table, a cupboard and a couple of chairs, and there were no windows. It was like being in a black box with a few bits and bobs thrown in.

The producer then interrupted my train of thought. 'Can you fix up the dartboard please, John?' she asked.

Now, that posed a problem. 'It'll have to be hung from a hook on the wall,' I told her. Even then, there was no way it would represent a true throw. 'It won't look very good,' I added.

The producer smiled and replied, 'Don't worry about it, John. It's only radio. No one will know.'

That wasn't what was bothering me, though. My understanding of Ali was that he was used to everything being perfect. I'd also been told that he might be a bit punchy and unsteady on his feet. I told the producer that I was concerned about how the great man would react to the wires all over the floor and a dartboard hanging by a couple of feet of garden string, but she had no time to respond.

The word came in from the control room: 'He's coming!' The moment of truth was upon us and, before I knew it, I was shaking hands with history itself, shaking the hand of the man who had destroyed so many famous boxers including Sonny Liston, Floyd Patterson, Joe Frazier, Larry Holmes and England's very own Henry Cooper. I was in awe of the man. Here was John Lowe, the coal miner's son from New Tupton, standing face to face with Muhammad Ali, my father's hero, my friend's hero, my hero.

As he walked into the studio, I was awestruck. A little taller than me, he was dressed in a double-breasted raincoat. Those eyes that had glared at so many opponents across the famous boxing rings of the world were looking straight at me. I felt incredibly good. 'You must be the champ,' he said.

Before I knew it, and to the delight of the production crew, who unbeknown to me had begun recording, I'd replied, 'No. I'm sure you're the champ, Mr Clay. Sorry – Muhammad.'

The programme was supposed to run for about ten minutes, during which time we would do the interview for about five minutes and then throw some darts for the remaining five. As planned, during the interview we discussed the problem of nerves. Ali said that he didn't suffer from them, that his opponents had enough for both of them. I said, modestly, that I didn't have any when I was on stage, although sometimes I wished I did, and eventually the Welsh lad confessed that he was too nervous to say anything!

The three of us then threw a few darts and, lo and behold, the Welsh lad threw the highest score. I think his nerves shook them in!

Then, to my amazement, the producer walked across and pinned a Polo mint to the dartboard and suggested that I show Ali how to put a dart through the hole in the middle.

Now, that trick was introduced to darts by the left-handed, ex-England darter Alan 'Ton Machine' Glazier, although in truth there was no trick to it; it was all down to accuracy and a little bit of luck. If you *did* put the dart right through the middle of the mint, it wouldn't shatter, but the slightest contact and it would disintegrate and pieces would fly around the room. While I'd often seen Alan do the trick, I'd never tried to do it myself before then, but of course I didn't tell anyone that!

Well, this was no time to suddenly find those nerves. Here was the greatest boxer of all time watching a darts player with, apparently, no nerves. At least, that's what I'd had told him just a few minutes earlier, but now I had to prove it.

I took careful aim and launched the dart through the air. It was like watching the throw in slow motion. The dart went into a high arc, flying ever nearer to the mint. Would it miss the target altogether? Would it hit the mint and shatter it? Would I be sweeping up the pieces after the show and suffering probably the greatest embarrassment of my life? All these thoughts sped through my mind as the dart hurtled towards the dartboard.

Then–

Thud!

The dart hit the mint dead centre – a perfect throw.

Ali's reaction was startling, to say the least. He took off his raincoat, turned to me and, with the producer looking on, mesmerised, shouted in that familiar Ali voice, 'I want to play with the champ!'

The programme overran by twenty minutes. The BBC even delayed the news. And no one was nervous anymore; the great man was doing what he was best at: being himself.

All the time we played, the Ali banter flowed. I did my best to show him how to play darts, but it wasn't easy. What he regarded as his natural stance was totally wrong. He was right-handed, yet he stood with his left foot forward to the oche line. I asked him to put his right foot forward with his left foot back, then watched his balance and reviewed his stance. I even had to hold down his left foot to stop it coming way off the floor when he threw the dart.

I eventually succeeded in teaching Muhammad Ali to throw all three darts into the board, and I assume he was impressed by this brief introduction to the sport of darts as he said to me, 'When you come to America, John, look me up. We gotta have a match. I'll get them to fix a board in the house.'

Now, that was some invitation, which I, of course, accepted, not actually believing that I'd ever meet the great man again.

By all accounts, the show was a tremendous success, and when it was over I was relaxed enough to ask Ali about his fights. It was then that I learned the truth straight from the man himself. 'Let me tell you, John,' he said, 'People try to put a show on outside the ring, because they have to attract the interest, but when they come into the ring the true person is shown. Muhammad Ali is himself when he climbs through those ropes.' I have never forgotten those words.

As he was about to leave, I asked him to sign a book for me. 'Oh, you bought my book!' he exclaimed.

'Yes,' I replied, 'I have, but this isn't it.' In fact he was signing a copy of my own latest book, *The Lowe Profile*. Thankfully, he didn't appear to mind. And as he left the studio, suddenly everyone around wanted his autograph. I could see, however, that many people were afraid to ask. Actually, 'afraid' might be the wrong word; perhaps they were simply too respectful or in awe of the man.

My son, who was only eight and so, of course, had no nerves at all, wanted his photograph taken with Ali, and when I asked if this was possible Ali picked Adrian up and sat him on his arm, then pulled back his fist as if he was going to punch him. What a photograph! I had it enlarged and today it hangs in pride of place in Adrian's home in Chesterfield.

As you might imagine, we left the BBC studios in very high spirits. The chatter never stopped, and before we knew it we were on the M1 and bound for home. Geoff turned to Adrian and said, 'You obviously enjoyed yourself. You know who that was, of course?'

Adrian smiled and replied, 'Yes. He's the man who advertises beefburgers on TV.' We'd forgotten that Adrian was so young he'd never seen Ali fight. He must have been wondering why we were all so excited about meeting him! So, of course, I had to buy all the Ali fights on video, and I had no trouble persuading Adrian to sit with me and watch them. How it reminded me of my father and me, sitting together and listening to the radio. Now, like his father, Adrian feels proud to have met the greatest sporting hero of all time.

DATE: 11 AUGUST 1996
VENUE: THE HOMESTEAD GOLF COURSE, WASATCH, UTAH, USA
Two English guys and a Mexican are on the eleventh fairway. Having won the last hole, it's the Mexican's turn to drive the ball.

Whack!

The ball flies 250 yards, but it's going right – right over a white fence and into the garden of one of many houses that line the fairway.

'Damn!' says the Mexican. 'Out of bounds. I'll take another off the tee.'

He does. The ball lands right in the middle of the fairway.

The three set off in their buggies to play their second shots. As the Mexican approaches the position where his ball left the course, he stops and looks across to where a lady is beckoning to him. 'Your ball is over here!' she shouts.

'Thank you so much,' replies the Mexican and goes across to reclaim his ball.

The next moment, the Mexican is over the fence, arms outstretched, and then the two of them are hugging and kissing each other as if they're long lost brother and sister. (Well, almost!)

The three guys were David Brook, Val Montayo and me. After a disappointing performance in the North American Darts Open in Las Vegas, where I was ousted at the top-sixteen stage, a party of us had gone off for a seven-day holiday at the Homestead, where we'd booked a house. There were five of us in total: David Brook, the Chief Executive of the Federation Brewery and my golfing buddy; Barry Twomlow, my neighbour in Chesterfield and the man widely regarded as the man who taught the world to play darts (he was Unicorn Products' roving ambassador, a highly respected man throughout the world of darts); Jay Tomlinson, another good friend of mine and editor of US darts publication *Bull's Eye News*; Bob Murdock; and, of course, me.

The order of the week was golf for David and myself and fishing for Barry, Jay and Bob, whose close friend Val Montayo (the Mexican referred to above) worked at the Homestead and had arranged everything.

We'd been at the Homestead for three days already, and that day we played our second round of golf on that beautiful course, 5,000ft above sea level. It was rather exhilarating because, due to the altitude, our drives were going an additional twenty yards, causing us to believe we were almost on par with the big guys.

But who was this woman Val currently had his arms around? 'Val!' she kept calling.

'Jean!' replied Val.

David and I walked across and asked, 'Anyone want to let us in on the secret?'

'Oh yeah,' Val said. 'This is Jean.' No kidding. 'We went to school together and were very close friends. It's been over twenty years since we last met. And if I hadn't sliced that ball, we probably would not have met again.'

When the pair of them had calmed down and returned to some semblance of normal behaviour, Jean asked, 'So what are you doing here, Val?'

Val explained that he worked at the Homestead as the senior valet.

Then it was Jean's turn to explain why she was there, and I couldn't believe it when she said, 'I'm Muhammad Ali's personal assistant.'

Now who was getting excited? I stood there, waiting for the next sentence in fear and trepidation, but soon I couldn't hold back anymore. 'Where is he?' I tentatively.

Jean flicked her head calmly and replied, 'He's in the house.'

Before anyone else could say a word, I blurted out the whole story of the BBC and the radio programme Muhammad and I had been on together fifteen years earlier.

'That's incredible!' Jean exclaimed, then added, 'Would you like to meet him again?'

I gasped and said, 'I most certainly would!'

'Well, he's sleeping right now,' Jean admitted, 'but tonight we're having a barbecue in aid of the American Boys Clubs. Muhammad's presenting the money raised from two days of golf to the charity. You're more than welcome to join us. It starts at five.'

A quick look at my watch showed it was already four o'clock, and we still had another seven holes to play. I looked at David. David looked at Val. Val looked at me. Then, more or less in unison, we chorused, 'Let's go get ready!'

We didn't even return the buggies; we just drove straight back to the house while Val went back to his home. After a quick wash and a change of clothes, it was back on the buggy to the clubhouse, where the barbecue was to take place.

When we arrived, there were about twenty-five people around the barbecue area, and I remember thinking that was a pretty small number for such a large charity event. I later found out that these were the specially invited guests; the rest of the people –

some 100 in total – wouldn't be arriving until 7:30 and would be going straight into the clubhouse for the presentation and a buffet.

I asked Val who these people were. I knew that he'd know, as he seemed to know everything (except, of course, the whereabouts of his old school friends). He said, 'Let me introduce you to a few of them,' then grabbed me by the arm and, with David close behind, walked me over to a small group of men.

'This is Desi Arnez Junior,' said Val, gesturing, and as the man turned to greet me I thought, 'That name sounds familiar.' Val introduced me to Desi as the world darts champion, and this seemed to go down very well indeed. (The Americans love meeting champions.) Desi and then I exchanged a few words before Val introduced me to another man who looked remarkably like someone I'd met in Las Vegas a few years earlier.

Eleven years earlier, when I'd just won the North American Open for the first time in 1985, Bob Murdock had introduced me to Jimmy Spade, one of his old-time friends from Chicago, whom Bob had invited along to watch the darts. Jimmy had loved it. Then, after I'd won the final, a few of us went to the bar to celebrate and Jimmy was there. He asked me when I was leaving for home. I told him I'd be off the next day, Monday. 'OK,' he said, 'I'll pick you up in Bally's Casino's new limo and take you to the airport.'

True to his word, Jimmy arrived at the front door of the Sahara Hotel at 10:30 the following morning in the biggest, brightest, whitest limousine I'd ever seen. He opened his door, climbed out of the driver's seat and called out, 'Limo for the champ!' I felt 10ft tall, but I was in for a greater shock when I got into the car.

When I climbed into the back, there was a man sitting in the back seat about 8ft from where I was. 'Hiya, champ,' he said and held out his hand.

'Hi,' I replied.

Before I could say any more, Jimmy stuck his head in and said, 'You don't mind if we drop Mr Martin off at Bally's, do you John?'

Mind? Did I *mind*?

'Fine by me,' I replied, as if I'd known Dean Martin all my life. Of course, two minutes later he was gone, but if I hadn't been a world champion our paths would never have crossed.

And now here I was, shaking hands with his son.

'John, David,' said Val, 'please meet Dean Martin.'

Again we had a few words and moved on. I stopped Val at this point and asked him, 'Are these guys who I think they are?'

'Of course,' replied Val. 'Desi is Lucille Ball's son and Dean is Dean Martin's son.'

Desi Arnez Senior, of course, had played Lucille Ball's husband in the US sitcom *I Love Lucy* series back in the 1950s and '60s, and Dean Martin...well, he needs no introduction.

Val then introduced us to a host of celebrities, although we recognised hardly any of them, as their fame hadn't really crossed the Atlantic. That was OK, though; we all joined in together. They thought we were celebrities in our own right. Little did they know that we were there for one reason only: to meet the great man himself.

We were standing there with Desi Arnez and another man when I received a tap on my shoulder. I turned to see a tall, clean-shaven man in, I estimated, his forties. He held out his hand. 'Nice to see you again,' he said, shaking my hand vigorously.

I was a little bewildered but replied, 'Nice to see you too.' I felt like adding 'for the first time', as I'd never seen the man before, yet there he was greeting me as if I was a good friend he hadn't seen for ages. Without another word, he smiled and then turned away, then walked over to another group and shook their hands. I heard him say, 'Thank you so much for your votes. It's much appreciated.' Then off he went again. It turned out that he was the Governor of Utah, complete with bodyguards. He'd obviously assumed that we were all residents and loyal supporters of his cause.

The barbecue at the Homestead was excellent. There were two chefs preparing food of the finest quality, and champagne flowed freely. It all made a pleasant change from the usual backyard affair. There was also a cocktail waiter who was mixing drinks the likes of which I'd never before seen or tasted. After about an hour, the guests were all talking to each other as if they were old friends. I had Desi's two-year-old son sat on my knee, trying to drink my Singapore Sling. Then I happened to turn to my right and look towards one of the houses, over a little fence that separated the clubhouse from the gardens. The door was open and, at that moment, a tall, athletic man appeared. It was, of course, Muhammad, about to make his entrance.

I stood up and watched as he walked slowly towards us. He appeared a little unsure of himself, the Parkinson's syndrome from which he suffered very noticeable, but he walked unaided. This was obviously a very proud man, and although he could no longer speak, he wasn't going to let his pride and dignity be taken away from him. His assistant, Jean, walked close beside him, ready to help if he stumbled, but he didn't need her this time.

Muhammad came right up to us as if he knew exactly who we were. He held out his hand to me and I returned his offer of friendship. At that moment I felt a lump in my throat and tears welling in my eyes – tears not of sympathy but of delight.

It had been fifteen years since I'd first met Muhammad, and I hadn't thought we'd ever meet again, yet here we were, shaking hands some 3,000 miles from that small BBC studio in London. I wondered if he still remembered me, and I asked Jean if she would ask him for me. She turned to him and asked him, 'Muhammad, do you remember John from England at the radio station?' She didn't mention darts.

Muhammad looked at me with those sparkling eyes, raised his arm and went through the motion of throwing a dart. I almost cried with joy; he remembered me. I walked over and gave him a big hug.

For the next hour, David, Val, Muhammad and I sat and enjoyed our barbecued food. We spoke to him while he simply nodded in return, then we posed for photographs. As I write, I'm looking at one of those photographs of us on my office wall and the memories come flooding back.

I remember asking Muhammad for his autograph then, not knowing if his condition would allow him to do so, but without hesitation he pulled a pen from his pocket, together with a religious tract bearing the legend 'IS JESUS REALLY GOD?', and signed his name. His signature looked exactly the same as that on Adrian's photograph, signed some fifteen years earlier.

What a day! I couldn't believe that history had repeated itself and I was again in the presence of 'the Greatest'. It was one of the most memorable moments of my life. I cared little that Muhammad was a Muslim; I, after all, had been brought up in the Pentecostal faith and believed that Jesus certainly was God, but I respect each individual's right to believe in whatever and whoever they please.

That August night in Utah, I remember thinking that here was a man who strode the world stage with enormous charisma, someone who had carried out his chosen sport better than anyone else, someone who had met presidents and heads of state all over the planet – simply, in my opinion, the most famous person in the whole world – and here he was, having a barbecue with a miner's son from New Tupton.

CHAPTER 10

How to Lose Friends, Faith and Your Money: The First Lesson

M any people who are successful in sport come to a point in their lives when they want to diversify, to try something else. They make some enquiries, put some money by and then suddenly become experts in other fields. Sometimes they'll branch out into opening a restaurant or investing in a sports shop, while many in sports such as boxing, football and darts find their way into the licensed trade and buy a pub.

In my case, it was the latter. After all, what more appropriate venture was there for a well-known darts player than to invest his money in a pub? As it turned out, while I and five friends embarked on the project with enthusiasm, it turned out to be our worse nightmare come true, resulting ultimately in fractured friendships and a loss of faith in human nature.

It all began one Saturday night at the stag night of one of my good friends, Peter Bradley. There were about ten of us in all, and I'd been put in charge of the kitty and so had a pocketful of money. The idea was to start in our local drinking house, the White Hart on Matlock Road, and then to move on after a few drinks.

Soon the drinks were flowing. We left the White Hart about ten o'clock for the Aquarius nightclub, where camp comedian

Duncan 'Chase Me!' Norvelle was appearing. I knew Duncan very well, so well in fact that I'd arranged with him to get Peter up on the stage while Duncan did his 'Teddy Bears' Picnic' routine. This was a really camp part of the show, and we all knew that Peter would have to be pretty drunk before he'd get involved.

What a show it turned out to be! Peter good-naturedly agreed to take part and sat on Duncan's knee in front of 800 people, as drunk as a skunk, all 6ft 6in of him. He was like a ventriloquist's dummy made of rubber, falling one way and then the other, and the audience were crying with laughter. We left the Aquarius that night at around two in the morning, pledging that anyone who didn't appear back at the White Hart at lunchtime the next day would have to buy the drinks for a whole night next time we all got together.

The following day, Sunday, the lads drifted into the White Hart one by one. When I arrived at about 1:30pm, one of my friends, Les Sheppard, was sat in his usual seat. We both had hangovers the size of a house. 'Morning John,' says Les. 'You all right?'

The only reply I could muster was something like 'Shut up, you sarkie git,' and that constituted the basic gist of our conversation for the next hour. True to form, though, all the lads made the session, but who could have imagined where that session would lead?

At that time, the White Hart had a new landlord and landlady, Alan and Jane, who we didn't know that well. All we knew about them was that he was tight – very tight. On Peter's stag night, he never offered him a drink, and I estimated that we'd spent about £150 in his pub that evening before departing for the nightclub. Many of the customers who knew Peter had left him a drink behind the bar, though, and he was doing his utmost to drink them throughout Sunday lunchtime.

After a while, Alan emerged from the Lounge Bar and said grumpily, 'What's this? Peter has one in every time a round is ordered!'

'Well, he does,' Les replied.

'How do I know that?' snapped the landlord.

This angered Peter and he chimed in, 'Do you think I would accept drinks that haven't been paid for?'

'I don't know,' Alan replied suspiciously.

Peter was livid. 'Well, if that's the way you feel' he said, 'I'll pay for my own.' With that he threw a £5 note onto the bar, and to our amazement Alan picked it up, took for a pint of bitter and handed Peter the change.

At that moment, Les asked Alan to order him a taxi.

'Where to?'

'The Star at Brampton.'

'OK' he said, smiling, adding, 'Are you meeting someone?'

'No,' replied Les. 'I'm going to drink there from now on.'

From that day on, none of us went into the White Hart again – at least, not while it was under Alan's management.

From that day on, our watering hole was the Anchor on Factory Street, Brampton, where the landlord and landlady, George and Rose Storer, accepted us with open arms.

One Sunday night soon after the affair at the White Hart, seven of us met up for a social drink at the Anchor. Just before closing time, Rose put seven brandy glasses on the bar, took the brandy from its optic and poured us all large ones. 'Cheers, gentlemen,' she said, toasting our good health. We thanked her and returned the compliment.

Having emptied our glasses, Rose immediately filled them again, which prompted us to ask what the occasion was.

'This is to you,' said Rose, raising her glass to us again. 'To all of you. Since you came to drink here, our takings have gone up by £700 a week!'

We all looked at each other but did not say a word. I wondered if we were all thinking the same. My mind was racing ahead of me, but that might have just been due to the brandy. I was thinking that, if we were putting that kind of money into someone's pocket, wouldn't we be better off putting it into our own?

With that, the seeds were sown, and soon we were all thinking of buying our own pub, our own place to drink, with no one telling us what to do and no change of landlord every couple of months.

The next Saturday, six of us met up at lunchtime in the Anchor. The conversation soon drifted back to what had been said the previous Sunday night, and it quickly became evident that we'd all been thinking the same for the past six days: why not buy our own pub? We sat down and kicked the idea around for a while, and by the time we left that afternoon I'd been given the task of finding a suitable outlet. I'd also agreed to contact my sponsor, the Federation Brewery, to find out if they'd be prepared to back the venture.

Over the next couple of days, I drove around the neighbourhood, looking at pubs that might suit our purpose, then made some initial enquiries into the available leasing, renting and possible purchase of the outlets that I thought would be right for us. To be honest, I wasn't encouraged; the ones I thought were right for us weren't on the market at that time, although of course the places that were totally inappropriate for our purpose were available tomorrow. Then, when I thought we'd never find an outlet, everything suddenly fell into place.

As I was driving down Goyt Side towards the Anchor, I noticed a boarded-up building on the left-hand side of the street. It was a pub, and it turned out that it had been empty for about a year. It had originally been known as the Furnace (probably because of the industry that was in the area at the time), and then it was taken over and became the Out of Town, a pub-cum-club that stayed open late. When that business collapsed, the establishment closed and was boarded up by the owners until a buyer could be found.

I stopped the car, got out and had a look at the building. As I was in the building trade before becoming a full-time darts player, I knew what I was looking for, and after a quick glance at the building I could see that it had recently acquired a new roof, maybe just a couple of years previously. I always say that a 'good hat' is a must when buying old property. If water can't find its way in through the roof, the rest of the building is usually in good shape.

For the moment I couldn't get inside, of course, but I was quietly enthusiastic about my find. However, this could come as bad news for George and Rose, as the old pub was only 300 yards from the Anchor. If we were successful in our venture, not only would they lose our custom but they'd probably find that a lot of their regulars would transfer to our new pub.

I reported my findings to the others as soon as I could, and to my surprise they were all supportive, with no negative vibes from any of them. We agreed that I should enquire further and find out who owned the outlet and where we could get access for a closer inspection.

After a few phone calls, I discovered that the owners were the Bristol Building Society, the company who had loaned money to the previous owner. Occasionally, being well known can help to open doors – and in this case my fame as a darts player did this quite literally. Within a matter of hours, I had the keys to the old building and I and a self-employed builder named Joe Mooney were able to inspect the premises without any agents present.

Inside, the building was in good shape. Predictably, it had suffered some vandalism, and there was evidence that a squatter or two had set up residence there at some point, but on the whole the place was structurally sound. In any event, we'd be gutting it and redesigning the whole internal layout. On discussing my findings with the others, we agreed that we should find out the purchase price and then meet again to discuss our plans.

We had a pleasant surprise when we discovered that the asking price for the property was only £70,000. I then drew up a number of floor plans (a skill I'd developed when I was a youngster in art class) and met with the others at the Anchor, where I showed them what I'd come up with. I know that sounds a bit cheeky, with George and Rose standing only a few feet away, but they thought it was all pie in the sky, that we were just fantasising.

When we chewed over my plans, everyone had their say – 'I think the bar should be over there', 'No, it'd be better over here', and so on. There were no real arguments, just creative input all round. Each of us had a lot of knowledge and skills to offer, plus we all came from different walks of life. We therefore had no difficulty in allocating tasks and positions of responsibility.

I then made contact with David Brook, chief executive officer of the Federation Brewery, and put our proposed plan to him, asking him if he'd submit it to the board of the brewery for consideration. We were looking to raise £140,000, half of which would go towards buying the place outright while most of the rest would be spent on refitting the place, leaving just enough to serve as start-up funds with which to operate the business. Our intention was to create a pub with a unique, friendly atmosphere, a good selection of entertainment and, of course, darts! At that point, we were very optimistic about the whole project.

Within a week, the Federation board had approved our plan, adding a few riders of their own to the agreement, one of which was that David Brook would sit on the board of our company to oversee the brewery's interests – ie their money.

We then held a meeting to hash out the formation of a new company to run the venture. I already had a dormant company, John Lowe Sports, sitting on the shelf, doing nothing, and offered this at no charge to the partners, although we all agreed that it should have a new name. After a lot of thought and a few beers, we agreed on the name Temperate 92 – temperate as in moderate, restrained, sober. What a name for a company dealing in alcoholic drinks! It was perfect, representing everything we aimed to be.

Before I go any further, let me just tell you a little more about the six others who were part of this venture with me. There was Brian Ashall, the managing director of Coalite Smokeless Fuels; Peter Bradley, a director of Protein International Technology; Peter Taylor, a self-employed consultant in the infrared photography industry; Pat Thornley, the owner of a newspaper and confectionery shop; 'Cockney' Les Sheppard, who worked in London for a courier service, and was therefore away from Monday to Friday each week; Joe Mooney, a builder; and me, the darts player. That list comprised six of our company's directors, while the seventh was David Brook of the Federation Brewery.

It seemed from the outset that we couldn't have chosen a better mix of people to run the business. Brian and Peter Taylor would deal with the accounts; Peter Bradley would provide financial advice and also set up the finance controls, arrange stock-taking, installing computerised tills, etc; Joe would oversee the renovation and repairs to the building; and Pat would be our first landlord.

Meanwhile, I would join Joe and help him out with the refit as much as possible, utilising my skills in carpentry and other aspects of the building trade, which would save Temperate 92 a considerable amount on labour costs. David Brook would help from the brewery end, providing us with all the backup we needed to put the business on a firm footing – for example, authorising promotions and discounts.

That left Les Sheppard. It was decided that his skills lay in promoting the outlet from the customers' side of the bar. In his capacity as 'bar liaison', apart from persuading his friends to come and drink in our pub, he was expected to keep the punters drinking while they were there. We all agreed that he'd be very good at this, and for a Cockney living in Derbyshire that was a compliment indeed.

And so, with all the roles and responsibilities farmed out, all we needed was a name. This was an issue that caused a few problems, as most of the guys wanted to retain the original name while I wasn't so sure and instead suggested an alternative. After much discussion, I had my way and it was agreed that we would rename the pub. For obvious reasons (to me, at least), I chose the name the Unicorn Tavern, after my sponsors, Unicorn Products Ltd. After all, I would be the person who would fill the pub on many occasions, with the name and the contacts to fill the outlet with players and visitors from around the country, and it would be Unicorn who would supply dartboards, mats and ready-made point-of-sale material. For a darts-orientated pub, it was an obvious choice.

However, I now hold my hands up and say that I was wrong and the others were right. I should have listened. Their reasoning had been that everyone in the area knew the place as the Furnace; even when it was renamed the Out of Town nightclub bar, the locals still called it by its original name. They argued that renaming the pub would cause us problems, and they were right – for two years, none of the locals knew where it was! But that, we would learn, was the least of our worries as we tumbled into our pub ownership blinded by the bright lights, stifled by the images of the packed-out bars at weekends and on exhibition nights, and deafened by the sound of ringing tills.

We set a deadline of three months from the date of purchase to the opening night. As expected, everyone mucked in. I dropped the ceiling and laid a new dance floor upstairs in the function room, constructed the two new darts throws, put up new studding walls and fitted the kitchen, plus many other joinery tasks too numerous to mention. Peter Taylor undertook major alterations to the electrical system while Joe Mooney organised and took care of any brickwork. The remainder of the team dealt with issues relating to the business side of the company by setting up an office and buying the right equipment that would minimise accounting time.

We succeeded in making the Unicorn Tavern into a town-centre pub. The bar was – and looked – superb, with plenty of room to accommodate customers, whether they preferred to sit or stand. Even though I say so myself, the décor was second to none, and all in all we did a fine job of turning the place into somewhere people could enjoy socialising. We installed four TVs, so there was always something for people to watch, but the sound was turned down after we'd been advised that if it was colour and it moved it would still draw the attention of the punters. We also subscribed to Sky TV, mainly for the sports, and that was an instant winner.

The Unicorn Tavern finally opened its doors on 10 April 1992. The event was advertised in *The Derbyshire Times* and the local gazette, as well as being covered by *Darts World*, and it was a grand affair. The board of the Federation Brewery came down *en masse* for the launch and the chief of the Chesterfield constabulary was also present. Local newspapers sent reporters to cover the event and Yorkshire TV turned up to film it.

This is where yours truly had an influence on the proceedings. It believe that my name helped to turn what would normally have been just another pub opening into a high-profile event.

We certainly opened in true style. Mark Roe, the internationally known golfer famous for signing the wrong scorecard in the 2003 Open when he was in the lead, pulled the first pint of bitter for Chesterfield's Lord Mayor. There was also a champagne buffet laid on and regular house drinks were all free of charge – well, up to a limit of £500, at least, after which it was time to start filling the tills.

A couple of other celebrities made an appearance. John Duncan, the manager of Chesterfield Football Club, and Nigel Bond, the snooker player, both turned up. Even George and Rose from the Anchor joined us for the celebrations, which we all thought was a nice gesture.

All in all, our new venture couldn't have had a better launch. From that germ of an idea discussed on that fateful Sunday lunchtime in the Anchor to the fabulous opening, we'd done everything right. With the golden glow of beer in our brains, we celebrated into the night, believing that we'd achieved what we'd set out to achieve and that from now it would be plain sailing. Even in our initial planning, failure had never been a consideration. Now that we'd come this far, we believed that nothing could go wrong and were confident that the Unicorn Tavern would be a success.

We couldn't have been more wrong.

For its first six months, the Unicorn Tavern did amazing business. The pub was full almost every night of the week, and weekends would see the place packed solid with customers, some playing darts or pool but most just socialising. The board members of Temperate 92 were overjoyed and, riding on the back of that success, we all became good friends. Brian Ashall and Peter Bradley did the book work every Saturday morning while a few of us would meet up regularly to discuss plans for promoting the Unicorn, take care of any little alterations to the pub and deal with those irritating problems that plague any new project. However, we were pleased to report that the ship had set sail and all hands were on deck, working hard.

Pat Thornley, who had taken the job as the Unicorn's manager, appeared to be enjoying his new position and effectively juggled his responsibilities with the pub with the running of his own newspaper shop. Unfortunately – both for him and, as we found out to our cost, for us too – Pat's marriage was going through a bad patch – so bad, in fact, that he and his wife eventually split up. As a result, Pat had left the marital home and was living at the Unicorn on his own, with apparently no chance of reconciliation.

Given that there were female customers in abundance, no one really expected him to stay celibate. He had an eye for the ladies, and there were plenty at the Unicorn. They liked him – and they liked him even more when the beer kicked in. Eventually, Pat decided to leave.

Next, we had to replace Pat, and fast. We needed someone reliable, someone we could trust. At that time, I was busy on the exhibition circuit and left this task with Brian Ashall and Peter Taylor as Peter Bradley resigned before the pub opened.

After Pat was gone, the chef, Mick, took over the Unicorn for a short spell. Strangely, he also broke up with his wife after a couple of months in charge. It seems that the licensed trade isn't a good one for keeping marriages together. I suppose that, when they've had a few drinks, some customers can't resist making complimentary remarks to the ladies behind the bar. Some can handle the compliments quite cooly, while others accept them with open arms – often quite literally.

When Mick decided to leave Chesterfield and move back to Hull, his home town, Brian and Peter Taylor asked Jean Robertson, the manageress of a local squash club of which they were both members, if she'd like to take over, and she accepted. So, within days of Mick leaving, the new manageress of the Unicorn was installed, with her husband, John – a professional coach at the squash club – providing a helping hand, doing all the heavy cellar work and keeping the lines clean – basically, taking on the role of odd-job man.

Our first impressions of Jean were that she looked and acted the part. She was smart, clean, efficient and friendly with the staff and customers alike, while her husband was the 'joining in' type, wanting to play darts and pool and generally become one of the lads. Of course, this was his prerogative; after all, he was employed solely on a part-time basis, and therefore what he did with his free time was his business. Personally, from the start, I didn't take to him, and I had my suspicions of him. He seemed sneaky, and I made my feelings known to the board. For a start, I'd regularly see John sneak out via the back door of the Unicorn to meet up with his mates in another pub. I didn't like the idea of our trade being taken elsewhere or the back door antics. Why did he have to behave like that? Why the apparent secrecy?

Despite my misgivings, however, things ran smoothly at the Unicorn for a year or so. Trade was stable. I brought the people in and would regularly play exhibitions. I'd play as many people as I could – even coach drivers – in the game of their choice: 101, 301 or 501. I booked Leighton Rees, 'The Gentleman of Wales' and the first ever Embassy World Darts Champion, along with Bob Anderson, 'The Limestone Cowboy' from Swindon, and famous left-hander Alan Glazier, 'The Man in Black'. I also brought in Jamie Harvey, Scotland's 'Bravedart', who can sometimes play better darts when throwing them backwards than when he throws them in the orthodox way! He actually scored 180 with his first three darts, thrown backwards, at the Unicorn against John Robertson.

The Unicorn had a fully equipped function room upstairs that was regularly packed out when any of these stars appeared to take on all comers. My son Adrian had his twenty-first birthday there.

My good friend Cliff Lazarenko and his wife Carol became regular visitors at the Unicorn. Cliff, a native of Wellingborough, Northamptonshire, would tell people that his local was 100 miles away!

Despite the apparent success of the Unicorn under the new management, the business still needed an injection of funds, so each of the remaining directors contributed £1,000. Although we had an overdraft at the bank and a couple of months' credit at the brewery, things looked in good shape. However, looks aren't everything, and one Saturday morning in 1995 Brian gathered us together and delivered a bombshell.

'Gentleman,' he said, 'I have some bad news.' In stunned silence, we sat and listened to Brian's declaration that we had 'lost' in excess of £9,000 over the previous six months.

To begin with no one replied. Everyone was too shocked to say anything. Then Brian continued, 'We seem to have been taken for a ride by the management.' He went on to explain that Joseph Dey's, our accounting firm since day one of the company, had discovered a discrepancy where money supposedly paid into the bank didn't correspond with the actual money written on the paying-in slip. It turned out that Jean would go to the bank with the takings, pay in, say, £2,500, and the bank teller would stamp the paying-in book. When Jean returned to the Unicorn, she would then doctor the book and enter a far greater amount in place of the first. Brian hadn't realised what was happening until it had become clear that we didn't have enough money in the account to pay the VAT. What could we do?

A meeting was called where Jean was invited to explain the position. She agreed to pay back all of the money, and she did so within a couple of weeks. I was surprised that someone who earned £200 a week could produce such an amount as quickly as she did, but what was even more surprising was that she carried on as if nothing had happened, as if she'd just paid off a bank loan. Joe Mooney and I wanted to sack both her and her husband, but the board decided that, in their opinion, the incident had been a one-off and that that would be the end of it. Jean was allowed to continue as manager and her husband stayed on in his part-time capacity.

Once again, things seemed to go smoothly for quite some time and the Unicorn kept a clean set of books. But then, in 1993, bombshell number two came out of the blue. Brian called the board to a meeting at the Unicorn only a few months later and, in the same tone as before, told us there was 'a small amount of money' missing. Well, it was hardly small; over £10,000 had gone missing! This time there was no interfering with the entries on the paying-in book, just a calculated misappropriation of takings against expenses deficit. Joe's and my worst fears had been realised.

What a dilemma. One option was to consider cutting our losses and dismissing the Robertsons there and then, or we could reason with them (if reasoning was possible) in the hope that they would repay – again. Jean was called to attend a meeting in the upstairs office at the Unicorn, where Brian explained the position to her. She admitted to being responsible for the irregularity and again agreed to pay back the money. She begged us not to tell her husband John, who apparently had no knowledge of her actions.

With hindsight, I can't believe that we agreed, purely in the hope that the money would be forthcoming. At that time we owed the Federation a considerable amount of money and were unable to pay them, while in addition we had an overdraft with the bank. All in all, things were looking pretty bleak for the Unicorn and its partners.

About six weeks passed and still no money was forthcoming from Jean Robertson, so I decided to pay them a visit, turning up at the Unicorn one Saturday morning. Not surprisingly, I was in a foul mood. I didn't like what was going on, and as far as I was concerned the Robertsons were laughing at us. We were still paying them a salary, and they had free accommodation, free telephone and free Sky TV while we were in debt to the tune of £16,000.

John Robertson was sweeping the tarmac in front of the Unicorn when I pulled up in my car. He smiled and said, 'Good morning.'

I let him have it. 'Good morning?' I yelled. 'Good morning? It'll be a good morning when you pay back the money you owe us!'

Robertson looked shocked. He moved towards me. 'What money?' he asked in a quiet, almost Mr Bean-like voice.

'You know very well what money,' I replied angrily, 'The money your wife has misplaced or, more to the point, stolen.'

At this he turned and went into the pub to confront Jean in private. After thirty minutes or so, he came out of the living quarters and told me that he would personally replace the money. Again, true to their word, the money was handed back within a few days.

Now we were faced with the same dilemma. Should we release them both or allow them to stay? We held a meeting the next Saturday morning to thrash out the management problems. Joe Mooney and I were against the Robertsons staying, while the rest of the directors thought it would be easier to retain them than possibly go through the same problems with any new management. It was a case of 'better the devil you know'.

This, it turned out, was a bad decision, as things began to go wrong again almost immediately. Trade had fallen off and soon the overheads were greater than the profit, and this time the financial directors of Temperate 92, Peter Taylor and Brian Ashall, didn't have an answer to the problems. The debt began to rise again, and the brewery began to ask for payment for products supplied. The management appeared to be toeing the line, but the expenses were for some reason far higher than before. Soon the debt was out of hand and it was not long before the Federation Brewery issued a demand for the outstanding amount of £25,000.

A board meeting was called to discuss this latest crisis. An urgent and immediate injection of funds was required but no one was prepared to cough up. It was suggested by Peter Taylor that the company be put into liquidation, a proposal that appeared fine on the face of it, except that we'd all given personal guarantees that any money owing would be met by those directors who could afford to do so. This let off a few who didn't have a good bank balance, but not yours truly. I would be top of any creditor's list.

I met with David Brook of the Federation Brewery and fellow director of Temperate 92 on 12 January 1997, where we decided that I would offer all the directors a chance to sell me their shares in Temperate 92 for a nominal fee of £1 per share, in return for which I would personally take on the outstanding debt. At first this proposal was met with a resounding no; the directors each wanted their stake back – £1,500 each in total. I told them that, if the deal wasn't accepted by Saturday week, I would withdraw my offer and they'd have to accept the consequences.

Over the next few days, there seemed to be a lot of doubt as to my intentions. I felt that the directors thought I was somehow going to make money out of the Unicorn by putting it on the market. Of course, this was absurd; the selling price of the business was dictated by the accounts, which at that time weren't good.

A few days later, with only Brian Ashall willing to sell his shares to me, the situation had reached a stalemate, so I withdrew my offer and informed David at the brewery. The brewery then drew up its own plan and on 23 January 1997 wrote a letter to the directors of Temperate 92 in which they stated that the brewery was willing to take over the Unicorn and release the directors from any personal guarantees given.

A week later, the brewery took control of the business. I had a meeting with the brewery secretary and David Brook and we came to an agreement that I would take over control of the pub and that David would remain on the board.

Not surprisingly, I suppose, this episode soured the relationship between the original directors and me. Brian Ashall went very quiet and more or less ignored me. Peter Taylor stopped speaking to me almost immediately. Les Sheppard said very little. Sadly Joe Mooney had been involved in a serious road accident and was too ill to take any part in the future of the Unicorn, although I did offer him a chance to join the board at a future date. Friends and friendships had been lost, and the task ahead for David Brook and me was a daunting one.

The Federation agreed to assist us by remortgaging the property, while we loaned a further £50,000, and soon the business was once again operating in the black. However, there were still questions outstanding. Should we install new management? How could we possibly turn the outlet around from making a big loss to generating a healthy profit? We sat together for countless hours working up a business plan. I trimmed all the expenses, cut the cleaner's hours and leased out the kitchen.

We decided to retain the Robertsons, although I cut John's hours and told Jean that she'd have to work the bar like any other landlady. David and I thought at the time that they'd never be so stupid as to loan, borrow or steal our money again.

As it turned out, we were the stupid ones.

CHAPTER 11

How to Lose Friends, Faith and Your Money: The Second Lesson (and the Third)

For the next year I worked myself into the ground, trying to restore the trade and profit margins at the Unicorn. I played exhibitions, invited coach parties, held birthday parties – anything to pull in the punters and make the business work. I've never been afraid of hard work, and believe me I was doing plenty of that. At the time, I was still out on the road, doing exhibitions and taking part in tournaments, but my main aim was to put the Unicorn in a healthy position. I was on a mission. It was 1997 when I took control of the outlet and I let everyone know it.

After a year, I produced a set of accounts that had David, our accountants and our bank manager smiling again; a loss of £25,000 had been turned into a profit of £30,000. The only ones not smiling were the management, as for the first time in a few years Jean and John had found out what hard work was all about. Not that it bothered them very much; they already knew that the smile would soon be wiped from my face.

Although the Unicorn was now enjoying a good trading period, my own private life was in turmoil. I was going through a dreadful time at home with my first wife, Diana, and the atmosphere was unbearable for the whole family. In 1997, I'd begun a relationship with Karen Rawsen, who had just divorced.

We became really good friends – and soon a lot more than friends. However, as I mentioned earlier in this book, through my friendship with Karen I developed a few enemies at the Unicorn, including Karen's ex-husband, Paul, who didn't like me seeing his ex-wife, even though he had one, two and then three new girls on his arm within a short period. Diana's friend, Sheila Cannon, also took offence to my relationship with Karen.

It later turned out that someone had rung *The Sun* newspaper to tell them I was cheating on my wife. My contact at the paper told me it was Karen's husband, Paul, who had contacted them accepting a payment of around £400 for the story. I confronted him and asked if it was true, but he adamantly denied it, arguing that it was probably my wife, Diana, who was responsible.

Anyway, one morning in October, I arrived at the Unicorn at about eleven o'clock to find a reporter and a cameraman outside. I instantly knew the score and decided that, if it was to be like this, I'd work the situation to my favour.

The reporter told me about the phone call *The Sun* had received and revealed that the caller had been a man, not a woman, which confirmed my suspicion about Paul – although of course this didn't rule out the fact that she might have been in cahoots with others to discredit me.

The guys from *The Sun* then asked if I'd pose for a photograph, and I obliged, although only on the condition that the sign for the Unicorn Tavern was also in the shot. They were OK with that. It wasn't much to ask, after all, and at least I knew we'd get some publicity for the business out of the whole sorry affair.

Then the questions were fired at me: 'According to Karen's husband, you've split them up by dating Karen and ruining any chance of reconciliation. Is that true?'

'Rubbish,' I replied. 'They split because of Paul's violence. He kicked her and ripped the TV off the wall in the bedroom and threw it at her. If you need proof, I suggest you visit the local police station. They have it all on record and, for that matter, Karen has photographs of her injuries. They're not a pretty sight, I can tell you. In fact, it's a wonder he didn't kill her.' The reporter had been looking for a story, and now he had one.

After he interviewed me, the reporter did go to the police station, but they wouldn't give him any information, telling him that, as it was a private domestic situation, only Karen or a magistrate could provide any details.

Then they went to my home in Wingerworth to see my wife. I was still living at home at the time, although Diana and I were sleeping in separate bedrooms and, indeed, hardly speaking to each other. It wasn't a pleasant atmosphere for anyone. I had put the house on the market and we both put on a brave front when anyone came to view.

Anyway, Diana confirmed Karen's husband's story, that I'd been going out with Karen for quite a while. Well, OK, I *had* been seeing Karen, but only since she split with her husband, and I fully intended to carry on seeing her, whatever happened. I found myself in love for the first time in many years. I didn't start the break-up of my marriage; Diana issued divorce proceedings against me within days of the reporter knocking on our door.

Because of all this turmoil, I had to delegate some tasks, so I drafted in my son, Adrian, to file the Unicorn's weekly accounts. The system was pretty straightforward. Jean Robertson would fill in a weekly sheet, a detailed list of expenses against takings, and Adrian would then collect the takings to be banked from the Unicorn each Monday, empty the gaming machines and leave the money with Jean after she'd signed for the amount counted. It seemed to me to be a safe and secure process, and I'd thought everything was going fine.

Then, in December 1998, I moved into my new house – bought from the proceeds of the sale of the marital home – and found myself with more time on my hands, and so took back the accounts. I spent a few hours checking through them, and it didn't take long for the alarm bells to start ringing. SHOCK! HORROR! SHOCK! Was I dreaming? I couldn't believe what I was seeing. 'Tell me it isn't true!' I yelled inside. I calmed myself, then checked and double-checked, again and again.

I was still at my desk at six o'clock the next morning. There was no more double- or triple-checking to be done. I'd gone over and over the figures, hoping against hope that it would go away, but there it remained, in cold black and white: a shortfall over the year of £32,000.

I felt a cold shiver go down my spine, followed by a hot sweat, as I realised that this could mean the end of the business. If the Robertsons were, as I suspected, responsible for the shortfall, they couldn't pay back that kind of money. How could they? They didn't earn enough to do so.

Instead of going to the Unicorn straight away, I decided to call David Brook at the Federation Brewery and ask him to come down to examine my findings, and the next day he arrived at my house, went over the accounts and immediately called Jean to arrange a meeting at the upstairs office at the Unicorn, where we revealed my findings to her. I expected her to be panic-stricken, but no; she simply sat there and appeared to be only a little unnerved. No panic.

I showed Jean a list of the weekly sheets and the results. I told her that £32,000 was missing. Her response was like hearing a recording from previous years: 'I'll pay all the money back, but please don't tell my John. He'll leave me if he finds out.'

David looked at me and I at him. We turned our attention back to Jean and explained that the only alternative to paying back the money was for us to inform the police and let them investigate the matter. Jean was unsettled by this and pleaded, 'Please don't do that. I'll pay all the money back, I swear.'

What happened next was nothing more than truly amazing. She and John had already planned to go on holiday four days after we'd informed her about the missing money, although I thought they might have cancelled their trip, given the circumstances. How on earth could anyone go away on holiday, knowing that they owed such a large amount of money? I asked Jean what her plans were with regard to repayment of the debt, and she said that she'd repay the money on the Wednesday before they left.

Confused? I was in a daze for the next two days. Then, on Wednesday, I contacted her and asked if she had the money ready. 'Come to The Unicorn at three and it'll be here,' she replied.

Three o'clock finally arrived, and at the top of the hour I walked through the doors of the Unicorn. Jean was standing there and immediately handed me an envelope that obviously contained a cheque – not cash. I opened the envelope, pulled out the cheque and saw that it read, 'Pay Temperate 92' and was for the sum of £10,000.

I was fuming. 'Jean,' I said, trying not to shout in her face, 'this is not the amount you owe us.'

Incredibly – I still can't believe it now, so many years on – she replied, 'Oh. I didn't think you'd want it all straight away.'

'Well, you should think again.' I said. 'When can we have the remainder?'

'Next week,' she replied confidently.

I didn't want to run the risk of her cancelling the cheque I had in my hand, so I said, 'Fine, but please make sure it's all here next week.'

I left the building, clutching the cheque made out for less than one third of the amount I was owed, and headed for the bank.

The Robertsons duly went off on their holidays as if nothing had happened. I honestly thought what Jean said was the truth and that John didn't know anything about the missing money. Perhaps I'd forgotten the conversation I'd had with him in the car park outside the Unicorn a few months earlier, when I'd revealed her earlier misdemeanour to him.

While the Robertsons were away, Jean put a good friend of theirs named Derek Wise in charge of managing the Unicorn, and I had no problem with him filling in. He was very well known by the customers and I knew he could be trusted. He filled in the week's balance sheet and handed me the money for the bank. When I checked the expenses against the takings, however, we were £400 short. By this time Jean was back so I took the matter up with her. I received a strange reply, along the lines of 'Don't worry. I'll have a word with him.'

That night, Jean handed me £400, saying that Derek had repaid the shortfall. I later found out that Jean had never mentioned the shortfall to Derek. She had, once again, performed some kind of miracle – or had she?

A few weeks went by and there was still no sign of the rest of the money from Jean. I was naturally concerned, so I asked David if we should perhaps bring the matter to the attention of Jean's husband. David advised me to give it another week then we'd meet again and decide what to do.

That week dragged on forever, and when we finally met again David and I decided to ask Jean once more if there was any chance we'd receive the rest of the money at some point in the near future.

When we spoke with her, Jean told us that she was waiting for her pension to be cashed from her last employment at the Brampton Manor Squash Club, which would apparently take a few more weeks, but that she would repay the money as soon as she received it.

Although we despaired at this further delay, David and I felt that we'd waited for so long now that another couple of weeks would do no harm.

Again the weeks went by, and again there was no sign of the money. It soon became clear that Jean couldn't raise the money.

Then, just when we'd given up all hope of ever seeing any of the outstanding £22,000, I received a phone call from Jean. 'I have some of your money for you,' she said calmly, 'if you'd like to come and get it.'

Needless to say, I was at the Unicorn in a flash, and when I got there I was handed another cheque, this time for £9,000. I was still concerned about the rest of the money, but it was a relief to get some of it back, at least. I told Jean that we still needed the rest of the money in the very near future, and she assured me that it would be with us in a matter of days.

Time was passing quickly. It was October 1999 – almost seven months since we'd first noticed the money's absence – and relations between the Robertsons and me were very strained. I'd taken over all the banking and had taken charge of the keys to the gaming machine a few months earlier. The only other source of cash that concerned me was the pool table, but we had to leave that in case any emergency change was needed. At this time, the weekly sheets were exact, week in and week out, and we were actually making a profit. For a while I thought that perhaps, just perhaps, the tide was turning.

Then, out of the blue, I received a phone call from John Robertson. 'I need to talk with you.' he said. 'Can you come down today?'

When I reached the Unicorn, I was surprised to see John with the results sheets spread out in front of him. I realised then that Jean couldn't raise the outstanding money and had decided to tell him. We spoke for a while and he explained that he'd known nothing about the missing funds, but assured me that he would personally find the money and repay us in full. He pleaded with me not to fire them, as this would finish them, leaving them with nowhere to work and, at that time, nowhere to live.

I said I wouldn't fire them, even though I'd terminated Jean's contract a few months earlier when we'd found out about the missing money. She was currently working on weekly employment terms. If any more money went missing, she knew she'd be out of the door.

To my complete and utter surprise, John paid the outstanding amount in full the following day.

I honestly believed that Jean and John thought that, now that they'd repaid the money, everything would be back to normal, but how could it be? I would always be watching them, waiting for another wrong balance sheet. I could never trust them again. This was, after all, the third time they'd taken us for a ride. Surely they didn't expect us to keep them on?

During this time, David Brook had resigned from his position at Federation and had decided to make his home in Phuket, Thailand. This left me with the unenviable task of running the Unicorn and still travelling the world on the darts circuit. I was sick to the back teeth of the place after all the trouble we'd been through with the Robertsons and decided the best course of action would be to sell it. I discussed this proposal with David and he agreed that we should sell up while we were still in a position to do so. And so, in November 1999, we circulated the details of the establishment to the major breweries, giving them notice of our intention to sell.

Interest in the premises was generated almost instantly. Within a very short time, David and I had agreed to a proposal from

Enterprise Inns that they would buy the Unicorn from us. We kept our knowledge of the missing money to ourselves – only David, the Robertsons and I were aware of it. I informed Jean and John that we'd done a deal with Enterprise Inns and that they would be able to remain at the Unicorn in a managerial capacity. If they thought a management position was on offer, I reasoned, they wouldn't try to cook the books before they left.

Instead of thanking me for preserving their livelihood, however, the Robertsons just said they'd consider it. That process took no time at all; very soon, John informed me that he and Jean wouldn't be taking up my offer, telling me that they both felt they wouldn't be able to make enough to have a reasonable living. He then gave me one week's notice, verbally, informing me that he and his wife would be leaving the Unicorn the following week. Surprises to the end.

Fortunately, as luck would have it, some friends of mine – Karen, Mourwyn and Steve Guest – had recently sold their house and, for the moment, had nowhere to live, so I suggested to them that they might like to take over the running of the Unicorn for the next month while we sorted things out. This arrangement suited both parties, and the Guests made plans to move into the pub as soon as the Robertsons were gone. None of the three had been in the pub trade before but I knew that they were all honest.

The Robertsons left in style in January. Coincidentally, it was John's birthday and he'd invited a few friends to the Unicorn for a celebratory drink. I told him I didn't mind, but asked him to make sure that, if they had a late drink, the curtains were closed, as there had been a little bother recently and, as I'd taken over the licence for the next month, I just wanted to be on the safe side. John instantly took offence, insisting that Jean was still the licensee. I argued the point with him, although in retrospect I should have rung the police and had him and his mates thrown out there and then. However, I decided that it would be better to try to ease the situation, as I didn't want my bar wrecked. After all, they'd be gone in a few days anyway.

That night will live in my memory forever. I was there with my new wife, Karen, and that caused some friction. Me, the licensee, being made to feel unwelcome in my own pub! One of John's yobbish mates – a friend of his daughter's, I believe – told me in no uncertain terms to clear off and live in America, adding that, if I was the licensee, he wanted his pint changed as it was foul.

Then another yob swore at Karen and me. It appeared that he'd been working behind the bar, and it was clear to us both that his little fiddle behind the bar was about to end. Karen was furious. Now, she can give as good as she gets and told one of the Robertson cronies, who was helping himself to a drink without paying, what she thought of him.

By that stage, I'd had enough. The mood in the bar had turned nasty and I decided that, discretion being the better part of valour, we should leave immediately. 'Come on,' I said to Karen. 'Let's leave while the place is still in one piece.' I put my arm around her and together we walked out of the Unicorn and into the night.

On the day the Robertsons left the Unicorn, I went down to the pub to accept all outstanding accounts and generally check the premises over. Jean was alone – at least, John was nowhere to be seen – and at first glance everything seemed to be in order, but I later discovered that the darts team's money – about £140 – was missing, after having been in Jean's custody. Some things, it appeared, never change. News of the missing funds had begun circulating around Brampton, but the Robertsons denied any involvement, telling everyone that they hadn't taken the money but that they were, in fact, going to court in order to retrieve it.

We sold the Unicorn to Enterprise Inns in March 2000 and found ourselves with a little money – around £16,000 – left over. It wasn't much of a profit for seven years' hard work. We'd opened the Unicorn in 1992 and had put a lot of effort and time into the venture right from the off. To walk away with so little meant only one thing: we hadn't lost. That in itself was a relief, but obviously we were disappointed that our venture into pub ownership had produced so little. And it wasn't just the financial side that I'd lost out on; I'd put too much of my time into the venture that my darts had suffered, too.

To be honest, I was glad to be out of the pub business. Now, with the Unicorn gone, my life settled down at last. I began to feel better in myself. No more worrying, and no more having to use the Unicorn religiously only to keep its trade; I could now drink where I liked. Most importantly, Karen and I could begin to make proper plans. We'd been married on 12 August 1999 and could now set about turning our home in Walton, Chesterfield, into one that we could live out our lives together. I was so happy and could not imagine that anything or anyone could possibly change that. I had at last exorcised the ghost of the Unicorn, and Karen and I had plans to make. Life was fine.

But then, a year later, in March 2002, I received a parcel that gave me the shock of my life. On opening it, I realised that the past had come back to haunt me. Just when I'd thought it was OK to get on with my life, along came the Robertsons to unmake my day. They had, it appeared, taken Legal Aid and, through their solicitor, were taking proceedings against me first and Temperate 92 second to recover 'their' £32,000.

I was stunned and sat down for several minutes in utter disbelief, then read through all the documentation contained in the parcel. It took me a full two hours.

The papers included a statement by Jean Robertson alleging that both David Brook and I had threatened her, telling her that, unless she paid us back all the money she owed, we'd call the police, who would first lock her in the flat and then take her to jail. More of the same followed. I just sat there and thought, 'These people just never change.' To say that they were being conservative with the truth would be the understatement of all time. The outrageous bottom line was that I should pay back the £32,000 or face the prospect of court action.

I told Karen about the papers that had been served. She was furious – and rightly so. 'You've all been so stupid!' she fumed. 'You should have fired the pair of them the first time it happened. They don't know how to tell the truth. They've dug themselves a deep hole and now they're looking for a way out.' She was right, and they were using the taxpayer's money to back up their concocted story.

I immediately made an appointment to see my solicitors and sought advice from them the very next day. They took everything on board and then we waited. Weeks, months, a year, almost two, passed. Letters were exchanged between the Robertsons' solicitors and mine. Court meetings between judges and lawyers took place to determine the next course of action. Bills – large ones – had to be paid on a regular basis.

We were advised to take a QC on board, which we did – even though he was very expensive – and he went to work with a vengeance. Of the seven cases against me, the judge eventually dismissed six. Only the case of extracting money through intimidation remained. The costs of two of the hearings – amounting to well over £12,000 – were levied against Jean Robertson, and although she had Legal Aid and could declare bankruptcy, the stigma of the outcome would still be hanging over her head for a long time.

Then, after many months and legal bills amounting to over £14,000, on 3 September 2002 I received a letter from my solicitors informing me that Jean had totally capitulated and would no longer be pursuing the matter. Although I found it hard to believe, it appeared that the case was over. No more lies. No more slander against Karen and me. I was presented with a letter stating essentially that, if any malicious words were spoken or written by the Robertsons against my good name at any time in the future, action would commence against them immediately. However, my solicitor also told me that one of the most common phrases used in law is 'do and be damned', meaning that, if they did say anything against us, it would be very difficult to take any action against them. Still, I decided that I wouldn't hesitate to take action against them if that happened.

Was this the end of the whole sorry affair? Were the Robertsons out of our lives for ever this time? Both Karen and I hoped so and began to rebuild our lives again on that assumption. As it turned out, it was the end of the matter for us, but the story still had a cruel twist.

I later learned that Derek Wise, the friend of the Robertsons who had temporarily stepped in as manager of the Unicorn while they were on holiday, had loaned the Robertsons £7,000. The £7,000 Derek had loaned them had apparently been part of the proceeds from the sale of his.

Derek, it seemed, didn't have a great deal of money left some time later and decided that it was time he was paid back. Reportedly, he subsequently had to commence legal action against the couple in an endeavour to claim back his money from them.

I named these last two chapters 'How to Lose Friends, Faith And Your Money: The First Lesson' and 'The Second Lesson (And The Third)' in order to summarise succinctly what happened over the years that I was part of the Unicorn's board of directors. If you were in any doubt about what that title implied when you started reading this section, you'll no doubt know exactly what I mean now and could well be wondering, as Karen did, how the hell we managed to make such a bad job of it. It was all down to trust – although some would say stupidity.

Something that had started out as an exciting idea, a dream created and developed amongst friends, turned into my worst nightmare. Along the way, friendships deteriorated, some to the point of extinction. My trust in people was irreparably damaged. A significant amount of my own money was lost for ever. The cost to my bank balance and to my personal pride was immeasurable. However, the pub project was just something that I had to do. Whether it was the Unicorn or some other pub, owning a pub was something I'd dreamed of doing. But now I've done it, and in the process I've been done. The lessons have been learned and I've now left the pub trade to others.

The only good thing to emerge from those seven years and the experience is that all the troubles I endured helped to strengthen my relationship with Karen, who stood by me throughout. Without her love and support, I doubt I could have got through with my sanity intact.

CHAPTER 12

The Five-year War

I suspect that many readers have been waiting to find out what I have to say about one of the most monumental events in the history of darts, what most people know as 'the split'. In my opinion, however, those two words completely fail to encapsulate even the essence of what was going on between 1992 and 1997, a period which I prefer to call 'the Five-Year War'.

In fact, in the beginning it was nothing like a split. All that was happening was that sixteen professional dart players had mandated a new representative body, the World Darts Council, to represent them from 1993 onwards. This didn't appear unreasonable to those sixteen players, and it was hoped that swift progress would be made. Ultimately, I believe the actions of the British Darts Organisation – and no one else – created the split in the sport of darts. However, before I give you the facts about the split, here's a bit of background of the events that led to that momentous change in the world of professional darts.

Although the split occurred in the 1990s, discontent with the way in which the sport of darts was being run by the BDO, its controlling body, had begun way back in 1975.

Before the 1970s, a few very good darts players, such as my great friend Barry Twomlow, had been able to make a living from darts.

155

Barry won the *News of the World* Individual Darts Championship in the 1968/69 season and was later snapped up by Unicorn and employed as a salesman for the company, eventually becoming known as 'the man who taught the world to play darts'. Other great champions of the past, Jim Pike and Joe Hitchcock were able to supplement their income from running a darts manufacturing company and a pub, respectively, and by taking on all comers on the exhibition circuit.

When the BDO, under the control of Olly Croft, turned darts into a TV sport in the mid-1970s, the professional darts player came into his – and, to a lesser extent, her – own. Players like Leighton Rees, Jocky Wilson, Bob Anderson, Alan Evans, Eric Bristow and, of course, myself became household names, and were somewhat successful, earning good sums of money for exhibitions and appearances. However, even in those early days there was an overriding air of discontent, the contention being that we felt we were being used by the BDO. Although we were all at the top of our game and were true professionals, we had no say in how the sport was organised or promoted or how it would be secured for the future.

In 1975, therefore, a players' association was formed. At first it didn't have an official name, but it consisted of a good number of those household names: Alan Evans, Leighton Rees, Cliff Lazarenko, Eric Bristow, Jocky Wilson, Tony Brown, Bob Anderson and yours truly – you could say, the world's leading players of that time. Its aim was simply to represent the players, who wanted to know the answers to the questions and concerns that were troubling us. For example, why did we lose money every time we played for our country?

Now, that question might sound strange, but it's a fact that, when a player represents his or her country, he or she is given only the value of a second-class train ticket and hotel expenses. OK, a breakfast is thrown in for good measure, but all other expenses are paid for by the player.

A typical example of this situation was the 1983 Darts World Cup, held in Australia. On that occasion, each British player had only their air fare and hotel, including breakfast, paid for by the organisers, and was allocated only £105 for expenses – that is, food (other than breakfast) and drink. I estimate that, including loss of work income, representing my country on that six-day trip cost me £600, which was an incredible amount of money back then. I'm sure no other sport treats its international players in that way.

Another niggling question was, why weren't we allowed advertising space on our shirts when playing in major TV events? At one stage, we all had to wear the WINMAU dartboard company's logo and name, which created a lot of dissent and, quite naturally, angered each of our sponsors, including my own, Unicorn Products Ltd, whose dartboard sales were restricted exclusively to NODOR models at that time. They were also paying me a great deal of money to promote their products, yet there I found myself wearing a rival manufacturer's name and logo – for free! It wasn't just wrong; it was, to my mind, a moral matter for each player. I almost gave up my international career and the captaincy of the England team over it. Luckily, Unicorn were very gracious in allowing me effectively to break my contract with them by wearing the WINMAU logo, but it was still patently wrong for the BDO to have put me in that position in the first place. I was furious.

And there were other questions that needed answering – for instance, why didn't the players have a say in the format of events? If the BDO answered some of our common-sense concerns, the players would have the sense that they were an important part in the overall development of the sport. Granted, the BDO did listen; we had quite a few meetings, usually before international matches or BDO tournaments and usually attended by the players mentioned above, as well as Dave Alderman, Olly Croft and Arnold Westlake or Sam Hawkins for the BDO. Yes, they listened many times, but it seemed as though they paid only lip service to our requests. What the BDO made absolutely clear was that *they* ran the sport of darts, that *they* decided how it was run and that *they* would continue to do so for many years to come. Well, no one can argue with that; they had absolute control over the sport of darts for a further eighteen years.

In 1979 the professional darts players – and now I'm talking about those already mentioned as well as a few overseas players, such as Sweden's Stefan Lord, Australia's Terry O'Dea and Nicky Virachkul from the US – attempted to introduce a professional division to the sport. We first held a meeting with the BDO at Primrose Hill, north London prior to the *Nations Triples* TV event, taking advantage of the fact that these prominent overseas players were in the UK to participate in that competition. About ten players sat with Olly Croft and offered their thoughts. Olly told us that he thought the idea of setting up a professional division was a good one and agreed that it was a natural progression for the sport at that time, but when I asked him to step down from his position as general secretary of the BDO and take over the running of the new division, he said he couldn't do that. Instead he said he would consider running the professional side of the sport within the BDO.

I then told Olly in no uncertain terms that that was impossible, that it would give the BDO a total monopoly of the sport. Not surprisingly, he didn't take too kindly to that and reminded me, 'The BDO put you where you are today.'

'Have you ever considered,' I replied, 'that I and the other professionals all helped to put the BDO where *they* are today?'

Olly opened and closed his mouth, speechless.

At this point Eric Bristow, who was sitting next to Olly, interjected, 'Hey, you can't speak to Olly like that!'

'Why not?' I shot back.

'Because he's Olly,' Eric retorted, 'and without him and his wife Lorna, darts would be nowhere.'

I sensed that to carry on with the discussion would be pointless. It was obvious to me that Eric thought of the Crofts as almost his own family. Meanwhile, Terry O'Dea and Stefan Lord were currently staying at Olly's, so neither of them would support me. The only players I could rely on to back me up were the Welshmen Alan Evans and Leighton Rees, so the meeting ended with the debate in limbo.

Actually, I suppose that Olly had won the first round without even trying, his loyal players, Bristow, O'Dea, and Lord, jumping instantly to his side. I knew when I left the room that my international place was in jeopardy, that I'd have to play my best and keep winning from now on to stay in the England team. I had dared to take on the boss of the sport, and that just wasn't on.

Not just as a result of that meeting but for other reasons, too, I could see that the united body of professional darts players was anything but united. Although the discontent between the players and the BDO didn't go away, it became evident that there were too many vested interests involved to allow any serious restructuring of the sport to take place. Olly Croft knew that if he kept the players, their managers and self-managed players divided, he would always win the day.

Olly knew how to keep certain players loyal to him. A lot of potential work for darts players came through the BDO's office at Muswell Hill – requests for certain players to do promotional work, undertake exhibitions, make personal appearances, etc, as well as enquiries relating to potential sponsorship arrangements.

First in line for any such work was Eric Bristow, who was managed by McLeod Holden, a management company run by Dick Allix, and if he couldn't oblige then another player who was close to the Croft brigade would be offered the work.

'How did you know all this?' I hear you ask. 'Is it just sour grapes, John?'

Actually, no. Far from it. I spoke with a number of company marketing managers at the time who were keen to use darts players to promote their products but were apparently stalled by the BDO. In the early 1980s, for instance, a representative of Unipart asked me one day, 'Why did you turn down the promotions we offered you?'

My answer was very simple: 'I never received your offer.'

At the time, I was ranked number one in the darting world, and I remember saying to fellow international Tony Brown (one of the world's foremost players of that time), 'The only way we'll ever get anywhere is when the work being distributed from the Croft office dries up. Then the managers will be looking for alternative work for their players. Then they'll expect us to stand side by side with them.' But would we?

During the 1980s, the BDO went from strength to strength. The Embassy World Professional Darts Championship, introduced by my good friend Mike Watterson – the most prominent promoter in the sport at that time – was an annual fixture on the darts calendar, and darts was on television almost every weekend and often on weekdays too. The players, however, were very quiet at this time; it was almost as though they were thinking, 'Let's take what's on offer while we can.' Behind the scenes, however, the discontent still remained.

In the late 1980s, things started to go wrong for the world of darts when TV production managers started to drop the sport from their schedules. The home international matches were the first to go, followed by the British professional championships, and before we knew it all that remained were the Embassy World Professional Darts Championship and the WINMAU World Masters. This wasn't a small decrease; it was the darts world's equivalent of the Wall Street crash!

The players and the managers were quick to realise the seriousness of the situation, and meetings were convened with the BDO so that we could ask Olly and his fellow directors what they were doing to safeguard the sport. We needed a united front; the world of darts was in a state of panic.

However, it didn't matter how many times we met with the BDO; the answers were always the same. Time and time again, we were informed that they were trying to secure more events but that sponsors were very hard to find in the pervading economic climate, etc etc.

Rubbish! The BDO had been told many times by management groups like McLeod Holden that darts was facing an overkill situation. It had been clear for some time that the viewing public didn't know which events they were watching, as darts matches were always the same format – 501. So, it was possible to watch a player on television one week playing a few legs of 501 and then switch on the TV the following week and see the same player playing a few more legs of 501. Of course, it was a different competition, but the regularity of it all made things confusing and

– dare I say it? – boring. What was needed was a comprehensive review of all events and professional guidance to set out a plan of action that would ensure the future security of the sport. But, of course, that would cost money, and it would also mean the BDO would have to listen to someone else. No need for that! Muswell Hill knew best.

Meanwhile, in 1985 a large group of players comprising almost all of the full-time professionals, including Leighton Rees, Alan Evans, Eric Bristow, Jocky Wilson, Rod Harrington, Cliff Lazarenko, Bob Anderson, Tony Brown, Nicky Virachkul, Stefan Lord, Terry O'Dea and me – about twenty-four of us in total – set up the Professional Darts Players' Association (PDPA), registering it as a company and appointing Roger Nickson – an official with the London County Team and licensee of the Star Inn at Peckham – as secretary. From its inception the PDPA was very proactive, making lots of noise and, most importantly, being taken seriously by everyone in the darting community – everyone, that is, except Olly.

The NODOR dartboard company asked if it could use the Association's name to promote its top-of-the-range dartboard. The Association was of course pleased to work with NODOR and came to an agreement with the company whereby it paid the PDPA £10,000 per year in order to promote their product. Predictably, this angered the BDO, who had signed an agreement with the WINMAU dartboard company, so they issued a notice to all players that they could not wear the name NODOR on any of their playing attire while involved in any BDO event or promotion. Thus another door was slammed shut in the face of the professional game. NODOR withdrew their offer after the first period of the contract.

By 1990, the situation was becoming somewhat desperate. Things weren't looking good at all for the professional players. Only the proven few, famous names such as Eric Bristow, Jocky Wilson, Cliff Lazarenko, Bobby George, Leighton Rees, Alan Evans and, of course, me, could command reasonable fees for exhibitions. That's not many, really, when you consider that by that time the PDPA had forty-four members. (I've included Bobby George in the list above even though he wasn't a member of the

PDPA, as he knew which side his bread was buttered and stood very close to the BDO, and Olly in particular.)

Management companies such as McLeod Holden, whose accounts were suffering too during this period of inaction, began to make noises, asking their players to stand firm, to confront the BDO and to press – no, to *demand* – to have a say in the future of the sport of darts.

In 1992, many meetings took place between the managers, the manufacturers and a couple of promoters, notably Craigie Taylor, the outcome of which was that it was decided that it was time to form a new body to challenge the authority of the BDO in general and Olly Croft in particular. They had decided that they would introduce new events to the sport and that those events would be offered to the BDO to run on a percentage basis. The new organising body was registered as the World Darts Council (WDC).

There's no need for me to go into any detail about how the BDO responded to this proposal. Just three little words will suffice: no, no and no.

Things finally came to a head in 1993 at the Embassy World Professional Darts Championship. The WDC and the players decided this was the ideal time to make their collective voices heard and on the third day of the tournament issued a statement to the national press that read, 'Sixteen of the world's top players have mandated the World Darts Council to represent them at all future darts championships, including the World Championship.'

I'm sure it's no surprise to learn that this action was totally unacceptable to Olly Croft and the BDO, whose flagship championship had just been hijacked and used to provide major publicity to another organisation and a bunch of professional players.

However, the Embassy's sponsors, Imperial Tobacco, didn't mind at all, as it meant their brand name appeared in all the national papers that covered the story. Indeed, I think that they received more publicity from that story than from the championship itself.

Of course, the BDO – or should I say Olly – replied in his usual fashion, to the effect that the BDO were the controlling body of darts and that the 'rebels' were trying to ambush the greatest tournament in the world for their own greed. I remember Martin Fitzmaurice, the BDO's master of ceremonies, saying to me in the dressing room behind the stage at Lakeside during the tournament, 'You lot [referring of course to the sixteen] are a load of fucking rubbish. You all want throwing in the bin. You're a load of selfish bastards.' However, it made little difference what Fitzmaurice or any of the other BDO's red-coated brigade had to say; at last it was time to stand up and be counted – and the sixteen were doing just that.

This united front was more united than those we'd tried to muster in the past. It was noticeable that we had new players in the PDPA who hadn't known what it was like to have been one of Olly's men – players like Rod Harrington, a man who tells it like it is, even if he's wrong, and Dennis Priestley, a man of principle who had just been made captain of the England team by Olly, I believe in an attempt to divide and conquer the professionals. Fortunately, Dennis can always be counted on to have the courage of his convictions, so he had no hesitation in joining us, as did Rod Harrington. The remainder of those famous sixteen players were Kevin Spiolek, Cliff Lazarenko, Mike Gregory, Peter Evison, Ritchie Gardner, Jocky Wilson, Chrissie Johns, Jamie Harvey, Keith Deller, Eric Bristow, Phil Taylor, Bob Anderson, Alan Warriner and me.

The mandate of the new organisation, signed and dated 4 January 1993, read as follows: 'We, the undersigned, members of the World Professional Darts Players' Association, mandate the World Darts Council to represent us exclusively on all matters relating to the 1994 World Professional Darts Championship. In particular, we recognise the World Darts Council as the only governing body empowered to commit our participation in any darts tournaments worldwide.'

The rest of that week at the Embassy at the Lakeside, Frimley Green, was unlike any other. Olly immediately stopped talking to the sixteen players and most of the officials spurned us as being ungrateful. The players, meanwhile, just got on with playing darts.

Personally, I didn't like the atmosphere at all. I would have preferred it if the dispute could have been settled there and then, but because we'd crossed the ruling body of the sport, and its leader, we couldn't expect any climbdown. It was obvious that battle plans were being drawn up to crush the rebels as we played the World Championship.

Despite being somewhat ill at ease about the situation, my week finished on a high when I beat Alan Warriner and became world champion for the third time. I didn't know at the time that later events would deny me the chance to return to Lakeside in 1994 to defend my title.

Over the next few weeks, the BDO sent out many letters all over the world informing members of the World Darts Federation (the worldwide arm of the BDO) that the WDC and the sixteen players affiliated with it were trying to take over the 1994 Embassy World Championship.

In addition, many people demanded that action be taken against the 'sixteen rebels'. For instance, the BDO branches in Yorkshire and Lancashire wanted the other BDO member counties to act immediately against the sixteen.

On 25 April 1993, the BDO held a full council meeting. It was there that they agreed to a proposal from Lancashire, which was seconded by Yorkshire, to introduce tougher measures against the WDC and its affiliated players for the purpose of lifting the threats made against the Embassy World Professional Darts Championship and the activities of the BDO. The following resolutions were approved by majority votes:

Any BDO official, or BDO player, who is associated with the activities of the World Darts Council shall forfeit the right to organise, attend or participate in any events under the jurisdiction of the British Darts Organisation, or its members, until written undertaking is given that they are no longer associated with the World Darts Council.

Votes for: 57

Votes against: 0

All member counties shall refrain from attending, or assisting in, any exhibitions involving the sixteen players named in the WDC statement issued on 7 January 1993, any players who have affiliated to the World Darts Council since that date, and any players who may affiliate in the future.

Votes for: 54

Votes against: 1

All member counties shall exclude any players who are affiliated to the World Darts Council from darts events under their jurisdiction.

Votes for: 60

Votes against: 0

These resolutions came into effect at midnight on Sunday, 25 April 1993, and so the 'Five-Year War' began.

A few days later, on 30 April, all sixteen players received a letter from the BDO solicitors Paisner & Co that read:

We are instructed by the British Darts Organisation (BDO) and the British Darts Enterprises Limited (BDOE), in relation to the current dispute between our clients, yourself and the World Darts Council (WDC).

We have advised our clients that your actions in, *inter alia*, mandating the WDC to represent you exclusively on all matters relating to the 1994 World Professional Darts Championship, and recognising the WDC as the only governing body empowered to commit your participation in any darts tournaments worldwide, give our clients a potential right of action against you, and the WDC, in the tort of knowingly and intentionally procuring a breach of contract.

The contract we refer to is, of course, the BDOE's contract with Imperial Tobacco Limited in relation to the sponsorship of the Embassy World Professional Darts Championship in 1994 and 1995.

As you are no doubt aware, your actions and those of the WDC are prejudicing the amicable way, but that you, through your affiliation to the WDC, have continually sought to delay its resolution.

Unless you withdraw your mandate to the WDC in relation to the Embassy World Professional Darts Championship 1994, and undertake to refrain from any actions designed to interrupt the 1994 and 1995 Embassy World Professional Darts Championship, in writing within fourteen days of this letter, we are instructed to commence legal proceedings against you immediately.

Now that the solicitors were on the bandwagon, the legal battle had well and truly commenced. The WDC's phones started to ring like crazy and many of the sixteen players were worried: 'Can they sue us? What is this contract we're supposed to have broken? What shall we do? Panic?' You could say that, as most of them did. It was a test of each player's character and resolve. If we could withstand this first attack without anyone breaking ranks, we'd have a chance.

At the WDC, we instructed our solicitors, Clintons, to act on our behalf. The WDC would pick up the cost of doing so, which would be a great help as only a few of us had any real money. Clintons advised us that, by sending us that threatening letter, the BDO and their solicitors were 'trying to break your solidarity. The letter carries no threat to you whatever. It states in the BDO's own constitution that any action brought against any member will have the right of appeal. They have not given that right of appeal, so they are in breach of their own rules and have placed themselves in a position of a counter-claim. They are guilty of preventing you from the right to carry out and perform your activities as a professional darts player, infringement of rights.' Clintons then put in a counter-claim against the BDO.

CHAPTER 13

The Most Delicate of Satisfactory Outcomes

The ball was rolling now but, as time would show, it rolled very slowly. The damage done by the BDO's ban against the sixteen players was catastrophic. Clubs wouldn't book us for exhibitions because their darts players were members of the BDO and, therefore, would not and could not attend. In some cases, relatives couldn't even support darts-playing members of their own family! The counties even banned the sixteen from entering BDO county matches. Fortunately for me, my own county, Derbyshire, didn't implement this.

And so it appeared that, while the BDO had acted illegally, they were getting away with it. The question, then, was how long could the players hold out before they had to return to the fold?

Not content with the actions they'd already taken, the BDO sought the approval of the World Darts Federation (WDF) for their illegal actions. A meeting was convened on 18 October 1993 in the Emperor's Ballroom at the Sahara Hotel, Las Vegas, its purpose to put a stranglehold on the WDC and its sixteen member players. There it was announced that two prior meetings had taken place between the WDF and executives of the WDC with a view to understanding the purposes of the WDF.

It was quite clear that many telephone calls had been made

from Muswell Hill prior to the meeting. The representative from Canada thought that the WDC was only attempting to look after the professional side of the sport of darts (well, they got that right), while those from Belgium and Wales stated that they resented the interference and attempts to take control of major events and insisted that the WDF should resist the WDC. Australia advised that they would have problems with sustaining government support if they were found to have dealings with an external darts body such as the WDC, and the Belgian representative stated that his country's darts players would not be intimidated by threats from any darts body. Representatives for the Czech Republic, meanwhile, queried the nature of the threat posed to the WDF.

Then Wales moved the debate along when they requested that Olly Croft, the BDO's secretary general, use the term 'former top players' when referring to those players who had joined the WDC. Belgium proposed (seconded by Bermuda) that the WDF statement be accepted without division. Votes for: twenty-four; votes against: three.

By this action, the door had been firmly closed on the sixteen players and the WDC, whose players found themselves in the position of being unemployed professionally and, at the amateur level, unable to take part in super-league, inter-county, international or any other major events.

Fortunately, the ostracising of the sixteen rebels wasn't total. One country that continued to allow us to play was America, and that was because the US federal government has strict laws that forbid anyone to take away the rights of others to work, including professional darts players participating in competitive events.

A crisis meeting was then held between the sixteen players and the WDC, where it was decided that the WDC would stage its own world championship in 1994 and also try to arrange and promote other TV tournaments, thereby securing a playing field for the players banned from BDO and WDF events. Major and rapid headway was made, and by the middle of 1993 the WDC was in a position to announce that lager manufacturers Skol would be sponsoring the new WDC World Championships, and that it was their intention to provide at least four televised tournaments during 1994. This was good news indeed, and was naturally welcomed by the sixteen professionals.

Coincidentally (ha!), Olly Croft changed his tactics. I've no idea whether or not all of the BDO's members had a say in this, but it appeared to me that Olly had decided to go it alone in his plan to break the sixteen players as he then proceeded to pressure some of them individually. First Olly contacted Mike Gregory and told him in no uncertain manner that, should the claims reach court and the players lose – which of course, Olly said, they would – Mike could lose his home. Next he approached Alan Warriner and promised him the earth if only he would go back to the BDO fold. Then Dave Alderman, the secretary of the Welsh Darts Organisation, rang Chris Johns and told him that he should consider leaving the WDC, as otherwise he would lose out on playing completely. Strangely, however, no one contacted me.

Not to be outdone, I wrote a letter to the BDO in which I professed that I no longer considered myself a member of their organisation, that I had no intention of ever playing in any BDO event and that I was free from all affiliation with them, thus ensuring that the WDF wouldn't be able to enforce their rule that stated I couldn't play in any world open events. The tactic didn't work, but it did make a lot of people put pen to paper. I received a ten-page letter from Peter McMenamin, the president of the WDF, in which he explained that, while he sympathised with my position, he couldn't go against the BDO.

Surprisingly, at that point in time, the players' resolve was firm. But then, at the end of September 1994, a bombshell was dropped when Mike Gregory announced through the media that he was leaving the WDC and going back to the BDO. He stated that his reason for doing so was that he thought it was the best way forward, but the other fifteen players with the WDC all knew that Mike had finally succumbed to the pressure exerted on him by Olly Croft. And when Chrissie Johns announced that he too was going back to the BDO and play for Wales, it looked as though Olly's plan was starting to produce results.

During this time, the WDC had secured a contract with BSkyB, who weren't happy when Mike and Chrissie turned their backs on the WDC, having already insisted that our contract would be void if any of the players named in the sixteen failed to take part in the championship. I wasn't the only one who thought that the TV company might pull out of the agreement, but thankfully they agreed that, as long as no one else withdrew from the championship, they would go ahead. However, it was a close run thing, as at one time it looked like Alan Warriner would also cross the line and go back to the BDO. Fortunately, though, his mates, and Rod Harrington in particular, kept him on board.

The time for the championship was soon approaching. It was decided by the WDC that the competition would have only twenty-four competitors, and as there were now only fourteen UK players affiliated to the WDC, the other ten would have to be made up of overseas players. A list of potential invitees was drawn up and invitations were sent out accordingly.

We agreed that the format of the championship would be 'round robin', in that there would be eight groups each comprising three players, who would play each other in turn. Points would be awarded for legs and sets won, and the player with the most points would progress through to the next round. After that it would be a straight knockout from the top eight (the quarter-finals) to the final.

That first WDC World Championship, held at the Circus Tavern, Purfleet, Essex, was a great success. Dennis Priestley was the first champion, and the people at Sky were delighted. However, the WDC didn't have sufficient prize money straight after the championship had finished, and many – including Dennis Priestley – had to wait for a long time before the coffers were full enough that they could receive what they were due.

The WDC upstaged the BDO by playing its championship one week before the Embassy, thus stealing a march on the main tournament's press coverage. Unfortunately, nearly all the stories that appeared in the media were about the breakaway from the BDO rather than the tournament itself.

The WDC requested that all meet at Lakeside before the BDO event began, the idea being to picket the Embassy World

Above left: Showing off my golf skills in the British Airways Golf Classic.

Above right: Former Spurs and Wales footballer, Mike Englands, holds the treasured Ryder Cup with me.

Below: The three Chesterfield lads! *From left to right*, Bob Wilson, me and Gordon Banks.

Another trophy I worked hard to win – this time the Beer Drinker of the Year Award! It was presented by Betty Boothroyd at the House of Commons.

Wedding Bells.

Above left: My son Adrian gets married to Karen.

Above right: My daughter Karen on the way to her wedding.

Below: A very happy day as I married Karen.

Relaxing in my free time as I sing with the band, *above* and a round of golf in the beautiful sunshine of Las Vegas.

Above: Snooker player, Willie Thorn has been a great friend of mine for many years.

Below: With Paul Lim and Phil Taylor having done the perfect nine dart game on television.

Above: Barry Hearn inducted Eric Bristow and I into the PDC Hall of Fame. We were the first players to achieve this.

Below: Unicorn presented me with a set of golden darts to commemorate thirty years as a professional player.

e had great fun doing a *Men in Black* pose for Unicorn promotional material.
ery smart don't you think?

Above: Karen and I enjoying a night out on the town.

Below: A proud grandfather for the first time. James Lowe was born on the 18th May 2005.

Championships – or, rather, the organisation that was running it. Consequently, a host of well-dressed darts players were depicted in the national press the following morning holding placards that read, 'THE REAL DEAL IS AT THE CIRCUS TAVERN' and 'WE ARE THE PROFESSIONALS', with a clutch of BDO officials and Mike Gregory watching through the parted curtains behind us.

The BDO went on the offensive and spent the whole week of their championship throwing mud at the WDC and the so-called 'rebel' professional players, describing us as being over the hill. It was all petty stuff – the sort of thing you'd expect of school kids – but the press loved it. I mean, how many times can you write, 'And the player scored 180,' or 'He finished in twelve darts'? Naturally, they much prefer to write about the dirt, the scandal and the untruths, which make good copy and are lapped up by the fans.

On 22 February 1994 I received a letter from Paisner & Co, the BDO's solicitors, in which they stated quite clearly that the BDO accepted they had acted wrongly by issuing the ban on the sixteen of us. 'We have previously made it clear to you,' the letter ran, 'that any suspension imposed by our clients pursuant to the Resolution passed by its members on 24 January 1993 (Resolution No. 1) has ceased to have any effect. You know this and we know this. The County Associations that make up the BDO also know this, but our clients will write to those Associations to confirm the position in order to avoid any doubt whatsoever, if this will be of assistance to your clients and yourselves.'

Could this be true? I could hardly believe my eyes. Were the BDO accepting that they had acted wrongly, even illegally? I re-read the letter – yes, they were! The BDO had had to accept that they hadn't given us the right of appeal, as stated within their own rules. (I later discovered that this letter wasn't circulated among the other member counties, where the BDO carried on with the ban regardless.)

But there was to be another twist. The BDO quickly issued new registration forms that had to be signed by anyone who wanted to play in the Super League. The form was basically nothing more than a statement of allegiance to the BDO. When it should have been checkmate, we actually found ourselves in a stalemate.

The BDO tried its hardest to attack the WDC and the fourteen remaining players at every opportunity. If Olly Croft couldn't do it himself, one of his henchmen would. Tony Green, the BBC commentator and a close relative of Olly's, had already tried to sabotage one of the WDC events, the World Matchplay, by writing to the event's main sponsor, Peter King, the managing director of Proton Cars, informing him that he, Tony, had written to the CEO of BSkyB, Sam Chisholm, with regard to a forthcoming 'darts show'.

Green's letter referred to the WDC players as players from a bygone era who could no longer compete in the current world of darts. He added that, while Eric Bristow, Jocky Wilson and myself had been great players in their day, they no longer had the right to call themselves the best in the world. He went on to say that Sky Sports was blatantly contravening every rule within the ITC, the ASA and the Trade Descriptions Act, although importantly he failed to include in his letter any reference to me being the last Embassy World Champion in 1993. It appeared that, within a very, very short space of time, I had become no longer the best. How could I have become that bad so quickly?

Green then went on to slag off his fellow (former) commentator at the BBC, Sid Waddell, who had transferred his allegiance to Sky but was doing other kinds of work for the station besides covering darts. 'Your link man for last weekend's draw was one Sid Waddell,' ranted Green. 'Was this the same man who just six months ago appeared on the BBC telling those watching a totally different story to the one stated last weekend?' What was all that about?

The letter – which was sad, malicious and very definitely actionable – went on and on, decrying the WDC and in particular the fourteen player members. It was a tirade of over 1,000 words from a man who made his livelihood from shouting, 'In one!' on TV's *Bullseye* game show on Sunday afternoons. In fact, Green should be thankful that Sid Waddell had left the BBC when he had, as Waddell's departure gave Green a job of work for many years to come.

Time went on and many letters changed hands. The solicitors' fees began to rise rapidly – £10,000, £20,000, £50,000. Where would it all end? After three years, the action had gone too far for either side to withdraw. The BDO had already accepted liability for their illegal ban and the WDC had decided to go to court and make the BDO pay, but the players just wanted an end to it all and to be allowed to get on with what was left of their darting careers.

When the date for the court case was finally set, things became rather hectic. We'd received a date by which full disclosure had to be made, so I had to supply our solicitors with all the correspondence I'd received or sent out during the past five years – and there was lots of it. I sat down and photocopied every page.

The court hearing was predicted to last for three weeks, at a cost to both sides of well over £100,000. The WDC had already contacted as many people as possible in order to drum up financial support for the case, and almost everyone they'd asked for support had come up with a loan. The players, manufacturers, promoters and management groups and even the PDPA had emptied their kitties in order to help. People recognised that it was paramount that the WDC should win the case, and everyone was confident that they would, yet at the same time we were all more than a little nervous.

The case eventually came before Judge Tomlin in Court 13 at London's High Court. What an opening day that was! When we got there, boxes and boxes of evidence in the form of letters, contracts, and other paperwork were piled on the courtroom floor. The opening ceremony was conducted, and then – would you believe it? – the case was abruptly adjourned. The judge ordered both sides to go to arbitration and sort out the problem between them and report back to him on the following Monday morning, which meant going to the buildings behind the Law Courts. There, each party would have a room of their own and offers and counter-offers would be passed between the two parties by the counsel or the briefs. The judge had given both parties two days to come to an agreement. I remember thinking at the time, 'If only the judge could have intervened five years ago!'

Cliff Lazarenko and I travelled down to the arbiters' rooms on Friday, as we were requested to be part of any agreement made between the BDO and the players. Indeed, Eric Bristow had already been there for four days. Our barrister was shuttling from room to room so quickly I thought that perhaps he was planning on going out that night and wanted a speedy conclusion!

The BDO were making concessions, but would we accept them? Bristow was saying, 'No. Screw them to the wall like they have done to us for the last five years.'

Then, at about four in the afternoon, the barrister came into our room. 'Gentlemen,' he said, 'we only have one point remaining: compensation.'

I knew then that we'd won the claim. However, still no one at the BDO wanted to back down.

Finally, an offer was agreed whereby the BDO would pay the WDC a considerable sum, in return for which the WDC would guarantee to hire BDO equipment, while the WDC agreed to remove the word 'World' from their name. (I remember that Eric Bristow fumed about this.)

The only other sticking point was the right of any player to take part in the BDO and WDC world championships. It was agreed in the late afternoon that anyone who played in one world championship wouldn't be allowed to play in the other for the next two years.

The next time the barrister came through the door, he had six glasses and two bottles of champagne. He looked at us and said, 'Gentlemen, we have won.'

That night I drove Cliff Lazarenko back to his house in Wellingborough, planning on staying with him and his wife, Carol, overnight but returning to London for the judge's summing-up on Monday. Neither of us was jumping with joy; we were both too exhausted. However, we did have a couple of bottles of wine and a Chinese meal, washing it down with a vintage bottle of Taylor's port.

The next day, Monday, 30 June, we were up early as we had to be in the court for eleven o'clock. Most of the fourteen players would be attending and a few other interested parties would also be there to witness the historic event.

Court 13 is only a small court and it only holds about 30 people. When we got there, we all took our seats, the players and

WDC representatives at one end and the BDO representatives – including Olly Croft, Dave Alderman, Mike Getty and Sam Hawkins – at the other. The barristers and court officials took their respective places and we were then asked to rise from our seats for the entrance of Judge Tomlin.

I remember so well how I felt when the judge entered. I could imagine all the people waiting for their prison sentences, only to see the judge taking his seat and then placing the black cap – the sign of the death penalty – on his head. It had happened many times in this very court. It was very eerie.

We resumed our seats and the formalities began. First, the judge asked the barristers if an agreement had been reached between the two parties. Of course, he already knew the answer, as he'd been given a copy of all the agreements earlier that morning.

The judge then began his summing-up of the case. First, he heaped praise on Olly Croft, stating that the sport of darts wouldn't be where it was today without Olly's hard work over the years, then went on to say that Mr Croft had dedicated his life to the development of darts and was to be commended. I looked at Cliff and he looked at me. I could see in his eyes that he was thinking the same as me. I leant over and whispered to him, 'Who the hell has won this case?'

The judge then went on to announce his findings of the action, which, in short, were in the players' favour. He found that their rights to carry out their profession as professional darts players had been unreasonably restricted. From that day on, every darts player would have the right to enter and play without restriction, and any party who tried to prevent them from doing so would be brought back before the court. All this took little more than thirty minutes to relate from start to finish.

After the court hearing, the WDC officials, the management representatives and those players who were present (not all of them could make it that day) left the court to have photographs taken outside. I remember Olly and his party walked very solemnly down the steps, looking sad and broken. Cliff turned to me and sympathetically remarked, 'If only they'd listened all those years ago, it would never have come to this.'

We then went across to the pub opposite, the George, to have our photographs taken for the national press and darts publications. Our barrister joined us there for a quick drink. It turned out that, because the case had come to a conclusion two weeks earlier than planned, he had time to take a short holiday, which was good for him, even though it meant he wouldn't be paid as much as he otherwise would have been for the case. Still, it was a win for him.

While we were there, I spoke with Dick Allix, who had put more effort into the case than anyone else and, more importantly, had made sure that we had the money to go to court. 'Did we win then, Dick?' I asked him.

'What makes you ask that?' he replied.

'Well,' I said, 'I don't much feel like jumping up and down. I expected the judge to tear a strip off of Olly and his merry men.'

'Well, that was part of the agreement made between the barristers,' Dick replied. 'We won, hands down, but it was made clear that no one would lose face in court.'

So that was how it had worked.

'By the way, how much did it all cost us?' I asked.

'Over £200,000,' said Dick.

Gulp. 'And will we recover our costs?'

'I'm not sure. I very much doubt it.'

At that, I turned to Cliff and said loudly and sarcastically, 'So much for winning. If we'd lost, we'd probably all be hanging from Tower Bridge!'

I could stomach only one celebration drink, as there didn't seem to be much to celebrate. It reminded me of a time when the son of a local landlord stole £1,000 worth of my darts equipment. When the case went to court and he was found guilty, he was asked to pay £150 court costs, while I was awarded £170! I'd won the case but lost £830! (The sad thing was his father had previously offered to pay me £1,000 not to take the case to court, but the police had encouraged me to go to court,) I'd felt cheated then, and now I felt cheated again.

I asked Cliff if he wanted a lift back to Wellingborough, but he said he was going to make a day of it and visit a few people he knew, so I said my goodbyes, thanked Eric Bristow for all the time he'd put into the final days at court and left for home.

The next day, I received calls from the *Nottingham Evening Post*, the *Derby Telegraph* and many other regional newspapers. I told them that we'd won the case, which meant that all darts players in the future would benefit from our action. I conveniently forgot to mention the part where the judge had thanked Olly Croft for all his time and effort over the years.

And so the case of *Eric Bristow vs the British Darts Organisation* was over – and yes, that's what it was called. Although everyone thinks the WDC took the BDO to court over the restraint of trade imposed on a bunch of professional darts players, the action was actually carried out in Eric's name. After all, it was the players who were suffering by the wrongful ban issued by the BDO, not the WDC.

The recommendations of the court concerning the case, known as the Tomlin Order, is available for all to read, but has it been universally respected and adhered to? Not at all; it's been broken more times than my coronation celebration mug. (I've always managed to piece together my mug, but the so-called 'agreement' is an entirely different matter.)

A few days after the court case, Olly and the BDO board began issuing new county registration forms, which were written in such a way that they prevented the fourteen players from taking part in BDO major events. I was told by one BDO official that the Tomlin Order was 'not worth the paper it's written on', and I think he might have been right.

But what happened to Mike Gregory and Chris Johns, the two professionals who at first sided with the WDC and then returned to the BDO fold? Well, it was only a matter of time before they were swept under the carpet. Did they really think they could cross Olly and the BDO and then go back as if nothing had ever happened?

The BBC, which still covers the BDO's Embassy (now Lakeside) World Darts Championships, filmed a thirty-minute documentary exposé of the BDO – and the Crofts, in particular –

as part of their *Blood on the Carpet* series, which aimed to achieve a balanced view of 'the split'. The programme featured an interview with Eric Bristow, who gave his side of the whole event quite well, in my opinion explaining things more clearly than Judge Tomlin did in court! The film depicted Olly and his wife, Lorna, as ruthless dictators who sought control of the sport of darts above all else and really didn't do them any favours at all. Maybe this was the finale that we in the professional ranks and the WDC (by then renamed the Professional Darts Council, then Corporation, as directed by Judge Tomlin) all wanted?

The Five-Year War was over, but it would be another five years before darts would resume full service, and it's thanks to the PDC that the sport of darts has been taken to heights never before reached or imagined.

If only the BDO had taken a more reasonable and open approach in the early 1990s to what the 'rebel' professional players wanted to achieve. If only Olly Croft and the BDO's directors had seen that the time had come to make better, more effective provision for those trying to earn a living from darts. We weren't seeking to usurp Olly's authority or bring the BDO to its knees; we merely wanted to take the professional game in what we professionals perceived was the right and proper direction. At last, we're finally achieving this with the Professional Darts Corporation.

All those years ago, we'd suggested to Olly and his crew that the darts world should have something akin to the football Premier League, and that we should all work together to achieve it. The BDO were invited to play but decided to take their ball home. In the intervening period, their door had slammed shut in our faces so often it damn near came off its hinges. The result was year upon year of grief, argument and counter-argument.

Five years after our successful day in court, Mel Webb of *The Times* wrote that the world of professional darts was still in 'a tortured state' and that 'the yawning schism that exists in the game is no closer to being resolved than it was two, or even five, years ago'. It's true; the pages of *Darts World* magazine are still littered with exchanges concerning a dispute that was legally settled in the Royal Courts of Justice in the summer of 1997.

I can't help but strike an analogy with the rift between the Five-Year War and the war in Iraq. That war officially ceased in April 2003, yet hostilities continue. In darts, the war was officially over in 1997, yet the snipers are still out there.

CHAPTER 14

The Bread-and-Butter Trail

My life story wouldn't be complete without a section about my journey around the world on what I call 'the bread-and-butter trail'.

Over the past thirty years, I've been fortunate enough to have visited many countries in the pursuit of my beloved sport and passion: darts. I have a story to tell about each and every one of those journeys, and I'd like to share just a few of them with you.

In 1981 I made my first visit to Japan. Bud Brick, then vice-president of the World Darts Federation, had invited me to Tokyo to play a few exhibition matches and also to try to secure a sponsorship deal with the Citizen watch company. Bud's wife, Eri, a Japanese lady, would be my negotiator and also the person who would set up my tour of Japan, while Bud rang me the day before I left for Tokyo to inform me that a television crew would be waiting to interview me at the airport when I got there.

As it turned out, travelling on the plane with me was Victor Borge, the comedian and pianist, and the two Canadian inventors of the board game Trivial Pursuit. Apparently we were all doing television interviews on arrival, which meant that three TV crews would be at the terminal gate.

I arrived at Tokyo Airport in good shape. Citizen had given me club-class tickets, and that made a lot of difference on such a long haul flight.

When I walked with the rest of the passengers up the aisle from the plane, I was amazed to see around twenty arc lights blazing away and three television cameras pointing in our direction. 'Wow! I thought 'These Japanese people know how to welcome you.' The aisle had been roped off in order to keep away the people passing through and to leave a clear space for the cameras.

As we approached the end of the walkway, a security guard stepped in front of me. 'Please wait there,' he said.

'OK,' I replied.

Then, to my amazement, who should walk up the next aisle, adjacent to ours, but Michael Jackson and his chimp, Bubbles! The TV people were going mad, dashing around like little school kids.

Two minutes later, Michael and Bubbles were gone – and so had the lights and the cameras. Victor Borge, the two Trivial Pursuit guys and I stood there in almost total darkness for a while, and then, almost simultaneously, we burst out laughing. We'd all thought the cameras were for us!

A few minutes later, I was interviewed for a local TV station in a small room, in front of one small camera. It took all of five minutes. As I left, though, Victor Borge was just going into the same room, to be interviewed by the same crew, and I thought, 'At least I've beaten the pianist!'

That first visit to Japan was a very rewarding time for me. Through Bud and Eri I secured a contract with Citizen, and I was also granted an insight into one of the world's oldest and greatest cultures. I went to tea-making ceremonies – nothing to do really with making a brew; more a discipline. It took thirty minutes to make two tiny cups of tea, and every stage of the process had a spiritual meaning.

I noticed that all the children in Japan go to school dressed the same, the boys wearing their hair cropped very short. When I asked why this should be, I was told that the reason was again rooted in discipline, in that no one goes to school thinking they're better than the others. I can't help feeling that such an attitude wouldn't go amiss back in the UK.

I have returned to Japan on three later occasions, each time finding new treasures and accumulating more fond memories. And I'll never forget a game the Japanese called 'pitchenko', which they play to release stress. Bud once showed me how it was played, taking me to a room containing around 100 machines, identical to the upright Allwin amusement machines I remember from my youth, into which you inserted a coin into a slot and a little ball-bearing then came out of a hole. On flipping a lever, the ball would then travel around a circle at a fantastic speed. When it slowed down, it would drop down the front of the machine and disappear into whatever hole it falls into. If you are lucky, your ball goes into the centre hole – 100 points – and then another ball appears and you do the same thing all over again.

Now imagine 100 Japanese playing this game at once in one place, all shouting and screaming at the machines at the same time. This, plus the noise of the balls spinning around, was deafening. I asked Bud what happened when the game was over, and he told me that, if a player has enough points, he or she goes to the control counter and exchanges them for cigarettes. I thought that this was strange; you visit the pitchenko room to have a good shout and scream and relieve yourself of all that built-up stress, and then you walk off down the street, smoking a Marlboro!

Then, on my third visit to Tokyo, in 1983, I was fortunate enough to be invited to the Diet Building in Nagata-cho, the core area of Japanese government administration. It transpired that one of the ministers who worked there had been injured in a road accident and as a result was confined to a wheelchair. Darts had become his passion, and although severely handicapped he could throw a mean dart. He had arranged for me to take part in a paraplegic challenge, to play sixteen players simultaneously, all in wheelchairs. I was fascinated and quite proud to take part in this challenge, feeling like a chess grand master.

I threw three darts on Board One against a player with one arm and one leg, then moved on to the next board and threw three more. I carried on down the line until I'd thrown three darts at each board. While I was doing this, the competitor at each board would throw his or her darts. When I reached the end of the line, I then went back to the first board and began my second throw, and so on.

I did win all sixteen matches, but that wasn't important. It was the attitude of the players that struck me most. They weren't just participants; they were committed, competitive players. Only a few of them spoke any English, so we communicated via the one thing we had in common: darts.

My last memory of Japan was one that will live with me forever. In 1983, I visited Osaka, where I'd once played an exhibition in a pub called the Sherlock Holmes, and Bud invited me along to one of the players' homes for a typical Japanese meal. There were about ten of us there that night, and we all sat around a small, low table that had what appeared to be a tea-light warmer in the centre below a shallow steel tray that had seasoned sake simmering in it. At the sides were various meats. I soon found out that the way to eat was to pick up a piece of meat with the chopsticks and dip it into the simmering mixture until it was cooked to my liking – so easy, and so very tasty.

At the end of the table there was a large serving salver containing round parcels of rice wrapped in seaweed, which, I learned, were the accompaniment to the meat. And right in the centre of the tray was one round parcel that looked almost like a small cake. It was bright orange in colour, and I noticed that no one touched this one at all. I asked Bud what it was.

'It's yours if you want it,' he said.

'How come?' I asked.

'You're the guest of honour. The one in the centre is always reserved for the main guest.'

By this time I was pretty full, and the food was almost finished, but nevertheless I took my chopsticks and held them above the orange parcel. The room went deathly quiet. Everyone was either looking at me or staring at the parcel.

Well, having tried almost every food in the world, from poisonous snake to ducks' feet, I thought that surely such a nicely coloured treat couldn't be too bad for me.

Wrong! I picked the parcel up and, with all eyes in the room following it towards my mouth, put it all in and chewed. I'd never tasted anything like it in my entire life. The food went down – and then came back up. Down, and back up again. It took an almighty swallow to keep my pride intact, to finish it off and not vomit.

Having achieved that, the Japanese guests stood as one and applauded me, bowing.

'Well,' said Bud. 'You've done it this time, Lowey.'

'What?'

Bud smiled. 'You're a hero now in their eyes.'

'Tell me what it was,' I demanded.

Bud replied, 'That was the paste of a sea urchin. And I'll tell you now that none of them here would contemplate eating it.'

I guess I knew why! Although it's supposed to be good for the brain cells, the taste of that 'sea-urchin paste' makes you feel quite fine with your cells as they are. It was obvious that the dish was set out for the main guest as a source of entertainment for everyone else present, and on this occasion the guest proved to be a worthy champion. Thus I accepted my new-found fame in the Japanese fashion: I stood and bowed to one and all and, through Bud's interpretation, invited them all to join me at the House of Karaoke, a local bar. (Incidentally, I've never eaten sea-urchin paste since.)

In 1996 I was invited to go to Madrid to film a live show called *Supressa, Supressa*, Spain's equivalent of Cilla Black's *Surprise, Surprise*. Running from six in the evening until midnight, it's the longest live show in the world, and I'd been invited to make an unexpected appearance on it after a very keen Majorcan darts player named José had hailed me as his sporting hero. At the time, playing the game with steel-tipped darts wasn't big at all in Spain, so the producer thought it would be a good idea if they invited José to appear and show the viewers how to play. The plan was that, while José was being interviewed, I would walk up behind him, throw a dart over his shoulder and scare the living daylights out of him. Easy? Well, it certainly sounded straightforward enough.

When I arrived at the studios on the outskirts of Madrid, I was amazed to see at least 2,000 people milling around outside. A carpet was laid on the tarmac from our car to the entrance of the studio and – just like in Japan – arc lights and cameras were set up. However, unlike that time in Japan, this time they really were there to film me and my travelling companion, Peter Lippiatt, walking into the studio.

When we reached the door to the studio, we stopped and looked back to where another car was pulling up. I said to Peter, 'Is that who I think it is?'

'Yes,' he replied. 'James Coburn, the guy from *The Magnificent Seven*.'

James left his vehicle, walked up to the studio and said to us, 'Hi, you guys.' Then he shook our hands and introduced himself.

I gave his hand a good firm shake (I'd always wanted to shake hands with a cowboy!) and then said proudly, 'John Lowe.' I don't think he had a clue who I was, and I almost added, 'Son of Frederick Lowe from New Tupton.'

The three of us then turned as yet another car pulled up. This time the crowd outside went mad, and when the car door opened and the man inside stepped out they were delirious. It was Ronaldo, the greatest footballer of the time, standing there and waving to his fans.

'Wow!' I said to Peter. 'This time we're mixing with real superstars.'

At least Coburn and Ronaldo spoke to us, unlike Michael Jackson back in Japan, who'd just walked straight past us without so much as a hello.

The show itself was a strange experience. James Coburn had to sit at the end of a makeshift cowboy saloon with his back to the door, while the man on the show who idolised him (and who, of course, didn't know that Coburn was on the show too) was instructed to enter the saloon with guns in both hands and call out, 'I've come to get my boy!' Well, so I was told, at least; everything was, of course, in Spanish.

When the man entered, brandishing his six-shooters, the other actors in the bar, all dressed as cowboys, dived over the bar, leaving just Coburn with his back to the gunslinger. Then Coburn swivelled round in his chair and faced one of his greatest fans and said, 'You'll have to get past me first.'

The fan almost collapsed. The guns dropped from his hands, his mouth fell open and he just stood there, trembling.

Coburn stood up and walked across and gave him one of his big handshakes, speaking Spanish – or so he thought. (Coburn had apparently told the producer that he could speak Spanish, but what he really spoke was Mexican, which isn't quite the same.)

Ronaldo's entrance was even more dramatic than Coburn's. The producer had set up a mini quiz, with the fellow who idolised Ronaldo being one of the contestants. The fan was asked how many goals Ronaldo had scored that season, and he then launched into a two-minute description of each and every goal. Then, when he'd finally finished talking, a football flew in from the back of the studio and Ronaldo followed, juggling another football with his feet and head. He called to the man, 'You missed one!', then turned and kicked the ball towards a goal mouth they had set up. 'That one.' He then gave his fan a signed shirt and a signed football. Needless to say, the guy was gobsmacked, so happy he was speechless.

Then it was my turn at last. They had José stand with his back towards where I would be making my entrance and instructed him to throw a few darts. He was very nervous; the studio audience numbered about 700, but there were millions more watching the show on their TVs at home. At the producer's cue, I came up behind José and threw the dart over his shoulder. He was surprised all right – I almost pierced his ear! The dart was so close that he spun round to see what manner of madman was throwing darts at him. Then a big grin appeared on his face as he recognised me and he flew into a Spanish greeting. I had to wait for the interpreter's voice to come over my earphones before I could understand what José was saying and form a reply.

I've looked at the tape of that show many times, and it looks really strange, like watching a reporter using a satellite phone live on Sky News. After each question from the studio, there's a delay for what seems like minutes before the reply comes through.

Peter and I left the studio quite late that night. Well, I guess anyone would. After all, it's not every day you have a chance to sit with and talk to a movie star and a world-famous footballer, is it?

In every nation I've visited, television has always been attracted to darts. Darts, after all, makes for easy TV. A game is simple to set up and can make two or twenty minutes of interesting television.

In 1990, I visited Moscow at the behest of my longtime sponsor, Unicorn, who intended to launch their products in the USSR and had made good contacts within the Russian government and the Kremlin. Barry Twomlow, Unicorn's roving darts ambassador, travelled with me.

When we left Heathrow Airport for Russia, I was quite surprised to find that we didn't have entry visas. Michael Lowy, Unicorn's sales manager, who was also travelling with us, explained that we'd been invited by the Russian government and that they would be overseeing the whole trip.

'Hmm,' I thought. 'Interesting.'

When the plane touched down at Moscow Airport, we disembarked to find huge queues waiting at the immigration desk. I thought it was going to take us a couple of hours to be processed, but to my amazement a tall Russian man dressed in what I thought was normal grey attire took us through a side door into a large room, where he asked for our passports before disappearing through another door. A woman present in the room then offered us coffee and tea, and then she left too, returning with our drinks along with a small bowl of ice cream. She quickly explained that they had no milk and that the ice cream was there as a substitute.

After a further five minutes, the man who'd taken our passports returned, handed them back to us and asked us if we were ready to leave for Moscow.

I had a look through my passport. No government stamp. Barry checked his, too – again, no stamp.

'How will anyone believe we've ever been to Russia?' said Barry.

'Don't worry', I replied. 'I have the camera.'

'Well,' said Barry, 'I suggest you be very careful where you point it.'

I understood where he was coming from.

On our arrival in Red Square, we were taken to a large theatre in a government building that was used for major lectures. There was an audience of about sixty people already waiting, most of them press. The television people had set up their cameras and Jerry Preski, our host from John Brown Engineering (the company who built the Channel Tunnel), had arranged for a dartboard to be set up.

I played darts with Barry for about an hour while we took it in turns to speak to the interviewer via an interpreter, hoping he was translating our English exactly! Later we discovered that we'd been on one of the country's two TV channels for an hour and that the viewing figures had been enormous, and the next day a feature about me was published on the whole back page of one of the two Russian newspapers.

I soon realised that the government had total power over the public. It wasn't so much that people liked or understood the sport of darts; the government controlled the output of both TV channels, so the viewers had no choice but to watch what was put in front of them. This was what I call the 'old Russia'.

This first visit to the Soviet Union was kind of experimental. It didn't boost Unicorn's sales dramatically, but it did give the Russians the idea of making their own darts. The problem they had was that they needed someone like Unicorn to promote the sport, and for some reason I was chosen to be the face of the company. Maybe my Derbyshire background had a few similarities with theirs. Whatever the reason for my being there, I didn't find it difficult to associate with the people, although verbal communication was obviously something of a barrier.

By the time I next visited Moscow, in 1991, Perestroika – the restructuring of the country – was certainly having an impact. What a different place it was! Just off Red Square, there was an American-style bar selling spare ribs and chicken wings and boasting pool tables and a dartboard, while next door were two nightclubs. Gone from the streets were the many Lada cars I'd seen on my previous visit, replaced now by Mercedes and BMWs that raced across the square.

On that occasion, I'd been invited to take part in a televised darts event in which I would play the Finnish champion over the best of nine sets of 501 – straight start, best of five legs to a set. When I was asked to make the week-long trip, I said I'd do it on the condition that they put me up in a top hotel, by that I meant (and learning from previous experience) one with hot water and toilet paper. I'd also asked the sponsors to provide a cultural tour for me, preferably taking in the Kremlin if possible. I didn't ask for any spending money; again, from my previous trips there, I'd learned that the Russian's didn't really have any – at least, none that was worth anything. The organisers agreed to everything I asked, and I was really looking forward to the trip.

On my arrival, I was taken to a fabulous five-star hotel close to the Moscow Dynamo football stadium. After I'd unpacked and settled in, I was driven to a large mansion house about twenty miles away where I was to have dinner with the government representative from the Olympic Sports Council and a few other dignitaries.

That night was another eye-opener for me. We started with champagne and caviar and then went on to a seven-course dinner, accompanied by some of the best wine I've ever had the privilege to drink. The meal and the evening were rounded off with the finest Napoleon cognac. I slept very well that night!

The next day was that of the challenge match with the Finnish champion. The venue was a restaurant, where a stage had been built in front of the diners. It was almost as if Lakeside – the home of the Embassy World Professional Darts Championship – had been moved to Moscow. It was very professionally done. I sat at a table next to a man who I gathered was very important, as he had two bodyguards standing at the corners of the room, watching everyone and everything. He knew little English.

When I was asked what I'd like to drink, I ordered a vodka, knowing that it would probably be served neat. This isn't a problem with Russian vodka, however, as it's not sharp and is usually drunk this way. Soon, a couple of bottles of vodka were placed on the table: one clear, the other a slightly brown colour. I tried them both and expressed a preference for the coloured one, and the next thing I knew, six other bottles were placed on the table in front of me. I remember thinking, 'What's the Finnish guy drinking? Nothing, I hope. Boy, is he in trouble!'

That night told a tale of woe for the Finnish champion when I beat him by five sets to nil. He won only five legs in the entire match. The restaurant was packed out with a capacity crowd of around eighty people and shot a ninety-minute show for television. The problem was, I'd beaten the Finnish champion in double-quick time and so had to make up thirty minutes or so with a darts 'clinic' in which I explained the rules of the game, the purpose of the doubles, trebles and bull, and talked about stance and style – in short, how to play.

At the end of the night, Jerry Preski, our host from John Brown Engineering, turned to me and said, 'How much did you win tonight?'

'Jerry,' I replied, 'you know as well as I do they don't have any real money, so what's the point in asking them for prize money? I've asked them for an all-expenses-paid week-long tour of Moscow, including a trip to the Kremlin.'

At this point Jerry, who speaks perfect Russian, introduced me to the man who had been sitting with me at the table. What a shock! He was the president of SovInterBank, the official bank for the Soviet car industry. He was the sponsor! And I thought they didn't have any money to pay me!

Jerry spoke for a while with the sponsor, and when he'd finished the man beckoned to one of his henchmen who came over, put his hand in his pocket and pulled out the biggest wad of money imaginable. He put the lot in my hand. Jerry looked at me and said, 'Just a bit of spending money for your trip.'

The rest of the trip was remarkable. I was given the full tour of the Kremlin, and at one stage I was within knocking distance of Gorbachev's office door, and the Sports Minister presented me with a medal that only the Olympic gold medal winners in Seoul had received. I then followed none other than Mike Tyson and his wife to a sports training facility where Mike was doing a boxing promotion for the Russian government, although I believe in truth that he'd been sent by boxing promoter Don King to explore the possibility of holding a world-title fight in the Soviet Union. And – surprise, surprise – I drank a great deal of vodka (although not in the training facility!). It's just a matter of joining in with a Russian tradition. Vodka does seem to be one product that they have a lot of.

Dining in Russia can be quite memorable. Anyone who makes a speech has to drink his or her shot of vodka straight down. Michael Lowy of Unicorn has never been known to be a drinker, but a speaker? Well, he just can't help it, and at dinner on our last night in Moscow, at a Georgian-style restaurant just off Red Square, it really was Michael's night. He made speech after speech. He was so merry – no, in fact he was drunk! By ten o'clock he was chatting up the Sports Minister's wife. If he'd tried that a few years earlier, he'd have undoubtedly found himself next morning on a train bound for Siberia.

As I left for home, my Russian hosts wished me well in their native tongue. I had no idea what they were saying at the time, so I simply nodded in acknowledgment, smiled and thanked them for their hospitality. I considered how amazing it was that a country had changed so much, so quickly. It seemed like one year it was Communism, the next Westernisation. The first time I'd been to Russia, I'd had to have ice cream in my coffee at the airport because they had no milk; then, two years later, they had an Irish bar there!

After I'd returned home and unpacked my things, I was staggered to realise that I'd kept all the roubles the president of the bank had given me – thousands of them. 'Now I'll have to go back,' I thought, 'as the banks in the UK won't change them.' In fact, it's illegal to take Russian currency out of the country.

It will be fascinating to go back and meet the many friends I made on my previous trips to Russia, particularly the people I'd dined with in that restaurant just off Red Square. I later found that, when they'd bid me farewell that night, they were actually saying goodbye to 'the Godfather of Darts'.

In my career as a professional dart player, I have visited the southern hemisphere on a number of occasions. Australia is one of my favourite countries in the world, and I love the city of Sydney and its many wonderful bays. However, no trip to Australia is complete without a visit to Sydney's seafood restaurant Doyle's. The first time I went there, back in 1986, there was just the one Doyle's, at Western Bay, but by 2004 this one had been joined by two others.

I'll never forget my first experience of Doyle's. I went there with Jocky Wilson when the pair of us were down under as guests of Channel 9 TV and our host was the cricketer Ian Chappell. We travelled from Sydney Yacht Club by water taxi, passing the bayside houses, each of which was worth millions. As we passed one house, we saw Robert Sangster in his garden and waved, but I guess he had no idea who we were.

We arrived at Doyle's and ordered mussels for a starter and fresh lobster for our main course. When they arrived, each of these huge lobsters overhung the large plate on which it sat by 3in on either side and must have weighed at least 3lb. Then, when the waiter came out and asked if there was anything more he could get for us, Jocky looked up and said, 'Yes. I'd like some chips.' No sooner asked than done. The waiter came back with a bowl of chips and poured them all over Jocky's lobster. Ian and I were in hysterics, but Jocky never even blinked. He squeezed the fresh lemon over everything, downed his beer and tucked in.

A couple of years later, I toured Australia again – or, at least, part of it; it's such a huge country it would take a couple of decades to do the lot. This tour was organised by Gary Churnside, a darts distributor in Australia who was trying to build up his business. Gary knew the darts people on the east coast very well and had put together a very well-organised tour that included a visit to Tasmania, the large island just south of Victoria (I say that for the benefit of any Australians, who sometimes forget it's there at all!), where I was scheduled to do two exhibitions. Gary and I checked in at the Point Hotel and Casino in Hobart.

The first night's exhibition in Tasmania was great, with a packed house, good darts and good company. When we arrived back at our hotel, we collected the keys to our rooms, had a nightcap and decided to call it a day. On our way to our rooms, however, we noticed that the floor in the corridor was soaking wet and could smell burnt wood. We did not have to wait long to find out why: the paint on the door to Gary's room was blistered, and the door to my room next door was in a similar condition.

Gary threw open the door to his room and then just froze. I peered over his shoulder. 'Bloody hell!' I said. 'I think there's been a fire.'

What an understatement! The whole room was burnt out. The windows had been smashed and then boarded up. I rushed over and opened the door to my room, expecting to find more of the same, but found the room relatively undamaged. Smoke had discoloured parts of the room, and the smell was truly awful, but fortunately all of my possessions were OK. But why hadn't we been told about the fire when we'd collected our keys?

We walked back to the hotel's reception, where Gary demanded to see the manager, who was very apologetic when he arrived and explained that he'd given instructions to the reception staff not to give out our keys but instead to call him so that he could explain the situation to us. Clearly, the staff had forgotten.

It turned out that the cause of the fire was the television in Gary's room, which, after we'd left that night, had burst into flames.

That experience left me thinking just how lucky we had been. After all, it's not unheard of to go out and leave the TV on.

I left for my bed after a few drinks with the manager, who had calculated that Gary was entitled to $10,000 compensation for the loss of his possessions. He had, after all, lost everything. However, Gary – an ex-CID man in the Australian police – and the manager weren't shaking hands, and Gary then pointed out that our rooms hadn't been fitted with fire alarms or extinguishers. I never did find out how much he eventually settled for, although I should imagine it was a considerable amount.

My darts took me in ever-increasing circles around the world, and in 1993 I arrived in Thailand for the first time in order to help launch the Federation Brewery's brand products in that country. The chairman of the brewery, Jimmy Ramshaw, and the CEO, David Brook, came with me on the visit, which coincided with the Pataya Open darts tournament and, three weeks later, the Thailand Open darts event. My exhibitions were organised in Pataya and Bangkok – all in outlets that had agreed to take the brewery's products.

My first experience of Bangkok was pleasant, to say the least. I remembered the publicity the snooker boys received on one of their trips to that city, when a reporter from one of the UK's Sunday tabloids followed their every move, later publishing his findings (which didn't make for pleasant reading for some of the players' families) on the weekend of the Thailand Open snooker event. Jimmy White came out of all this very badly, although his mates probably thought he was a hero. I felt a little more than sorry for them all.

I was booked in to play at American Jack's bar in Pat Pong, having never been to Bangkok before and not knowing what to expect. On my arrival, I was asked to wait outside the bar for a few minutes while a photographer for the *Bangkok Post* and national newspapers took my picture. I was posing for the shots, holding my darts in the usual way, when the next thing I knew I had ten girls swarming around me – leaning against me, kneeling down in front of me and hanging around my neck. The photographer snapped away as I looked at the camera, not knowing what the hell was happening.

Then I realised there were about 200 people watching this display – and it didn't take long to find out why: the girls were totally naked. Nice? You bet! But all that night I was thinking, 'What if that photograph makes the daily press back home?' I knew that my marriage was a bit rocky at the time, but that kind of disclosure would have sunk the ship there and then. Eventually, the girls disappeared just as quickly as they had arrived and I was left to play sixteen matches of 701, so I honestly never tasted authentic Thai, so to speak. The truth of the matter is that I was actually very dubious about them, as they appeared to be so readily available, so easy. I've always preferred a challenge when it comes to women.

So that was my introduction to Thailand, the country of smiles. Indeed, there were plenty of people smiling one week later at two in the morning on our night out after I'd played yet another exhibition in Pataya. At the end of that night, David Brook, Jimmy Ramshaw and I were on our way out of the bar where I'd been performing when we almost bumped into a passing elephant that was on its way home to the farm after a busy night of posing for photographs for the tourists.

'Stop!' David called to the elephant's driver. 'Quick! Get a poster on him.'

Jimmy, who was carrying the posters for the exhibition tour, nipped back into the bar and returned with some sticky tape – and a lot of people.

While the driver muttered something in Thai, Jimmy stuck the poster to the elephant's side. David then told me that I was going to sit on top of the elephant and have my photograph taken for the brewery's in-house magazine. (It's wonderful how the mind works when it has alcohol rushing about inside it.) The elephant was only a baby, so it didn't look too hard to climb onto its back. The driver brought the elephant down onto its knees, and I was supposed to stand on one of its front legs, and then, when the elephant stood up, it would lift me up and onto its back. Simple, right?

Well, no. When the elephant decided to stand, instead of going upwards I went backwards and smashed straight into the wall, cracking the face of my beloved Omega watch in the process. The elephant had also done damage of his own, kicking out its back leg and catching one of the thirty or so mopeds parked beside us at the side of the road. Over went the bike, and the rest went down like dominoes.

That was it for me; I was well and truly pissed off. The hands of my watch were stuck on 2:22 and no drink in the world was going to make me feel better.

The driver of the elephant wasn't amused, either, and he wanted paying.

'Give him some money,' David said to me, so I pulled out a fifty-baht note and held it out.

In a single swift movement, the elephant's trunk came over, sucked up the note and delivered it to the driver, who then tapped the elephant on the ear. This signal must have meant that fifty baht wasn't enough, and so the elephant promptly dropped the note. I then pulled out a 100 baht note, and again the elephant picked it up with his trunk and delivered it to his boss. This time the driver kicked his heels and they were off back to the farm.

I carry that memory and story everywhere I go. I often think of the sight of all those mopeds falling over and then despair when I remember how much it cost to have my Omega repaired, but I wouldn't change a thing.

I've visited Thailand quite a few times since then and now have my own charity golf day firmly established at the Phuket Golf and Country Club. Central Hotels and Resorts are one of my sponsors on the darts circuit in that country, and they give good support to the golf classic.

At the 2003 John Lowe Golf Classic I auctioned off a set of gold Unicorn titanium darts that I'd used in the world championships. There was quite a large gathering for the presentation, with all the competitors and sponsors of the tournament convening on the terrace outside the Karon Village Hotel. I informed everyone that the darts were special and that I expected them to raise around £150 at auction for a local children's hospital, then opened the bidding at 10,000 baht. An arm shot up straight away, and we were away – '15,000 from the man in the white hat', '20,000 from the guy in the corner', and so on.

At 80,000 baht it was down to just the man in the white hat and the local tailor. The tailor then bid 90,000 and I said to white-hat man, 'Go again. Another 5,000 will do the trick.' He nodded his approval. I then tried to get the tailor to make it 100,000 baht, but he demurred. The auction was at an end.

'Ladies and gentlemen,' I announced, 'please give a round of applause.'

By now the Thai waiters were just standing and staring. They couldn't believe the sums being bid for my darts. After all, 95,000 is worth about £1,200 – about six months' wages to those waiters. I imagined their thoughts: 'Who is this guy? He must be very famous!'

That night I was very pleased, not only because we'd raised a lot of money for the charity but also because we'd raised the profile of darts, as the money we raised for those darts was a record amount for darting memorabilia. Even so, I hope that it'll be broken soon and that even more will be raised for worthy charities in this way.

If I make all this globe-trotting sound like one continuous laugh, it's because that's how I'd like to look back on it – as a good time I had while doing my job. However, the serious side – the exhibitions and competitions – can be equally as rewarding, and I've been fortunate enough to have won a record fifteen world open darts tournaments. Now, that takes dedication, serious practice and many hours of competing. After all, the players who reach the finals are usually those who play the most.

My trip to Thailand in November 2003 was intended to be a holiday, a time to recharge my batteries for the busy period ahead. I was planning on spending the time just sitting around the pool all day, making a start on this book. And so I arrived in Phuket armed with three Papermate pens, two A4 notepads and what I thought was enough memories to fill the latter many times over.

To my surprise, when it was time to put pen to paper, there was nothing there. I couldn't link a sentence together, never mind a page or a chapter. The pages stayed resolutely blank. So I decided to do the usual things – sunbathe, swim and generally laze around – intending to have another go the following day.

Well, the following day came and still nothing. The same thing happened for the next three days, so in the end I gave up.

Later that week, I was invited by David Brook to meet with some of the ex-pats on the island and have a few beers. We met in a bar owned by one of the Brits but run under his girlfriend's name of Kaan. From my seat near the door, I spotted a Buddhist monk outside just sitting and looking into the sky. Curious, I went over to him and engaged him in quiet conversation, and to my surprise he spoke very good English. It turned out that he'd been educated in England and returned home to Thailand to join the Buddhist faith.

The monk then asked the reason for my visit, so I explained to him that I was primarily on holiday with my wife but that I'd also be playing a few exhibition matches around the area. He understood darts very well and likened it to a form of Zen.

Then we talked about my proposed new book, and I told him how I'd been unable to find any words so far on this trip. At this point his Buddhist teachings manifested themselves. 'You know,' he said, 'The reason you are unable to find the words is quite simple. They are in there, but they have become mixed together with many other words. Like a computer, the brain can store only a certain amount of information. Once capacity has been reached, something has to be taken out to make room for new information. Or maybe the information already stored has been placed into the wrong file. When you sit to write your thoughts, they come out mixed with other thoughts and do not make sense.'

Well, he'd really hit the nail on the head there. 'What do you suggest I do?' I asked.

'Nothing,' he replied. 'Relax and refresh the body. The mind will refresh with itself and automatically place all thoughts into the correct file.'

I understood but decided to ask more. 'How do I free up some space in there so I can absorb more?' I asked.

'You must dispose of the thoughts that you do not need. They can take up the most room. Jealousy, greed, hatred and selfishness – they can consume and totally exhaust the human brain and they are the most difficult to remove. Sometimes they keep returning and can be likened to the modern-day computer virus that keeps rewriting itself.'

'Wow!' I thought. There I was, many thousands of miles away from home, talking to a monk and yet hearing what my mother had said to me in my teens. Obviously she'd used different words, but she'd told me the same thing: 'Don't fill up your mind with useless information.'

I thanked the monk, said goodbye and returned to the bar to refresh my glass. I did not tell my friends what we'd spoken about, although they did ask when I was joining the order.

On that trip I'd arrived in Phuket armed with pen and paper, but in the end I didn't write a single word of this book. Instead I simply did what the monk had advised me to do: relax and recharge my batteries.

Now, I hear you say, 'All this globe-trotting, visiting interesting and exotic countries, is all well and good, Lowey, but what of life on the trail in the UK?'

It's a good point. Well, when I think about touring the UK, one incident immediately springs to mind and brings a huge smile to Old Stoneface. As Simon and Garfunkel once sang, 'And here's to you, Mrs Robinson ...'

The Fiesta Club, Stockton-on-Tees brings back many memories of the early professionals. At that time, Barry Dennis and Cameron's brewery were responsible for taking darts to a level never seen before. 'Walk-ons' (ie players walking onto the stage while accompanied by their own signature music) are now common practice in all divisions of the sport, but it was Barry Dennis who introduced the very first walk-ons nearly thirty years ago, featuring attractive girls, music and flashing disco lights.

The Fiesta Club became the home of the Strongarm Cameron's Classic from 1976, a tournament that was run over sixteen weeks, during which the club – a 400-seater venue – would always be packed. The very best players took part in this tournament and the darts played was of the highest quality. I won this event in 1977, but it's not the tournament itself that sticks in my mind from that year but the guest house in which I and most of the other players stayed: the Pendelphin, run by a Mrs Robinson.

The Pendelphin was only a few yards from the Fiesta Club and was known in entertainment circles as 'pro-digs', a place where all the entertainers who appeared at the Fiesta stayed. Top English comedian Freddie Starr, pop group The Fortunes and UK comedian Dick Emery had all stayed there. In fact, the list of well-known names who lodged under Mrs Robinson's roof was very long. Then, in the 1970s, it was the turn of the darts players to join this prestigious list.

I remember my first stay at the Pendelphin as if it was only yesterday. Mrs Robinson made me very welcome. She was a fan of mine, and she showed it. She asked me into the Robinsons' own quarters, and on that and future stays I was given one of the best rooms. In those days, of course, there were no en-suite rooms; the toilets were down the corridor, just off the landing.

Not surprisingly, the entertainers didn't usually return to their digs until the early hours of the morning, and when they eventually stumbled through the front door, they'd find vacuum flasks left by Mrs Robinson on a table in the hall, labelled 'coffee', 'tea' and 'drinking chocolate'. Even the milk jug and the flask containing water would be labelled.

As I got to know the ways of the Pendelphin and Mrs Robinson, it didn't take long for me to realise that she labelled everything. The toilet had a notice over it that read, 'Please do not pee on the floor' and 'Please put the seat down when finished', while the pull-cord light switch bore a sticker that exhorted the night-time user to please switch off the light. It was impossible to look anywhere without seeing a sticker or label telling you to do or not to do something. The lads used to laugh at Mrs Robinson and her strange habit.

I remember sitting in Mrs Robinson's kitchen one afternoon when she told me that the singer Tony Christie had recorded a cover version of the Paul Simon song 'Mrs Robinson' especially for her. (Good old Tony – never one to disappoint the ladies!)

I also remember staying at the Pendelphin one night at the same time as UK comedian Freddie Starr and his band, on the last night of his three appearances at the Fiesta Club. Freddie was – and, indeed, still is – famous for his practical jokes, and he'd become quite friendly with the bar manageress, a woman called Christine. Although Christine was clearly fond of Freddie, too, she was also a little scared of him – understandably, as no one ever knew what he might get up to next.

On this night Freddie was on his best behaviour and invited Christine to his dressing room for a drink before he went on stage. Christine was convinced that nothing untoward would happen, and so she accepted, bringing with her to the dressing room a bottle of champagne and two glasses, as Freddie had requested.

When Christine got there, Freddie was sitting at a table in the centre of the room, and she placed the bottle of champagne and the glasses on the table and sat opposite him. Freddie then leaned forward, opened the bottle and poured two drinks, and then he stood up and proposed a toast to Christine, thanking her for looking after him and the band for the last four days. However, as she raised her glass in acknowledgement of the toast, the wardrobe doors around the room burst open and out spilled the members of Freddie's band – all completely naked and lunging towards Christine. Not surprisingly, Christine dropped her glass and fled in horror. You could hear the laughter down in the main concert room.

Freddie later apologised to Christine, who took it in the spirit in which it was intended and no doubt has never forgotten that Starr story ever since. But I digress …

That very same night, after Freddie's last show at the Fiesta he returned to the Pendelphin in the early hours of the morning. I'd been out playing an exhibition with Leighton Rees and had arrived back at around 2am, about the same time as Freddie and his band. Someone produced a bottle of whisky, and soon we were sitting in the lounge of the Pendelphin, drinking scotch out of coffee cups. Freddy was again on top form and was taking the mickey out of Mrs Robinson's notices, which were attached to everything in sight. Eventually, at about four o'clock, we all drifted off to bed.

The next morning – or, more accurately, lunchtime – I packed and went downstairs to pay my bill. Leighton was still in bed and Freddie and the band had already left. I went into the kitchen and found Mrs Robinson absolutely fuming with rage. 'Something wrong?' I asked.

'*Something wrong?*' she yelled back. 'You would not *believe* what that Freddie Starr has done.'

I waited with bated breath. What could have possibly made her so very angry?

Drawing a deep breath, Mrs Robinson told me, 'He's been to the toilet to do a number two, collected a big turd, taken it to his room and placed it in the wardrobe, where he's put a straw in it with a notice attached to it reading, 'Please do not crap in the wardrobe.'

I wanted to burst out laughing, but I could see Mrs Robinson was not amused and somehow held back. I could imagine this turd sitting in the wardrobe with its sail attached, like a ship in the night, to confront Mrs Robinson when she opened the wardrobe door.

I paid my bill and left the Pendelphin. It was a two-hour journey back home to Chesterfield and I laughed all the way, wondering if Mrs Robinson took down any of her notices after Freddie's prank.

Back on the trail, the best exhibition I ever played took place in the UK, at Durham's Argus Butterfly in 1983. On that occasion, I was up against fourteen players over a series of matches, each comprising one leg of 1001. The list of contenders featured quite a few Durham County players, and I knew it would be a tough night. As it turned out, however, I needn't have worried; that night I could have thrown the darts over my shoulder and they would have still landed in the treble-twenty bed. I beat all fourteen players and on the way scored twenty-three maximum 180s.

At the end of that night, one player came up to me, shook my hands and said, 'Thanks, John. You've just finished my ambitions of becoming a good darts player. I've never scored 180 in thirty-two years of playing.' With that, he threw his darts down on the table and left in despair.

Nowadays exhibitions are changing. The resurgence of darts as a major TV sport has brought a new dimension to the game. The PDC, with their razzmatazz and their new vision of darts as an exciting sport, have created a spectacular game that draws in more and more viewers. Unfortunately, this hasn't convinced people to rush down to the shops and purchase Unicorn darts with the aim of becoming high-earning professionals; instead they're rushing out in their thousands to buy tickets for the Circus Tavern and the PDC World Championship at Blackpool and the World Matchplay – and more!

Nowadays many people come to darts exhibitions for the same reason: they like to watch good darts and they love the atmosphere created by a good darts match. I tour quite a lot, doing a 'Legends Night' with my old sparring partner, Eric Bristow, and our aim for each night is to entertain, which we do by playing people from the audience, finishing with a head-to-head match between the two of us over the best of thirteen legs of 501. We don't run quizzes or play disco music; that's not what the punters come to see. They want to see the players they watch on TV doing their stuff. I don't think I'm being over-modest when I say that, even today, Eric and I are the best-known faces in the world of darts.

So those are some of the stories I've accrued during my time on the bread-and-butter trail. It's good to know that, at the age of sixty, my bread is still being buttered – probably not as thick as it used to be, but nevertheless nicely, thank you.

CHAPTER 15

Relentless Darts: The North American Open Darts Tournament

I've pondered long and hard over which darts tournament out of all of those I've played in is the hardest and most difficult one to win. This chapter is about that tournament.

Many people would instantly say that the *News of the World* Individual Darts Championship was the most difficult tournament to win, taking the form of the best of three legs of 501, from the very first round in your local pub right through to the Grand Final. In that contest, there was no chance of falling into bad form and hoping to pick up in the next set, because there wasn't one. And you have to remember that the players in the *News of the World* Championship represented only England, Scotland, Wales, Eire and two invited countries: Sweden and America.

I'm not saying the *News of the World* Championship didn't rank right up there; it did. After all, it was the biggest event in the world of darts back in the 1940s, '50s and '60s, and countless numbers of participants took part in clubs and pubs throughout the UK. However, as other tournaments became established in the 1970s, it lost some of its acclaim, the number of entrants dropped off and eventually, when sponsors backed out and the newspaper itself had a change of policy towards the sport, it was lost to the darting fraternity. The tournament was reintroduced briefly for one season in the 1990s but is seemingly now lost for all time. We will never see its like again.

I always believed that I would never be classed with the greats of the sport unless I won the *News of the World* Championship, and I was determined to do so. My neighbour and close friend Barry Twomlow had won the title in 1969, and I realised that that one win had made him almost immortal. My home county of Derbyshire also had a double *News of the World* winner in Tommy Reddington, who had won the trophy in 1954/55 while playing out of the New Inn, Stonebroom, in the process beating Johnny Bell of the Sun Inn, Waltham Abbey, Essex, two–nil in the final. Tom's second success was in 1959/60, when, representing the George Hotel, Alfreton, he beat Dai Jones (Cambrian Hotel, Aberystwyth) two–one. I realised that, if I was ever going to be recognised in my home country, I needed to put my name alongside Barry and Tom's.

In 1976/77 I made it through to the semi-finals of the *News of the World* Championship at Alexandra Palace, London, where I played in front 13,000 spectators. What a crowd! Few other sporting events could command such numbers. Surprisingly, I wasn't nervous. Mind you, I had steadied myself with a couple of beers! However, it proved not to be my year when I lost in the semi-final to Mick Norris from the King of Denmark, Ramsgate, and that was after bursting on 140 to win the match. The only solace I could draw from that defeat was that Mick went on to win the title, beating Bob Crosland (Blackamoor Head, Pontefract) two–nil in the final.

I returned to London in 1980, this time to the Empire Pool, Wembley, where again I reached the semi-final of the *News of the World* Championship, but again I lost, this time to Stefan Lord from the Stockholm Super Darts Club, Sweden. Again, I had been beaten by the eventual champion, with Stefan going on to beat Dave Whitcombe (Naval Club, Chatham) two–nil. I vowed that I would return and take the crown.

I returned yet again in 1981, this time playing for the Willow Tree at Pilsley. I made the journey to the Empire Pool, Wembley, for the finals, and as usual there were thousands of spectators present and countless millions watching on TV. It made me feel good, as it seemed to me that the majority were rooting for me, chanting, 'Lowey! Lowey! Lowey!' I was the bookies' favourite to lift the trophy this time, but I knew that it wouldn't be easy. This was, after all, my third attempt, and although they say, 'Third time lucky,' I knew there were some good darters in the draw. Scotland's number-one player at that time, Rab Smith, was the one I was most worried about.

In the first quarter-final I'd drawn Cam Melchiore, the US Open darts champion. He drew first blood, shooting out on 115 to win the first game. We matched each other in the second leg and Cam had a chance to beat me, but I won that game and the next to set up a semi-final match against Rab, who had put out Stefan Lord two–nil in his quarter-final match.

I remember *Darts World* reporting that that semi-final 'had everyone on the edge of their seats', and it turned out that I'd been right to worry about Rab. He won the first leg with a 100 game shot and then came back at me in the second, leaving himself 120. His first dart hit the treble top, leaving him needing only a single and double top to finish me off. He hit another treble and burst.

I had forty left to get. I missed double top, missed double ten but hammered in the double five to level things up. I then won the toss to start the decider and in seventeen darts secured my place in the Grand Final. I knew then that it was my year.

The nice thing about the final was that my opponent was none other than Mick Norris, who had beaten me back in 1977, giving me a chance to exact a little revenge. Mick hadn't lost a leg up until the final and had a chance to win the first leg of what was an ordinary game by our standards, but he missed the double twenty to finish. I then walked up and checked out on double sixteen.

In the second leg, Mick seemed dejected and threw some indifferent scores while I piled in 41, 140, 100, 100, 100 and double ten (first dart). This time I had made no mistake and had taken the title with ease. *Darts World* quoted me as saying afterwards, 'Now I can be happy for the rest of my career.' I went home knowing that I could now stand tall in Derbyshire. I was on the list that mattered most. I was the *News of the World* champion, and I felt like I was champion of the world.

So I hear you say, 'Why do you have such a problem ranking the hardest tournament in the world to win? Surely that story tells it all?' Wrong!

In 1977 I made my first visit to America after my sponsors, Unicorn Products, had asked me to play in the North American Open Darts Tournament (NAODT), which was being played on the HMS *Queen Mary* at Long Beach, California. I was really excited at visiting America and even more so at being able to take part in the biggest darts tournament in the USA. But there was a shock in store for me.

The first week of my visit, I stayed with Tom Fleetwood, the NAODT's tournament director, and his wife, Della, at their home in Bellflower. I would sit in Tom's den and talk to him about darts America, where it all started, how it was run, etc. He was always very obliging and had no problems answering all the many questions I put to him, but when I eventually asked him what he'd done for a living before entering the world of darts, I was surprised to learn that he was an ordained Methodist preacher. I was even more surprised when he told me that he'd played the part of the bartender in long-running cowboy TV series *The High Chaparral*. However, I wasn't at all surprised when he told me that he'd been a quarterback for the Green Bay Packers, as he was a very big man, weighing over 30st.

Before we went to the *Queen Mary* for the NAODT, there was a pre-warm-up shoot in Santa Monica known as the Santa Monica Open, a very prestigious event well attended by darts players mainly from the West Coast. (Incidentally this is where Eric Bristow got his nickname 'the Crafty Cockney', from a bar of that name in Santa Monica whose logo was a UK flag behind the image of a British policeman.) I became aware at this event that it was important to be part of a good team of players, as the weekend included doubles (both men's and mixed [the ladies' doubles round wasn't introduced until 1983]), a four-person team game and open singles.

I also learnt that time was of no concern to anyone. The weekend would start with blind-draw doubles, where each contestant would pay his or her entry fee, and a few minutes before the start of the matches a draw would be made to determine partners. You might be lucky and draw a good player or you might be unlucky and draw a first time player. The logic behind the 'blind draw' event was that it would introduce new players to the sport and at the same time give them a chance to play with and against the very best. At the time, I thought the concept was a great one, and indeed the more I played darts, the better I liked it.

The blind-draw doubles would begin around 7pm and finish when the final was over, which might be midnight or even 2am! As I said, time wasn't an issue; the weekend was all about getting people up playing darts and partying. It certainly didn't take me long to get used to both.

After Santa Monica it was back to Tom's for a couple of days, and then, on the Wednesday before the NAODT, we made our way to Long Beach to the HMS *Queen Mary*. The ship, which could accommodate over 2,000 people, was full to capacity, but that first year I had a room to myself. I'd been entered in an American team comprising of Jody Simkins, Javier Gopar and Andy Green – all fine 'shooters', as they call dart players over there, and all ranked right at the top of American darts. I knew that to win anything we'd have to play outstanding darts.

The Brits, meanwhile, had a couple of good teams, one in particular that included the pairing of Leighton Rees and Eric Bristow. Although I was playing with the Americans in the team, I'd paired with Tony Brown from Dover in the pairs and I really fancied our chances to do well in this event.

Let me tell you about the format. The men's singles and doubles took the form of the best of three legs of 301, with a double to start and one to finish. That leaves no room for mistakes. If you don't hit the opening double quickly, before you know it you're left way behind, while if you *do* get away and reach the double first, you must finish in three darts to guarantee winning the leg. Once you've both hit the starting double, your opponent is never far behind. On each leg, regardless of whether or not you won or lost the previous leg, you go for 'cork' (the US terms for the centre bull) to decide who throws first.

Now, this is some game of darts, and not for the faint-hearted, where concentration is of the utmost importance. With one slip, lasting for as little as eight minutes, you could become a spectator for the rest of the event.

That first visit to the NAODT was memorable, to say the least, as on that occasion I won my first event on American soil (or I should say water?). The team of Simpkins, Gopar, Green and Lowe won the team event, and things got even better when Brown and Lowe won the pairs. Then, at 3:30am, Alan Glazier, 'The Man in Black', from London, one of the best left-handed darts players of all time, won the men's singles match and Maureen Flowers, from Staffordshire, won the ladies' singles. The line up of winners also included Andy Green and Vicki 'Sticky Fingers' Williams from California, who won the mixed doubles.

To be honest, I'm surprised I can remember any details about the event, as the darts and partying were relentless and the days and nights blurred together. We started the blind-draw doubles on Friday night at 7pm and the final of the men's singles 301 was over by 5:30pm on Sunday. I estimate that I'd been in my bed for a total of only seven hours throughout the whole event and had managed to consume only six hot dogs, two beefburgers and a plate of French fries. Nevertheless, I'd enjoyed the experience. It was no effort for me to play darts for ever, but the partying was something I decided that I had to get used to for the following year. I learned that it was no good saying you didn't want to join in, as participation was compulsory.

I returned to the NAODT every year for the next twenty-three years, my goal being to win the hardest darts event on the planet – yes, even harder to win than the *News of the World* Championship. I battled away each year, getting ever closer to that goal, and in many matches missing one dart at the double only to see my opponent take out a big score with three darts and win by two legs to one. I chalked up more victories at the NAODT than any other player, winning twelve events in total, but it was

1985 before I achieved my ambition of winning the singles event.

I remember talking to Cliff Lazarenko on the night before the 1985 tournament's singles final. By that time, the tournament had become so big that a new venue had to be found, so after the World Cup in 1979 the Space Center in the Sahara Hotel, Las Vegas, became the home of the NAODT. The venue has a capacity of 10,000 (with 4,000 present that year) and was the biggest room in Vegas that didn't have a supporting roof pillar.

Anyway, Cliff and I were sitting at the bar below the Space Center that night and I said, 'I don't think I'll ever win this event. This will be the one missing from my legend.'

'Nonsense,' Cliff replied. 'If I don't win it tomorrow, you will.' And believe me, Cliff was quite capable of winning.

That night I broke my golden rule and, instead of going to bed at midnight, stayed up until around 4am with Cliff and some good friends of ours, BJ Clark and Howie Reed. We even had breakfast before we went to bed. Don't ask me why; it just seemed a good idea and, indeed, is something the Americans do regularly in Vegas.

The singles match started at about eleven o'clock the following morning. I was in the Space Center early that day, practising for around two hours. I felt good, but at the same time I'd conditioned myself that, if I lost, it would not be a disaster. After all, I'd been losing at some stage in the event for the last eight years.

As it turned out, I actually made good progress throughout the day. I was using double 14 as my double-in with great accuracy, and I even hit a perfect leg of 301 in six darts. I reached the quarter-finals and conceded only one leg. 'Big Cliff', who had been knocked out in the top sixteen, was giving me all the support I could ever ask for, while BJ Clark kept asking me if I needed a drink and a whole bunch of ex-pats were shouting me on.

After two hours of play, I reached the semi-final. This, along with the other semi-final, would be played on the floor – ie on the regular boards used for the knockout stages. My opponent for this match was Bobby George, who I was told had been playing well all day. Well, I never needed winding up to play Bobby, and I produced great darts to take him out to the tune of two–nil.

I was now in the one final I'd always wanted to play in, ever since my win at the *News of the World* Championship in 1981. This was my chance to add the NAODT to my ever-growing list of tournament wins.

My opponent in the final was Lane Helgeson from St Paul, Minnesota. Lane was the surprise of the tournament; an outsider amongst such world-class players, he'd made it because he hit those doubles in and out. I must admit that my confidence rose a little when I knew I was up against Lane, who'd had to borrow a shirt with a collar (stage regulations) before he was permitted to play in the final. Besides, the money was on 'Old Stoneface'.

The men's singles event was always played after all the other finals, which meant we had to wait around five hours after qualifying. This, for me, was the most worrying thing. What do you do for five hours? Practise? Not a good idea after playing so well all day. Go for a meal? If I did that, all I'd want to do was sleep. I decided the best way to prepare was to get out of the room for at least a couple of hours, then come back and start practising as if it was a new day.

No points for guessing where I headed: the bar near the bottom of the elevator, where I'd been until four o'clock that morning. Cliff and BJ Clark kept me company.

We were stood there, enjoying a screwdriver, when a man with a lived-in face approached us and said, 'Hi guys. How are you doing?' I remember thinking, 'Why is a Brit talking in an American drawl?'

'Fine,' we replied. 'How are you?'

'Better now I've met you two,' the man said, looking at Cliff and myself.

'On holiday?' I asked.

'No,' he answered. 'I'm working here.' He held out his hand and introduced himself, 'Micky Gunn, Hartlepool. No need to tell me who you are. I've been watching you on TV for ages.'

I asked Micky what he did and he replied, 'I'm a comedian. I'm the man who invented spoonerisms, reciting *Cinderella* backwards and mixing up the words. I'm playing the revue bar opposite the elevator.'

'In that case, we'll come and watch you tonight,' I said. 'But first I have a little business to take care of upstairs.' I didn't tell him I was in the final of the NAODT.

Soon it was three o'clock and time to prepare for the final. When I went back into the Space Center, the ladies' pairs had just finished; Judy Campbell and Karen Lawman Smith had won. Judy came across and wished me all the best for the final and gave me a huge kiss. (I've tried to keep that one quiet, lads!)

I started my practice routine but found I had no rhythm. Had the break not worked? How would I find my throwing style before the final began?

The practice area was behind the stage, cut off from the audience by a curtain. While I was there, a lot of my American friends asked me to have a drink. Not wanting to seem impolite, I ordered a brandy on ice each time, not realising that the drinks were then handed to Cliff, who lined them up on the table as he watched me throw. So when it was time for the final, I suddenly realised there were about a dozen large brandies, all in a row.

'Better have a drink, Lowey,' said Cliff.

I managed one – well, OK, probably two or three – and then it was time for the introductions.

I turned to Cliff and asked him to sit where I could see him from the stage, behind the curtains. Then I asked him to watch my throwing action carefully, instructing him that, if it changed from a consistent one, two, three – darts timing – he should raise his arm up and instruct me by going, one, two, three – just like an orchestra conductor.

Two minutes later, the final was under way. I'd forgotten that it had been five hours since I'd thrown competitively, but I was in the final and I wasn't going to lose.

When I was one leg up and waiting to throw for the cork, I looked across to where Cliff was sitting and had to smile – something I rarely do in a match, but who wouldn't? Cliff was sitting at the table behind the curtain with a row of large brandies in front of him. He had one of the drinks in his right hand and with his other he was doing the one-two-three action. I almost started to sing. I will never forget that moment as long as I live. I went on to beat Lane two–nil and lift the coveted trophy, the hardest one in the darts world to win.

Winning that first singles event seemed to open the door for me and I won it again in 1987, this time beating my old friend Barry Twomlow in the semi-final two–one and Craig 'Dusie' Dusenberry in the final by the same score.

Now, at this point I hold my hands up and say that my averages for the semi and final weren't good when compared to today's averages regularly seen on our TV screens. In the semi-final my three-dart average was sixty-five and in the final it was sixty-three. Shock, horror! But don't forget that we had to start on a double in each leg as well as finish on one, so missing with three darts at the starting double could bring your average crashing down. A twelve- and thirteen-dart leg of 301 – double in, double out – is therefore quite a respectable result. Admittedly, it wouldn't win matches all day, but at certain times you might hit a purple patch where you're getting on clean and finishing clean, bringing up your average dramatically. I'm told by my friend BJ Clark, who followed my every match in 1987, that my average for the singles was around 10.5 darts per leg thrown, and I'd take that average anytime!

It was another thirteen years before I walked onto the stage to take part in my third NAODT in 2000. By that time, the format of the tournament had changed to the best of five legs of 501. On that occasion, I defeated 'Rocket' Ronnie Baxter in the semi-final after Ronnie found that he couldn't hit those doubles. I could, though, and won by three legs to two.

In the final, I was up against Texan Rudy Hernandez. I honestly believed that it would be a formality, but I should have known better. Just because I'd beaten Colin Lloyd, Alan Warriner and Ronnie Baxter, that didn't make my opponent in the final any less worthy. After all, Rudy had been busy beating the other top Brits in the other half of the draw.

The tournament's organiser, Tom Fleetwood, and his crew had sold the rights to the tournament to the PDC, and Tom was also trying to wind down and spend more time at home – well deserved after almost thirty years in the organiser's seat. At least a month before that year's event, the PDC had introduced a register-and-pay entry system, and in addition they'd changed the 301 double-in, double-out format to the best of 5 legs 501 straight start. This proved very unpopular, and the Americans who liked to enter and play on the day didn't approve of the change, many voicing their dissent. I thought that the PDC had done a fine job, however, and although mistakes were made I was sure that the tournament would continue the following year.

However, it wasn't my job to worry about the format of the tournament; it was to get on that stage and win for the third time, fifteen years after my first NAODT victory. If I succeeded, it would be a 'world open win' for me in four decades – something I was striving for – but it was not to be. Rudy played a superb game and was the better player in the final, beating me by three legs to two.

I was asked if I would make a farewell speech after the presentation on behalf of the players and the PDC, which I duly did. I remember thanking the American people for all their support of the event over the last twenty-three years, the period in which I'd taken part, and for their support for the tournament, which had been running for a total of thirty-one years, then went on to mention how I'd made many friends and great friendships at the tournament. I was unaware at the time that this would be the last speech ever made by anyone at the NAODT, as the tournament held in the millennium year turned out to be the last ever held. Then the curtain came down on one of the greatest ever darts tournaments.

It would be two years before the PDC would enter the American market again, and then it would be with a brand-new event taking place at the MGM Grand, Las Vegas. This was, of course, the Desert Classic, which at the time of writing is in its fourth year.

Obviously the PDC, in their wisdom, decided that the NAODT had to be put to bed, possibly because they couldn't hope to follow in the footsteps of Tom Fleetwood and his organisation. They would always be seen by some within the US darting fraternity as being the Brits who came to America and took over the country's number-one tournament and ruined it, and this viewpoint could be well justified. My father always told me, 'Don't mend it unless it's broken.'

I feel that some of the finest American darts players who ever played the game did so at the NAODT, and here I'm talking about Joe Pacchainelli, Bob Thiede, Ray Fischer, Frank Ennis, Al Lippman and Joe Baltadonis, who were just a few of the great male players of American darts, while Gerry Dover, Kathy Karpowich, Kathy Maloney, Sandy Reitan, Lori Verrier and Stacy Bromberg, ably represented the American ladies.

The Brits made the annual visit to participate in the NAODT in large numbers, knowing that, if they formed a team of four and shared their winnings, they would almost certainly come home with money in their pocket. That was the sensible way to approach a four-day tournament like the NAODT, as being four days of relentless darts and parties. I still miss it.

Even now I know that I'll always be able to cross the Pond to visit the long-time friends I made at the tournament – a tournament known as the one at which friends meet up.

After almost thirty years playing the sport of darts as a professional and thirty-nine years of play in total, I honestly believe that the NAODT was the hardest of all tournaments to win, because of its format of 301, double in, double out, and its open draw from round one onwards. I am proud at having won the competition. Of course, I would have been proud to say I'd won it once, but in fact I ended up winning it twice, which is something I will be able to tell folk when my darts have long been put in their case for the final time.

Sadly, Tom Fleetwood passed away on 25 April 2004. I think it's only fitting that Tom be remembered for all his many contributions to the sport of darts, not least of which was organising and running the NAODT, the toughest ever darts tournament in the world.

CHAPTER 16

Socialite Lowe

The sport of darts has not only made my life a happy and rewarding one; it has also introduced me to many people around the world who have since become good friends. Darts has also opened many doorways that have been interesting to walk through. From being a little boy in New Tupton, I have, like everyone else, had my heroes – the people who you look up to as a kid and wish you could be just like. They usually remain in your memory, and you might still dream of meeting them, yet seldom are one's dreams realised.

I've been fortunate over the last thirty years not only to have met many of my boyhood heroes but also some of my father's heroes, too. In this chapter, I'll introduce you to a few of them, and through my personal experiences you can mingle with the celebrities of bygone and present years.

When I was a young boy, my father would take me to Queens Park in Chesterfield to watch Derbyshire play cricket. I was only five years old when I witnessed Freddie Trueman hitting the ball out of the ground and onto the main road beyond. I remember him holding his bat like a machine gun and miming shooting the pigeons on the pitch. My father used to say, 'He's a great bowler, son, and a slogger with the bat.' I agreed; I thought Freddie was a good player, and he also made me laugh.

My father used to listen to the test matches on the radio, and like many people I think that cricket is sometimes better enjoyed when heard on the radio than watched on TV, as the commentators work overtime to keep you interested. My father used to get quite excited when England were doing well, especially when Dennis Compton was at the crease. Compton was my father's favourite batsman of all time, so you can imagine how I felt many years later, in 1979, when I actually met the great man.

In that year I was the Embassy champion, having exacted my revenge on my great friend Leighton Rees, who had beaten me in the inaugural final the previous year. As a result of my success, I'd been invited to appear on *The Sports Review of the Year*, the BBC's annual celebration of sporting success and endeavour.

When I reached the BBC studios at Shepherd's Bush, London, I was taken into a large reception area, where all the celebrities were gathering before the show began. Peter Dyke from Embassy came across to me and introduced me to Nigel Mansell, whom Peter had signed to race for John Player Special. Willie Carson, the famous jockey, was standing with him and Steve Davis, the world snooker champion, was just behind him. I was quite amazed when everyone said, 'Hello John,' as if they'd known me for years.

I asked if anyone wanted a drink from the bar and Willie said he did, so off I went to fetch two halves of bitter. When I reached the bar, there were quite a few people standing around it, so I pushed my way to the counter and ordered the drinks. As the waiter pulled the beers, a voice to my right said, 'Please, let me buy those.'

I turned, and what a shock I had! The voice had been that of Dennis Compton, my father's cricketing hero.

'No,' I said. 'Please, allow me to buy you a drink.'

'No,' Dennis replied. 'I offered to buy you a drink for all the enjoyment you give us on TV.'

I accepted his offer but went on to tell him that he was my father's hero, not noticing at the time that the two gentlemen to his left and right were England wicketkeeper Godfrey Evans and Colin Cowdrey, one of England's finest cricketers.

At this point we were called into the studio. I felt very pleased, sitting there with all the famous sporting personalities, even though darts was regarded by many – most, in fact – as a pub game, a pastime. Those who spoke to me, like Dennis Compton, showed great respect for the skill of playing darts.

As I sat there in the studio, sport after sport was shown live to the nation. I received about three minutes' worth of exposure on the screen and received a warm round of applause from the sporting superstar audience. I remember thinking at the time that the sport of darts had come a long way very quickly.

When I arrived home the next day, I told my father who I'd met, and his eyes lit up when I mentioned Colin Cowdrey's name.

'Did you tell him he's the best batsmen who ever played for England?' my father said. I told him that I had, but also that I'd told Colin that my father had said so. That didn't just make my father's day; it made his year! He told everyone he met. It didn't matter whether they liked cricket or not; they still had to listen.

That was the first time I'd ever met any really famous people, and I must say that they didn't seem like I imagined. Most seemed just like ordinary folk.

The next year, I was again invited to the *Sports Review of the Year* show, and on that occasion I took along with me Bud Brick from America. The reception room that night was again full of sporting celebrities. From the world of Formula One motor racing were James Hunt, Jackie Stewart and Sterling Moss, while boxers Frank Bruno and Henry Cooper were in attendance together with a host of First Division footballers. Olympic gold medallist Sebastian Coe was there, too, as were Jayne Torvill and Christopher Dean, the world ice-skating champions, plus many, many more champions of sport.

I was delighted to be among such a prestigious crowd. This was my second year at the BBC for this event, and I still felt that it was a privilege to be there among the real sporting icons. My self-given tag of being 'only a darts player' was beginning to fade, and I really did feel as if I belonged there. Darts had finally arrived on the sporting stage, and it was there to stay.

When we all took our seats in the studio, Torvill and Dean were on my left and big Frank Bruno was on my right. When it came to darts' turn to be shown on the TV monitor, the cameras focused on me and I felt 10ft tall, only coming down to earth when big Frank patted me on the back and said, 'Well done, John. You're great. Know what I mean?'

After the show had finished, I went across to Bud, who had been sitting in the seats reserved for the non-sporting people present, and said, 'What about that then, Bud? It's not often you meet so many famous people in one place.'

'I only knew one of them,' he replied. 'Seb Coe, the runner.'

Of course! I'd forgotten that, living in Tokyo, Bud knew only those UK sporting celebrities he saw at the Olympics.

'But you know me,' I admonished him.

'Oh yes,' Bud replied. 'That's two, then.'

A few years later, in 1984, the UK tabloid newspaper the *Daily Star* awarded me a special Gold Award for my services to sport, and I was invited to the Hilton Hotel, London, to attend a special ceremony and to receive my award, which would be presented by then Prime Minister Margaret Thatcher.

I arrived at the Hilton in plenty of time, as I was quite excited at the prospect of meeting the PM, although not for reasons of politics; I was brought up the son of a coal miner, and choices of political persuasion never came into question in those mining villages. It was accepted that you voted Labour, the party of and for the working man. Conservative politics were only for the people who had money. However, I must say that I grew up with a more open attitude towards who I thought would give me a better chance in life. Although inwardly I'm a Labour man, I confess to voting for the Tories for a few years. Mrs Thatcher was disliked immensely in New Tupton, more so by most of my friends, and for that reason I kept my politics private.

However, I admired Mrs Thatcher for who she was and where she'd come from – a Grantham grocer's daughter who became the first female UK Prime Minister. I guess I have always been a people supporter, an admirer of people who've gone from rags to riches. After all, it was my aim to emulate other's successes that had set me on the path on which I now found myself, and just being at these awards placed me very high up that ladder.

There were quite a few other nominees for the Gold Award in attendance that night. Bob Geldof had been nominated for one for Live Aid, Seb Coe was in the running for his Olympic success and Roy Castle's name was in the hat for his service to entertainment. There was also a young lad named Gary Plane who was up for an award for his courage after having had his feet amputated following a road accident, while a policeman who had dived into a canal to rescue the trapped occupants of a car was up for another. It was a very prestigious affair – indeed, it had to be if the Prime Minister was to make time in her heavy schedule to spend a full afternoon out of Parliament.

Before dinner, we were all asked to line up to be presented to Mrs Thatcher. Bob Geldof was first in line and his live-in partner, Paula Yates, stood next to him. What a sight! Paula arrived in slippers and with curlers in her hair and scarf tied around her head. I asked Roy Castle, who stood between Paula and me, 'What's with her?'

'Not sure,' Roy replied. 'Maybe she's dressed up, or maybe she doesn't like Mrs Thatcher.'

Mrs Thatcher approached the line and extended a hand to Bob Geldof. Before she could say anything, he threw a tantrum. 'Mrs Thatcher,' he railed, 'you can keep your Gold Award. I want my VAT back from the sales of the 'Do They Know It's Christmas?' record.'

So that was what all the dressing down was with Paula: it was a statement, a protest.

Mrs Thatcher calmly replied, 'Mr Geldof, I have a cheque in my handbag for £70,000. It's from the VAT office, who have agreed to return the VAT deducted from your charity. And now you've finished your gallant deed, please feel free to call round at Number Ten, where I have many more worthy causes that need your attention.'

'Wow,' I thought. 'That's why she's Prime Minister.' What a slap-down for old Bob!

Mrs Thatcher then turned to Paula and handed her the Gold

Award. Again, she showed her quick wit when she said to Bob's partner, 'How nice to see you, Paula. You must be exhausted with all this charity work. You should take a few days off. Maybe go to bed for a while.' Another bull's-eye!

Next it was Roy Castle's turn, but to my amazement he'd disappeared! Before I knew it, the Prime Minister was talking to me.

'Hello John,' Mrs Thatcher said. 'It's great to see you here. I've watched you play on my TV. Dennis speaks very well of you. Keep up the good work.

'Thank you, Prime Minister,' I replied, and then she was off and into a long chat with Seb Coe.

I turned to look what had happened to Roy and found him standing behind us, near the wall. After the awards had taken place, I went over to him and asked if he was feeling ill.

'No,' he said. 'I just couldn't accept the award from her.'

'Don't you like the Conservatives?' I asked.

'It's not that,' Roy protested. 'It's the principle. I read this morning that she'd been the chief negotiator behind her son signing a contract with Philip Morris, the tobacco manufacturers, to promote their cigarettes in South Africa.'

I still didn't understand. 'Is that a problem for you?' I asked.

'It is,' said Roy. 'I was diagnosed with lung cancer only two days ago, caused by passive smoking. I've got only one year to live.'

I was dumbstruck. I could not find the words to express how I felt and was only able to say, 'Sorry Roy' before we had to take our seats for dinner.

Roy's words put a dampener on the proceedings for me, making me feel inadequate. Although I've never smoked in my life, I've worked in many smoke-filled working men's clubs in the same way Roy himself spent a career performing in venues where the danger of inhaling others' smoke was never recognised. I couldn't help but think, 'That could have been me.' What made it worse was that Radio 1 DJ Simon Bates sat at our table and lit up a large cigar after we'd finished eating. I felt like telling him to stub it out or tell him about Roy, but in the end I kept quiet. I knew that Roy had told me about his cancer in confidence, as the news of his illness hadn't yet reached the national press.

My gloom turned to happiness, though, when Mrs Thatcher brought young Gary Plane over to meet me. 'John' she said, 'Please meet Gary. You're his hero.'

I sat and talked to both of them for a good thirty minutes. I felt a lot better knowing that Gary had battled his way through a terrible tragedy and was now walking with artificial legs. Without doubt, he was the true hero of the day.

Actually, Mrs Thatcher isn't the only Prime Minister I've met. In 1979, David Wickens, the chairman of British Car Auctions, offered to sponsor me, providing a car in exchange for advertising his company, and invited me to join him for lunch at the Savoy Grill, London.

I arrived at the Savoy dressed in my Sunday best – after all, it's not every day Frederick Lowe's son gets the chance to walk into such a grand place – and David was waiting there for me. He looked a million dollars, standing about 6ft 4in tall with a manicured moustache and wearing a suit that looked like it would have cost me a year's wages. David was a well-built man out of the Howard Keel mould who turned heads whenever he entered a room.

Just as I walked over to shake David's hand, there seemed to be a lot of people walking in from the Embankment side of the Grill. David put his arm on one man's shoulder, turned him gently towards me and said, 'Mr Callaghan, meet John Lowe.'

Prime Minister Jim Callaghan shook my hand and, to my amazement, told me how much he enjoyed watching darts on television, especially my attitude towards the sport. Then he was gone for a bite of lunch before going back to Westminster.

For me, meeting and mixing with the famous became almost normal. Because I was a world champion – and I've always been told that you're not just a world champion for one year, you're a world champion for ever – I was invited to many social occasions where fellow champions and superstars would be present. I never had the chance to speak to all of them, but I found the ones who liked darts – and, perhaps surprisingly, that was almost all of them – would go out of their way to find and talk to me.

My association with the government seemed to repeat itself

quite often, as the House of Commons bar has stocked Federation beer for decades, so it was arranged for me to make a full tour of both the House of Lords and the House of Commons, complete with a trip to the top of the tower housing Big Ben.

For those of you who aren't interested in visiting these great establishments, think again, as this tour is possibly the best in the land. It takes at least a couple of hours and starts in the House of Lords, then crosses through the entrance of the House of Commons (something no current member of the royal family has ever done) and proceeds on through the House of Commons. I sat in the Speaker's chair (forbidden, I know, but I did it anyway) and noticed the name of my local MP, Dennis Skinner, on one of the chairs. (I later found out that you could reserve a chair only if you went to the chapel on the day of sitting. Full of surprises, our Dennis.)

I was then invited to take the stairs to the top of the clock tower. Now, that's something I wouldn't recommend to the faint hearted. There are literally hundreds of steps, and the climb to the top is truly exhausting.

After seeing Big Ben, I went into the Strangers' Gallery to watch Prime Minister's Question Time. The Prime Minister at the time was John Major and the leader of the opposition was Neil Kinnock, and on that day the Strangers' Gallery was packed. I was enthralled by the banter between the two leaders. It was mayhem, but very entertaining. John Major would stand up to talk, and the Labour MPs would boo and jeer. Then the Speaker, Betty Boothroyd, would shout, 'Order! Order! Order!' At that they'd all go quiet for a couple of minutes, and then off they'd go again. No wonder there was a fifteen-minute limit for each question.

When the Prime Minister stood up to leave the chamber, the man sitting next to me asked me how I was and if I'd enjoyed the session.

'Yes,' I replied. 'Very much. What an eye-opener!'

I then realised that I'd spoken to the author Jeffery Archer, who would later become probably the most famous Lord ever to go to jail for perjury. I asked him why he was sitting in the gallery.

'Working on my next novel,' he said.

'Well,' I said, 'I guess you can fill a few pages of interesting reading in here.' Then I shook his hand and went to the Commons bar for a game of darts with John Prescott.

'Name dropper!' I hear you cry. Actually, no; I was playing the current Deputy PM in a charity darts match, organised by the House of Commons Social Club, set up to combine elected members' interests outside the political arena. After all, there are many people who work at the Houses of Parliament who aren't MPs, including secretaries and librarians, all of whom have access to the club. My membership of the club (I'm member number 501) came about through the Federation Brewery's association with the Commons.

On that occasion, I was playing John to raise money for his favourite charity, the Royal National Lifeboat Institution, in a match of one leg of 1,001. For every point John needed when I'd finished the leg, the brewery would donate £1 to the RNLI. When we left the Commons at midnight I left him on 700, so £700 went into the charity's coffers. I did hear that 10,000 pints are consumed each week in the Parliament bars, so in theory there should be some good darts players there!

My next visit to the House of Commons was in 1997, when I was invited there to attend the annual Parliament Beer Drinker of the Year Awards, a celebrated occasion attended by over 300 MPs. All the major brewers are represented there, and the awards featured include those for Best Newcomer of the Year, Most Innovative Brewer, Finest Brand and, the most prestigious of all, Beer Drinker of the Year, awarded not for drinking the most beer in a year but for services to the brewing industry. In 1996, the award was won by footballer Jack Charlton.

During the ceremony, I sat with David Brook and Jimmy Ramshaw, CEO and chairman (respectively) of the Federation Brewery; Alan Milburn, MP for the Northeast; and the Prime Minister's personal secretary, whose name I think was McWinney. The rest of the crowd comprised Peter Lippiatt and a few more representatives from the brewery.

After dinner, the awards began. Black Sheep from Masham in

Yorkshire won the Most Innovative Brewery Award, while Bateman's of Wainfleet, Lincolnshire, won the Brewery of the Year Award.

Then, after thirty minutes or so, it was time for the final award: Beer Drinker of the Year. At that moment, a big screen dropped from the ceiling and footage of that year's nominees – Daley Thompson, Sebastian Coe, Frank Bruno and many more who had been in the spotlight that year – was played. Then, right at the end, 'Old Stoneface' appeared. Yes. Me.

The video showed the whole of my nine-dart perfect game, and the applause from the room when I threw the final dart was something I'll never forget and made me very proud. I remember at that point I looked at Peter and he smiled and said, 'Darts has finally made it, John.'

We then listened to the club secretary announce the nominees for the award. He listed all the personalities in the video bar one: me. Then a hush descended on the room and the Speaker of the House, Betty Boothroyd, announced, 'The winner of the 1997 Parliamentary Beer Drinker Award is … John Lowe!' Everyone in the room rose to their feet and applauded and cheered as I made my way down to accept my award.

What followed was the first and, probably, the last speech I'll ever make in front of such distinguished people. Representatives of all the brewers came over to shake my hand, first of all George Bateman. Then, when everything had calmed down, Betty Boothroyd asked me, 'Did you get any of that wholegrain mustard from Young's, John?'

'No,' I said, a little bemused. To be honest I had no idea what she was talking about.

Then Betty was gone, only to return two minutes later with a jar of mustard in her hand, which she handed to me. 'Take that home, John,' she said. 'It's the best. Young's send it round to the House for me.'

You know, I kept that jar of mustard for years. To this day, my Parliamentary Beer Drinker Award – a pewter desk tidy with two inkwells and pen holder – stands proudly on my office desk, bearing the Houses of Parliament's coat of arms and the inscription 'Presented to John Lowe by the Speaker of the House, The Rt Hon Betty Boothroyd, MP. Tuesday 24th June 1997.'

Whenever anyone in the media asks me who my heroes are, I always answer, 'Muhammad Ali and Niki Lauda. You will already be aware that Ali is my ultimate sporting hero, and that I managed to meet him a couple of times (as described earlier in this book), but I also dreamed of meeting Niki, and thankfully my dream did come true. Remember I told you that I'm a great believer in fate? Well, like my encounter with Muhammad, I ended up meeting Niki purely by chance.

In the early 1980s, I was captain of the Marlboro Team of Champions, a team of top-flight dart players that included Leighton Rees (Wales), Tony Brown (England) and Rab Smith (Scotland), with Colin Baker (England) as reserve. We were the envy of all of the other darts players in the country. Dressed in the red-and-white colours of the Marlboro racing team and travelling in a specially personalised team coach, we travelled the country, taking on representative teams of the major breweries. The aim was to promote the Marlboro brand of cigarettes, thus ensuring that they found their way onto the breweries' stocking lists.

I soon became friends with George Makin, the chairman of Marlboro's parent company, Philip Morris, through our liking of motor sport, and he would invite me to the British Grand Prix at Silverstone and fly me in by helicopter. At that time, John Watson was the top Marlboro McLaren driver, and on one occasion George asked me if I'd like to visit the pits just before the race began. Would I!

We went through the tunnel under the racetrack and into the glamorous world of Formula One. Girls! Wow! Where did they get them from? They were everywhere. 'If only my dad could see me now,' I thought.

George then took me to an enormous red and white trailer unit, knocked on the door and then we were face to face with John Watson.

'Hi, John. Good to see you.'

No, that's not me speaking to him but the other way round! We sat and had one of the most interesting conversations I've ever had. John answered all my questions and asked me a few, too. George and I then left his trailer, offering our best wishes and good luck in the race ahead.

Then George asked me if there was anyone else I wanted to meet.

'Can you arrange anything?' I asked.

He replied, 'When you sign a cheque for £5 million in sponsorship, you can do a lot.'

'Right,' I said. 'In that case, I'd love to meet Niki Lauda.'

'OK,' said George. 'This way.'

Within two minutes, I was speaking to one of my all-time heroes. Just like John Watson had been, Niki was as cool as a cucumber. You'd never have guessed from his demeanour that he was about to be driving a car at incredible speeds for two hours – and to make matters worse, it was beginning to rain. Niki, however, made his profession sound like any other job of work, although he did say to me that it was 'probably not as dangerous as your father's occupation'.

Next stop was the black-and-gold trailer of John Player Special. This time it was the legendary Mario Andretti who met us with one of the strongest handshakes I've ever received. 'Good to meet the champ!' Mario bellowed out.

I knew straight away that Mario was a guy I could really get to like, and I was just about to sit down and listen to some of his many stories when a horn sounded outside.

'Sorry, champ,' Mario said. 'Got to go to work.'

It seemed there were only twenty minutes before the start of the Grand Prix, so I returned to my seat in the stands a very happy person. At the end of the race, though, I came back down to earth when I realised that the helicopter I'd arrived in had left without me. Instead I was picked up by Peter, my driver, who'd been the guest of Marlboro for the day, although not in the VIP section. Then, of course, we had to queue for two hours just to get out of the car park! But did I mind? Not at all. It was one of the best days of my life.

In 1994 I joined Paul Gaskell on his celebrity golf tour. I'd been playing the game for a number of years and thought I was a fairly efficient golfer, although many say, unfairly, that I'm a bandit. Now for those of you who aren't familiar with this golfing term, a 'bandit' is someone who lies in wait and then steals the game. It's like someone saying they can't play darts very well, then step up to the oche and score 100, not just once but repeatedly. Well, I can play off my golfing handicap of sixteen quite well. Most of the single handicap players I know can't play to theirs, or at least do so only very rarely, but that's a subject I could go on about for hours!

After running corporate golf days for a few years, in 1994 Paul decided to bring in a celebrity to play with each three-person team entered. The new arrangement worked like a dream, and the celebrities jumped at the chance to enjoy a round of golf and afterwards entertain the sponsor's guests at a presentation awards dinner. Another big draw to the sponsors and participating teams, meanwhile, were the courses at which Paul chose to play the events, including the Belfry (home of the Ryder Cup), the Forest of Arden, Carden Park, Druids' Glen in Ireland and many more of the best courses in Britain.

Paul ran his company from the Isle of Man and we would visit there once a year to play a corporate event sponsored by the Stakis Casino and Manx Airlines.

The reputation of Paul's tour grew very quickly and soon a host of famous golfing celebrities wanted to be part of it. Big names from the world of show business included Jimmy Tarbuck, Dennis Waterman, Robert Powell and Sir Norman Wisdom, while from the sporting domain there was Howard Kendall; ex-Manchester United captain Willy Morgan; Great Britain rugby league captain Frank Myler; boxer John Conteh; dartsmen Eric Bristow, Keith Deller and Steve Beaton; and snooker players Dennis Taylor and Willy Thorne. Meanwhile, TV drama actors Tim Healey, Johnny Briggs and Tony Barton also signed up, as did comedians Frank Carson, Stan Boardman and Mickey Gunn. Even musicians such as John Miles and Rick Wakeman took part. There were so many famous names that participated on Paul's tours that I just can't name them all. I know everyone raved about the after-dinner shows, which would go on sometimes for two hours.

Paul's Pro-Celebrity Golf Tour was, and still is, simply the best organised golf event in the UK. Not only does it give golfers a chance to meet with celebrities but it also offers the opportunity to raise millions of pounds for worthy charities. There's always a good atmosphere, and you'll often find a group of us around the piano at the Carden Park Hotel, near Wrexham, the night before the actual golf day with John Miles playing while everyone else is trying to sing.

There's also a famous father who regularly joins the tour, namely Peter Conway, better known as Robbie Williams's dad. Peter is a good entertainer in his own right, and one thing Robbie can be sure of is that he'll look just like his dad when he's forty (although he probably didn't want to know that!).

I've enjoyed many memorable times on Paul's tour. For instance, on one occasion in Spain, while playing in a three-day golf classic at Benalmadina in aid of the Kadeca Hospice, Paul asked Sir Norman Wisdom, Willy Thorne, Tony Hateley and me if we would represent the tour by going to dinner at one of the sponsor's restaurants, to which, of course, we all readily agreed. When we arrived at the restaurant we found it was on the third floor. As we looked for the lift, Sir Norman turned to me and said, 'Race you up the stairs, Lowey?'

'Not on your life,' I told him.

'OK,' he said. 'See you later, then,' and off he went.

The lift arrived a couple of seconds later and took up a couple more people to the third floor.

When the doors opened, there was Sir Norman, not even panting, having run up the stairs – all sixty of them – to the third floor quicker than the lift could get there.

'Well, what's so impressive about that?' I hear you ask. Well, Sir Norman was eighty at the time!

We enjoyed a good meal that night, and at one point Norman stood up and sang his song 'Don't Laugh at Me ('Cause I'm a Fool)'. We left about one o'clock in the morning and we were out on the first tee at nine.

A really funny thing happened at Blackpool on one of the Roy Castle 'Train of Hope' golf events. On this occasion, Micky Gunn wanted to go to the bathroom at about three o'clock in the morning. Half asleep, he got out of bed and opened what he thought was the bathroom door, carefully closed it behind him and then – now fully awake – found that he was standing in the corridor, locked out of his room. He had to make his way downstairs to the front desk and ask the night porter to let him back into his room. The porter looked at him curiously, and no wonder – Micky was stark naked.

Now, Blackpool has a bit of a reputation for attracting men 'on the other bus', as it were, so the porter wasn't taking any chances, telling Micky to go back to his room via the lift while he took the stairs. Then, having let Micky back into his room, the porter returned to the front desk.

Thirty minutes later, the porter was confronted by another naked man. This time it was Tony Hateley, who'd done exactly the same thing as Micky.

You can imagine the porter's face on confronting two men standing stark naked in front of his desk within thirty minutes of each other. I believe that might be some kind of record!

That morning, the fire alarm went off at 4:30. I honestly think that was the porter's attempt to wake everyone up so he wouldn't have to spend the rest of the night taking naked men back to their rooms!

Over the years, I've heard many great quotes from the celebrities I've played golf with. Here are just a few:

Howard Keel, singer (while talking to me at his own Darts Classic in Manchester, England): 'Can you hook or slice a dart, John?'

Jimmy Tarbuck, comedian: 'Are you still throwing them point-first, John?'

Gary Player, professional golfer (after playing at Lytham St Annes): 'I guess a nine-dart game is like doing nine consecutive holes in one.'

Muhammad Ali, the greatest sportsman of all time (while at the BBC to record a radio programme about nerves): 'I want to play the champ. Boy, am I nervous!'

Freddie Starr, comedian: 'Lost the wife last week, John. Some game of darts that was!'

Engelbert Humperdinck, singer (in his hospitality room after his show at Bally's, Las Vegas, after beating Jocky Wilson at darts): 'If you're an impersonator, Jocky, you're a bloody good one.'

Barbara Windsor, well-endowed actress and comedienne (while playing in the Yorkshire TV Pro-Am darts tournament): 'You get the big numbers, John. Just leave the double tops to me. I know where they are!'

Sid Waddell, Sky TV darts commentator (known, among other things, as 'Hissing Sid'): 'These players miss with pinpoint accuracy.'

Barry Twomlow, 'the man who taught the world to play darts': 'Darts is like sex: a reasonable start, a good performance in the middle and a quick get-out.'

Roy Castle, all-round entertainer (at the launch of the Children in Need charity at Hemel Hempstead, when Roy was instructed to blow his trumpet until I hit a bull's-eye. After a long time, and with Roy looking purple-faced, I finally hit one!): 'John, you almost blew that one!'

Freddie Trueman, arguably the most famous cricketer in England: 'John, this game is not cricket.'

Sir Henry Cooper, British champion boxer famous for decking Ali in his prime: 'If only accountants could add up, they'd make great darts players.'

Kenny Ball, jazz musician: 'Darts is like jazz: you miss a few notes and hope no one notices.'

Ronnie Corbett, famously diminutive comedian: 'Double three is my all-time favourite.'

Telly Savalas, movie and TV star (at Combe Hill Golf Course): 'I once played a game of darts on set. Lasted thirty-two takes. A whole day! Who loves ya, baby?'

Steve Davis, world champion snooker player and master cueman on the green baize: 'What's your safety like, John?'

Golf introduces you to many people from all walks of life. It's probably the only sport outside of darts where labourers mix with doctors and bricklayers with bankers. Naturally, I always carry my darts with me when I go to the golf course. If I have time after the game, I go to a local pub and have a practice on the board with Karen.

On one such occasion, I was in the Carden Arms at Carden Park, near Wrexham. This is a nice, friendly pub with a good darts throw. The walls are covered with photographs of the regulars at race meetings, most of them holding up large cheques.

That night, the landlord of the Carden Arms introduced me to a guy he called 'Budgie'. We had a long conversation over a few drinks, during which I discovered that Budgie was a friend of Leicester strongman Geoff Capes. I knew Geoff from a few public appearances we'd done together for a building company, so the conversation became more interesting. Budgie, it appeared, bred budgerigars, as does Geoff, hence their acquaintance.

The conversation then turned to horseracing. I was told that Budgie's mother, Iris, had died the previous year and left him a little money, £6,000, which Budgie had used to purchase a racehorse, which he named Iris's Gift in memory of his mother and was trained by former champion jockey Jonjo O'Neill.

Budgie told me that JP McManus – until recently a major shareholder in Manchester United Football Club – had offered him over £300,000 for the horse, but he'd turned him down! 'One day soon,' said Budgie, 'that horse will be a big winner.'

When we left the Carden Arms that night, I told Karen to make a note of the horse's name, telling her, 'We'll have a few bob on it when it runs again.'

Well, it next ran at Bangor a couple of weeks later. On that day, I went to the local bookies' to put a few pounds on it, but when I saw that the odds were eleven to one on, I changed my mind. It eventually won by twelve lengths.

Since that day, Iris's Gift has won at the Cheltenham Festival and at Aintree, amassing over £150,000 in winnings to date. Everyone connected with the horse is understandably happy, and Budgie will always remember his mum's gift, while we will always remember Budgie.

Golf is undoubtedly one of my passions, and I've been fortunate to have played with some great players, including Sandy Lyle, Eduardo Romero, Colin Montgomerie – in fact, most of the Tour golfers of today. I really enjoy their company and the large galleries of spectators they command. They often tell me that I should be used to big crowds, at which I reply, 'Don't you believe it. When we play darts, we have our backs to the audience. With golf, the spectators are always in your field of vision.'

My claim to fame in golf is that I once beat Gary Player on the eighteenth at Lytham St Annes in 1997. On that occasion, Gary had recently played in the British Open Seniors' event and came out and played eighteen holes with me the next day. He was fantastic company and a great ambassador for his sport, and after the round he gave me his driver. (Actually, to be honest, I won only the last hole. Gary actually beat me by a country mile!)

I also had the privilege of getting inside Eduardo Romero's ball on the long par three at Stoke Poges. The two hundred or so spectators around the hole gave me a massive round of applause when I walked onto the green, passed Eduardo's ball and marked my own, which was only 12in from the hole.

I've also had my fair share of wins on the Pro-Celebrity Tour. For instance, I was presented with the Howard Keel Trophy at

Manchester Piccadilly Hotel by Howard himself; I won the Les Dawson Trophy; and I won the Tour Order of Merit in 2000, the prize for which was a £7,000 week-long holiday in the Caribbean. As fate would have it, though, unfortunately the holiday company went bankrupt and I finished up with nothing.

In fact, I love golf so much that I have my own golf classic in Phuket, Thailand. It's played in December each year and all proceeds go to the local children's hospital. Teams now enter the contest from Canada, Australia and the UK. Mike Inman, the general manager of the Central Village Hotel, is a great sponsor of the event, and I hope in time that it will become a truly international date on the golfing calendar.

The game of golf is, of course, very much like darts: it requires a lot of concentration and you must keep your head still to make a good shot, which I feel is one of the most important skills to have in playing good darts. The one advantage golf does have over darts is its handicap system, enabling the very worst players to compete with the very best and still stand a chance. At darts, of course, this is impossible; a top player will beat a lesser player 99 times out of 100. Maybe we'll see a handicap system introduced into the sport one day; a start of, say, 100 for the lesser player, or a seeding system that would see players of the same standard compete in different categories. Please, though, not just yet; I need all the help I can get!

At the time of writing, I've been playing golf for twenty-four years, and during that time I've never achieved a hole in one, while almost all of my mates – including Eric Bristow – have achieved them and continually remind me about it. I do have the last laugh, though, when I remind them that, as Gary Player observed, on 13 October 1984 I once achieved nine 'holes in one' on the dartboard – nine perfectly thrown darts to win a perfect game of 501.

That shuts them up.

CHAPTER 17

Two and a Half Minutes of Magic

Y̶ou can do a lot of things in two and a half minutes. Just ask in any bar or at any mixed social evening. I guess sometimes the ladies will be the ones replying and the guys (they know who they are!) will be the ones with the red faces, but thankfully that's not what this chapter is about!

What I achieved in two and a half minutes on 13 October 1984 changed my life. It was also a moment in darts history, the day I scored the first televised perfect nine-dart game of 501. To this day I'm asked about that historic feat, and hardly a day goes by when I don't think about the moment that ninth dart hit the final double and – some say for the first time ever – 'Old Stoneface' allowed himself a smile.

I achieved my greatest darting feat while playing Keith Deller in the MFI World Matchplay Championship at Slough, and in just two and a half minutes on that day I won the staggering amount of £102,000 – a record then and still a record today.

Before I take you on a journey through that memorable experience, I'd like to express my disgust at Sky TV and its commentators, particularly Sid Waddell, for the injustice they I believe bestowed upon me at the World Matchplay in Blackpool in the summer of 2002. On that occasion, Phil Taylor was playing Chris Mason in the top eight. 'The Power' was on top form and had been predicting all week that he'd achieve a nine-dart game in the championship.

We didn't have long to wait; after just a couple of legs, Phil was throwing at double twelve with his ninth dart. The dart went into the double as clean as a whistle.

Over in the commentary box, Sid Waddell went berserk. 'History!' he shrieked. 'History! Phil 'The Power' Taylor has just created darting history! He's scored the perfect game of 501 on TV – the first player ever to do so!'

OK, so it's fine to get carried away for a few minutes, a few days even, but when the dust had settled and the PDC, BSkyB and the commentators had had time to reflect, did they recognise the fact that the first nine-dart game recorded on TV in this sport had, in fact, been thrown by yours truly back in 1984? No. And did they recognise that the second nine-dart game had been Paul Lim's televised performance in the 1990 Embassy World Championship? No. Did they even recognise the third televised nine-dart game by Shaun Greatbatch in 2002, the first to be achieved live on TV? No.

No, in much the same manner as the BDO refused to accept champions of the past like me even existed back in 1993, now these guys did exactly the same. There's no mention in the PDC's records of the three perfect games that had been thrown on TV over the previous twenty years; according to the video footage on the homepage of their website, history began at the World Matchplay in Blackpool in July 2002. Talk about rewriting history!

To be accurate, that great achievement by Phil 'The Power' Taylor – and no one can deny him that – was the fourth televised nine-dart game. It was also the second nine-dart game to be shown as it happened on our TV screens and the first to be achieved live on TV in the UK. And while I'm on the subject of records, the prize money of £100,000 that Phil picked up that night wasn't a record, either; twenty years earlier, at the Fulcrum Centre, Slough, I received a cheque for £102,000 from Derek

Hunt, the chairman of MFI, for my perfect nine-dart game of 501, the scores for which were as follows:

180

180

141

For the record, my last three darts were treble seventeen, treble eighteen and double eighteen.

I have been asked thousands of times over the past twenty years about that nine-dart game. How did it feel when I needed the double? Was I nervous? Was it the most memorable moment in my darting career? These and many more questions I simply never tire of answering, and I've had more arguments over that match than I had with my first wife! So many people are convinced that I finished on double twelve, often becoming quite annoyed when I tell them I finished on double eighteen. I know. I was there! One thing I tell everyone who asks, though, and which I honestly believe, is that fate played a big part in that wonderful experience.

On 6 October 1984, I travelled down to Norwich from my home in Chesterfield to play in a series of exhibitions booked by my good friend John Carmichael. I've always had a strong liking for Norwich, not just because it has 350 churches and even more pubs but also because I've made many friends there over the years.

The Marlborough Hotel in Stacey Road is owned by one such friend, Eddie Harvey, and this becomes my home whenever I'm in the area. My only concern about staying at Eddie's is that his Italian wife, Maria, fills my dinner plate to the top at mealtimes. 'Come on, John,' she'll say. 'Dinner's ready.' I love her to bits, but I find myself thinking, 'Oh no! Its five o'clock now. After four hours of Maria's pork chops and four vegetables, I won't be able to play darts properly until nine o'clock!'

I always enjoy my visits to the Harveys, though, and I remember calling in to see them one day in 2002, after my divorce, while I was on my way to Great Yarmouth, where I was taking part in the Vauxhall Darts Weekend. That day was a sad one for me, as John Carmichael had suddenly passed away in

Spain. Eddie had been a lifelong friend of John's and was understandably very upset. That day I introduced my new wife, Karen, to Eddie and Maria and we sat there, reminiscing about John, for around two hours. We had many stories to tell, like the one of the night when John drove us to an exhibition a few miles away in East Dereham.

That night turned out to be a good one. The drinks flowed freely, and I know that John – our driver – was a little worse for wear. On our way back to Norwich, I was sitting in the back seat of John's Jaguar while Eddie was in the front. As we approached a ninety-degree bend on one of the many narrow country lanes, John turned round to me and commented on what a good night it had been.

Not a good idea. Instead of going around the corner, we went straight through a hedge and into the field. My life flashed before me, but John just turned the wheel, accelerated, made another hole in the hedge a few yards around the corner, drove back onto the road and carried on driving.

Silence reigned in the car for a few seconds, and then Eddie took his cigar out of his mouth and said, 'I really enjoyed that, John. Maybe we should do it again.' Nervous laughter then filled the Jag.

Then we noticed a loud knocking noise coming from underneath the car, and I asked John if he thought he should stop and take a look.

'No,' he replied confidently. 'It's just the exhaust pipe come loose.'

When we reached Norwich, we decided to have a late dinner at the Savoy Hotel there. We pulled up, exited the car – and I couldn't believe my eyes. There was grass between the wheel rims and tyres, and the bodywork of the car seemed noticeably twisted. We must have hit one of the dykes (ditches) that run along the road, and the impact must have been pretty severe to cause that much damage to a two-ton car. In his usual, calm way, John just shrugged and said, 'Let's go and eat. I'll have a look at the car in the morning.'

Halfway through our meal, John suddenly stood up and left the table, making his way to the exit. When he returned a few minutes later, we asked where he'd been.

'Just taken care of the car,' he replied. 'John the German has taken it away.'

Did this mean what I thought it meant? Then I realised that this was my first night in Norwich, and because I'd been late arriving I'd thrown my suit carrier and my luggage into the boot of John's car. 'John, what have you done?' I moaned. 'All my gear's in your car!'

'Don't panic,' said John. 'I'll give you a couple of hundred quid and you can get some new stuff tomorrow.'

I remember thinking, 'Oh, great.' My embroidered darts shirts for the Ladbrokes British Open were also in the car. How was I going to replace them?

Then Eddie ordered another bottle of wine, hoping that a drink would help matters a little. It was no good worrying about my missing gear, of course, as it was too late to retrieve it.

Then Mr Lucas, the owner of the Savoy, came over and offered us a drink, so we sat with him, talking about his family for an hour or so. When we were finally ready to leave and goodnights were being said, Mr Lucas turned to me and said, 'John, don't forget your things in the other room.'

'Things?' I queried.

'Yes,' replied Mr Lucas. 'The luggage John put in there earlier.'

The air went blue for a couple of minutes. (My mother would have never forgiven me if she'd heard my ranting!) I'd sat in that restaurant for an hour and a half, wondering if I should head home tomorrow to pick up some more shirts and clothes, when all the time John had taken them out of the car and put them in the restaurant! (By the way, I never did find out what happened to the Jaguar.)

After five good nights of exhibitions in Norwich – all good practice for the Matchplay – my last night in the city was free, so we planned to visit Eddie's local pub, the Woodman, and have a few games of cribbage. Eddie loves his crib, and so do I, and we often play for £1 stake and drinks.

Anyway, that night, at around ten o'clock, one of our friends, Sweeney, walked into the pub and, on seeing us, asked us if we were going to the opening of the new disco/bar one of the lads had bought.

'No,' I said. 'I have to be in Slough tomorrow for the World Matchplay.'

'Well, you can just have one and then go,' said Sweeney.

I knew all too well that there is no such concept as 'one and then go' in Norwich – at least, not in the company I kept. I was adamant that I wouldn't go to the new bar.

Predictably, at eleven o'clock that night I found myself shaking hands with the club's new owner, who thrust a large glass of champagne into my hand. I remember thinking at the time, 'Not to worry. We'll just stop for an hour and I can still be in bed by half past one.'

Well, it was 2:30am when Eddie eventually turned to me and said, 'I reckon we should go, John. You've got to be fresh for the big match tomorrow.'

I just looked at him, that big smile wreathing his face, and we got up to leave. If only we'd known what was to happen over the next few days.

The next morning, I left Eddie's house at seven after having only three hours' sleep, and I was not looking forward to the long journey to Slough. I shook Eddie's hand, gave Maria a big kiss, poured myself into the car and drove off at a disgusting speed towards the A11.

When I reached the Fulcrum Centre, I wasn't feeling too good and just wanted to go to bed. That was impossible, though, as a good friend of mine, Garry Churnside, had come all the way over from Australia. He'd fixed an exhibition tour for Cliff Lazarenko and me the previous year, and Garry and I spent the next hour looking at the hundreds of photographs of that tour that he'd brought with him.

I remember Garry talking about the best Australian darts player, Russell Stewart, and placing a bet with him that Russell wouldn't make it through the first round, especially as he was playing Mike Gregory. Garry went on to suggest that maybe Terry O'Dea – another Australian dartsmaster – would meet Russell in an all-Australian final, but I gave that suggestion no chance as Terry had to play Eric Bristow in his first game.

At four o'clock the players were practising in groups or, more correctly, cliques. Those who drank together would practise together (some things never change). I could hear Eric Bristow winding someone up, Jocky Wilson chatting to his manager, Mel Coombes about the prize money on offer. Jocky had missed the double twelve in the Embassy World Championship to record a perfect game of 501 and he thought he could do it this time and pick up the dough.

Nicky Virachkul was drinking Jack Daniels out of a Las Vegas plastic tankard. Keith Deller was trying to ruin the treble twenty on his practice board, hitting ton-forties and ton-eighties for fun. Cliff Lazarenko was in his usual place at the corner of the bar and I joined him for a couple of straighteners.

There was an air of expectation. Everyone knew this was the biggest tournament in the world. OK, it wasn't the Embassy, but it carried by far the biggest purse to date: £100,000 for the first perfect nine-dart game of 501 along with a further £2,000 if it was achieved while the cameras were rolling. A couple of players had been very close to achieving the nine-darter during the previous six months; like I said, Jocky Wilson had come close but missed double twelve, and likewise Nicky Virachkul had missed his last double. In any event, most people thought it was about to happen and, not surprisingly, Eric Bristow and Jocky Wilson were the bookies' favourites to do it.

As always, the bookies seemed to have the upper hand. No sooner had the Matchplay begun than Garry Churnside ran into the practice room from the arena. 'You're one bet down, Lowey,' he said. 'O'Dea has just beaten Bristow.'

Terry, it seemed, had dumped the Crafty Cockney out of the competition two–one, which cheered me up, as it meant that Eric was now out of the way. I bought Terry a drink and carried on practising.

Only an hour later, Garry came back into the room with another big smile on his face. Russell Stewart had put Mike Gregory out of the championship, two–one, and Bob Anderson had ended Jocky's hopes, two–nil. Good news? I should say so. There were only four seeds in the event and two had gone within an hour.

By this time, the effects of my long night in Norwich were beginning to wear off (I wonder why?), although I still had to beat the quite brilliant Thai Nicky Virachkul. I knew he wouldn't be a pushover, but my confidence was growing by the minute.

We took the stage at nine o'clock. Our match wasn't the best but I just edged it, two–one. By then I couldn't wait to leave the Fulcrum Centre and fall into my bed.

The following morning, players had to be at the Fulcrum Centre by 10:30am. Hard to believe, I know, but it's true – darts players don't just come out at night. Major competitions demand early starts and late finishes. In the case of the MFI World Matchplay Championship, the quarter-finals and semi-finals were to be held on the same day, and this meant that the successful players would be in the venue for no fewer than twelve hours. (Now tell me you don't need to be fit to play professional darts!)

It was very quiet when I arrived in the practice room, which I thought was strange.

As if reading my thoughts, Terry O'Dea asked, 'Why do you think it's so quiet, John?' I said I didn't know and then Terry said, 'It's obvious. Take a look and see who's not here.'

I immediately understood. Bristow was missing. Wow, that was great! Now the remaining players would be able to get on with their practising without hearing any of his interminable wind-ups.

My second-round opponent at the Matchplay was Keith Deller, who had beaten Welshman Peter Locke two–one in the first round. I spotted Keith over at the practice board, continuing in the same form as the previous night, hitting the treble-twenty segment as if it was magnetised.

I decided to start my day with the same routine I'd followed the previous night, so I went over to the bar and joined Cliff Lazarenko for a few drinks. Yes, I know, drinks at 10:30 in the morning! But that's what we did. That was part of our lives. It didn't matter what time of day it was. I estimate that around ninety-eight per cent of all professional darts players at that time would take a drink or two (or three, or four) before a match, whatever time it was to be played. It was the norm, our way of relaxing – our drug, if you like.

Unlike anabolic steroids, however, alcohol isn't a performance-enhancing drug. Ask any red-blooded male.

I sat with Cliff because we had many things in common, firstly the drink and secondly life in general, by which I mean our similar family backgrounds. We'd sit and talk about our mothers, who both went through long illnesses, and then our fathers. There was always plenty to discuss about Cliff's dad, Maxi. After that, and being duly relaxed, we would put the flights in our darts and find an empty practice board, where we'd practise together for the next hour.

I was very much aware that my match with Keith was going to be a tough one. He was in superb form and no one was going to be disappointed with his performance. The match eventually started at around 1:30pm, and – although I say it myself – it was a great match, with 140s followed by 140s and 180s answered by 180s. It was a match in which, if either of us scored 100, we were disappointed. After three games I was leading Keith two–one and was one leg up in the fourth.

Then came two and a half minutes of pure magic.

My first three darts all hit the treble-twenty bed, and I remember standing there on stage, wondering what Dave Lanning was saying in the commentary box. The first dart of my next throw was, again, perfect – another treble twenty – and then the second hit the spot, too. However, I was in a little trouble as I didn't think I could get another dart into the sixty bed, as the second dart had caught the first and landed in the segment at an angle, obscuring the target. I thought, 'Should I go downstairs to the nineteens?' but with that little matter of a potential £100,000 pay day, I decided, 'No. Have a go. Nothing ventured, nothing gained.'

I moved at least 6in to my right on the oche to obtain the optimum view of the only corner of the treble that was available, aiming the dart to go up and over the second dart. I concentrated so hard and threw that third dart with as much precision as any shot I've ever played, before or since.

Bingo! The dart found the spot with pinpoint accuracy. The perfect game was still on.

With 360 points scored and a 141 remaining, it all somehow

looked easier – but what about all that money? £100,000 rested on my next three darts! That was more money than anyone I knew could earn in a year. Thoughts were tumbling through my mind. £100,000. I tried not to think of that one missed dart that would turn the dream back into grim reality. But just a moment: I was 'Old Stoneface', the coolest darts player on the block, the guy who never smiles. The man who just does the business.

A few years earlier, I'd made up my mind that, if the opportunity to score the perfect game came my way, I'd do it the John Lowe way: two scores of 180 – six treble twenties – followed by treble seventeen, treble eighteen and double eighteen. I'd worked out that, after the first two ton-eighties, by starting with the treble seventeen on the right hand side of the board I'd only have to raise my eyes slightly to be looking at the treble and double eighteen. Now here I was, staring right at the treble seventeen, ready to start off on that sequence.

The first dart left my hand and I knew instantly it was on target. *Thump!* Straight in the centre of the bed.

I lifted my sight-line a few inches and viewed the treble eighteen, held the next dart firmly but not tightly and launched it at the target. *Thud!* Treble eighteen.

With only one dart between me and darting history, I was oblivious to the money; only that double eighteen mattered. Out of my view Keith Deller was gesturing to the large audience to be silent.

I steadied myself for the throw that would make me immortal in the darting world, and I can still feel that almost unbearable tension, even today. I was not shaking, though; actually, I was more confident at that point than at any other time during that now-famous leg of 501. I was ready to hit that double eighteen because it meant so much.

The dart left my hand and I swear that before it hit the board my arms were raised high in the air. I heard caller Freddie Williams announce, as if from the next room, 'Game!', then 'Ladies and gentlemen, history has been made here in Slough today.'

I felt unbelievable and shook hands with everyone in sight. There was some kind of blockage in my throat and my eyes filled with emotion. Of course, the place erupted. Keith shook my hand and we embraced each other. A few minutes later, we had to continue the match and I had to get on with the task of beating Keith.

With £102,000 secured, you might have thought that winning the championship was no longer important to me, but to me that nine-dart game was the icing on the cake. If I wasn't going to be called 'Lucky' by my fellow professionals, I had to get back out there and win the tournament. I went on to win the third leg of the fourth game and therefore beat Keith three–one. Keith did nothing wrong, and it was a match that he can look back on with pride; he just happened to catch John Lowe at his very best that day.

When that quarter-final match was over, I found myself surrounded by TV cameras. Jim Rosenthal wanted a quick interview to go out on air a few minutes later, but I told him I should phone my wife, Diana, thinking that if she'd watched my performance on TV without knowing the end result, she might have a heart attack! Jim begged me to do the interview first, though, and I reluctantly agreed. It was a very relaxed interview for Jim, but not for me. I wanted to sing and shout and – to be honest – find the bar and celebrate.

As soon as the interview was over, though, I found the nearest payphone and called Diana to tell her the great news. She sounded dreadful. She was ill and hadn't been watching the darts as she'd been spending most of her time in the toilet. Well, I thought, this would surely cheer her up. I said to her, 'I have just beaten Keith.'

'Oh good,' came the rather disinterested reply.

'And guess what else!' I added.

'Hold on a moment,' said Diana and the phone went quiet. She was off to the toilet again. When she returned, I told her that I'd her just won £102,000.

'What for?' she asked. In my excitement I'd forgotten to tell her about my perfect nine-dart game.

I had to ring off at that time as I was wanted by the ITV people. *World of Sport* anchorman Dickie Davies had rung to congratulate me and offer a bottle of champagne – the first of many. I couldn't resist a few glasses, although I knew I had to play Bob Anderson in the semi-final that same night.

I took to the stage that night to rapturous applause. I was the King of Darts, the champion, the man who had achieved the perfect game, and everyone who had witnessed my triumph was saying, 'I was there.' However, Bob Anderson had other things on his mind. Having beaten Jocky in the first round and taken out London's Dave Lee three–one in the quarter-final with checkouts of 154, 151 and 137, he was very confident. I also think he thought that Lowey wouldn't be at his best, his concentration perhaps a little shot to pieces by his full pockets and champagne-fizzing brain. He probably thought that now was the time to bring Lowey back down to earth.

In his pre-match interview, Bob had almost written me off! Big mistake. Not only did I end up beating him but I did so convincingly, four sets to nil. In addition, during one of the games, I finished on 161, which was later to earn me another £1,000 as the highest out-shot of the tournament. Bob's misery was complete when he was informed after the match that his car had been stolen while we'd been playing.

That night, champagne consumption was resumed. Earlier that day, I'd asked Garry Churnside to call the hotel and put their entire stock of bubbly on ice, deciding that it was only right that all the BDO officials, including Olly Croft, had something to remember of their greatest moment. At one point a toast was raised, and everyone had a glass in their hands – all except for Cliff and me. We had a bottle each.

The final was a classic, two mates – me and Cliff – playing for keeps after he'd won the other half of the draw to meet me in the final, having beaten Bobby George two–nil in the first round, then taken out Terry O'Dea three–two in the quarters and demolished England's Dave Whitcombe four–one in the semis. (Dave had actually beaten Russell Stewart three–nil in his quarter-final match, thus putting paid to Garry Churnside's outrageous prediction of an all-Australian final.)

Nothing had changed that morning. On 14 October 1984, Cliff and I were as usual having a drink in the bar, followed by a practice on one of the two boards. I was pleased for him and he likewise for me.

I asked Cliff if he'd like to share the prize money for first and second place as I thought I'd won enough. Besides, £9,000 each sounded like a nice arrangement. Cliff said that that would be great but that he had to make sure it was OK with his manager, Dick Allix, as of course the manager receives a proportion of all prize money.

Dick said no. Just like Bob Anderson, he thought my pockets were full enough and that I was vulnerable. He also moved Cliff on to the other practice board.

I didn't understand his attitude. I didn't care about the money; I was playing for pride, and I had heaps of that left.

During the final, I remained in good form, coming from behind twice after some great darts from Cliff to level with him at three–all. Cliff's scores of 100 were just not good enough that day, and with my ton-plusses I pulled away to win the championship by five sets to three.

I'll never forget the presentation at that tournament, and to be honest there's never been another like it. Not even the great Phil Taylor has received so many cheques after winning an event. Derek Hunt, the chairman of MFI, presented me with a cheque for £100,000 for the nine-darter, and then he gave me another for £2,000 from the BDO for achieving the perfect game on TV, then another for £1,000 for the highest out-shot of the tournament and then – finally – the cheque for £12,000 for winning the tournament itself, making a grand total of £115,000.

That night I celebrated with Irish coffees as the Holiday Inn at Slough had run out of champagne. I was joined by my good friend, defeated finalist and truly great guy, Cliff Lazarenko.

So there you have it, the story of how I made darting history and the most magical moment in the sport of darts since the first formal rules were issued back in the 1920s. And I take this one final opportunity to remind those at Sky, Planetdarts and Sid Waddell in particular that the first televised perfect nine-dart 501 was achieved by Frederick Lowe's son from New Tupton in the MFI World Matchplay at the Fulcrum Centre, Slough, on the

13 October 1984 and ask them to amend their record books accordingly. Thank you!

CHAPTER 18

Support and Loyalty

This chapter is named after two very important elements to being successful. One cannot work without the other, and both have been vitally important in my career as a professional darts player. My background and upbringing taught me to respect the people who helped me throughout my life. The builders Bob and Arthur Lowe gave me my first real break and saved me from a life down the coal mines. That one deed of kindness has stayed with me all my life and I will always be grateful to them.

When I first realised that I was very good at the art of throwing darts, I believed at the time and resigned myself to the fact that it would only ever be a pastime for me, a hobby. Never once way back in 1966 did I ever envisage that one day I would be a professional darts player, let alone a world champion.

Barry Twomlow, another darts player from Chesterfield, won the *News of the World* Individual Darts Championship in 1969, representing the Red Lion, a town-centre pub run by former British heavyweight champion boxer Peter Bates. That year, Peter told Barry that if he qualified for the *News of the World* tournament grand finals at Alexandra Palace, he would take him and his wife Margaret down to London, and if Barry managed to win the championship then he, Peter, would give him £50, which in 1969 was a great deal of money.

Barry, of course, went all the way and defeated Cornwall's Paul Gosling in the final. That win was to change Barry's life. At the time, Unicorn Products were looking for a player who could represent them, and Barry fitted the bill exactly. With his knowledge of selling (he was an office-furniture salesman in partnership with his brother-in-law, Billy Newton), he proved the ideal choice. So Barry signed a small contract to use Unicorn products exclusively, and then they employed him full time as he travelled the globe, preaching the Unicorn darts gospel.

For over thirty years Barry quite literally taught the world to play darts. Although he never won a world championship, his influence on the growth of darts across the planet over four decades earned him the respect of everyone in the darting world. Barry was the perfect example of those two words at the head of this chapter: support and loyalty. In return for the support that Unicorn gave him, he gave back double in loyalty. He was a good friend of mine and helped me to obtain support at the right time. Sadly, Barry passed away in 2004. My personal tribute to this great darts ambassador and friend can be found towards the end of this book, in Chapter 22.

Back in 1974, Barry asked me if I would be interested in using Unicorn darts and being part of their team. Barry was very much a part of the modern development of Unicorn, and they expected him to ensure that the players he recommended were of the highest calibre, not only in skills but also in respectability; they didn't want to take on anyone who would harm their good name.

I jumped at the chance. Unicorn Products was the biggest dart company in the world. Every player knew who they were. So Barry took me down to Forest Hill in southeast London, and there at the Unicorn factory I met the Lowy brothers: Stanley, the managing director, and Michael, the sales director. I was given a tour of the factory and lunch in the canteen, and Stanley and Michael then offered to supply me with all my darts equipment – darts, stems, flights, etc – free for the next three years.

I accepted their generous offer, and to be honest I was thrilled.

I was actually joining Unicorn. We never spoke about any financial payment. There were few, if any, professional dart players at that time, and no one was making a living out of the sport apart from the manufacturers. Even in the early 1970s darts was still only a social game, yet it was being played by millions of people in pubs and clubs the length and breadth of the country.

Shortly after my trip to London, the team I was with at the time, based at the Park House Hotel, Danesmoor, were booked to play a team a few miles away at the Corner Pin, Stonebroom. It was a cup match, Tuesday night, and all the lads turned up in the usual jeans and T-shirt (except Dennis Bradbury, who never wore T-shirts). And then I walked in wearing my new gold blazer with the Unicorn badge on the pocket. You can imagine the reception I received! OK, I was overdressed, but I didn't care; I was telling everyone I was a Unicorn player.

The rest of the team were all pleased for me – well, almost all of them. Ronnie Allen, the captain, thought he was the bee's knees and made it clear that he didn't like being upstaged. In truth, Ronnie very rarely lost a league match, or any match for that matter. He was also a good captain, especially when it came to putting the team down in a winning order, but would he have made it to the very top? I doubt it.

I didn't ask Unicorn for lots of darts and accessories. In fact, they asked Barry to keep in contact with me to find out why. The truth was that I was used to having a set of darts for a long time. (Remember, I was brought up in an era of 'make do and mend'.) On the other hand, Unicorn wanted me to use as many of their products as I could and thereby advertise their brand as much as possible.

It was quite strange. Here I was, contracted to the biggest manufacturer of darting products in the world, and yet I went to Redgate's sporting shop in Nottingham to buy my first set of tungsten darts. At the time the use of tungsten in the manufacture of darts was a very new innovation. Barry had what we believe to have been the very first set, made in 1970. I, of course, wanted to try the new tungsten darts out for myself and saw this as an opportunity to do so.

I bought a set of 'Tommy O'Regan' Maid Marion 18g copper tungsten darts. (At that time, Tommy was under contract to the Harrows Gameshot darts company and was one of the first darts players to have a signature set of darts.) With the purchase of these new darts, my game improved immediately. I had this great sense of being able to balance a dart by using the correct stems and flights for the barrel shape and weight, and I still have that skill.

After a couple of weeks of using my new darts, I contacted Unicorn and told them I was coming down to London to see them. They knew it had to be important, as it's a long way from Chesterfield to London, and it meant I had to take a day off work.

When I got down to London, I picked up a few bits and pieces at the Unicorn factory, had lunch in the canteen and then went back to Michael Lowy's office to show him my Maid Marion darts. I was a little nervous as they were made by a competitor and I didn't know what his reaction would be, but when I showed him the darts he just said, 'They look very good, John.' I could tell that he was thinking: 'If we've contracted this guy, why is he using our competitor's products?'

I replied, 'Yes, they're very good, and I would like you to make some like them and name them 'John Lowe' darts.'

At this point his attitude changed, and I knew then that I'd timed my request just right.

Michael produced a pen and a piece of paper and asked me to draw the dart, and I obliged. I kept the barrel the same length and then added a grip of seven rings. The dart I drew wasn't of the same design as the Maid Marion darts Tommy threw; those darts had a raised part on the barrel, whereas mine were designed to have a smooth barrel with no protrusions. I asked for three sets of the darts to be produced, each in different weights: 18g, 19g and 21g. When I headed home to Chesterfield that day, I remember thinking how well the meeting had gone.

Within one week, Unicorn had produced the 'John Lowe' dart. When they arrived at my home, I was like a school kid breaking up for the big holiday. I was on the dartboard for hours on end with the new darts before eventually settling for the 19g set. Then I set out to beat everyone in sight.

My association with Unicorn was cemented in 1977 when the company asked me to sign up with them again, this time under a new contract that guaranteed a payment to me of £500 per year and that they would supply me with all the darts, shirts and accessories I needed. I knew that this was a significant move.

Unicorn also knew through Barry Twomlow that I was beginning to play world-class darts, and Barry knew that I wasn't afraid to leave Chesterfield in my quest to make it to the very top. Inspired by the confidence Unicorn had shown in me, I repaid their support with interest!

Five years later, with a bagful of world titles to my name, my loyalty to Unicorn was rewarded when they invited me to sign an extended contract. This time, my yearly contract fee went up to £5,000.

In those five years, Unicorn Products and I had become a team. They were repaying me for my success, which had boosted sales of their products – particularly the 'John Lowe' darts and flights – and that was to be the pattern of our association right up until today.

It is now over thirty years since I first joined that great company. Stanley and Michael have now gone and been replaced by Stanley's sons, Edward and Richard, who, like their father, are taking the company onwards and upwards.

Thirty years is a long time to be involved with sport, especially in such a competitive sector. I've maintained my world ranking status and have played in every Embassy World Championship since the very first one. I could have left Unicorn and joined another manufacturer, and I've not been short of offers, quite a few from America and manufacturers of soft-tip, electronic darts. A couple of these were very good offers indeed, and many players would have taken them, but I chose not to.

I feel that I've repaid Unicorn's support of me by remaining loyal to them. Likewise, Unicorn continued to support me through the quieter times of the late 1980s, when the sport was in turmoil and sales were falling fast. I'm not saying that it would be the right stance for everyone, especially in these days of rapid economic change; companies, after all, are sometimes not as successful as the players they contract, and it often becomes necessary to change. I was fortunate, though, that Barry Twomlow introduced me to a company that has maintained their position in the world of darts and rightfully uses just five words to describe their company: 'Unicorn: The Big Name in Darts.'

Support is necessary in other departments besides darts products. For example, for a professional darts player travelling is very costly and is one of the factors preventing so many good darts players from making it to the top. They simply cannot afford to travel to the many competitions around the world that are necessary to play in and be seen at in order to develop their level of experience and raise their personal profile.

My first break in the travel department came in 1979 when I received a phone call one morning from Eric Johnson of BCA (British Car Auctions). At this time I was travelling around 30,000 miles per year. Anyway, Eric asked me if I had a car, and coincidentally I'd taken delivery of a brand new Ford Granada that very day. 'Would you be interested in BCA providing you with a car?' he asked.

I told Eric that I'd just bought one, but he was persistent and went on to say that his company wanted to give me a car free of charge to drive to exhibitions and competitions. Now, that was different!

I asked Eric what model car it would be. After all, I didn't want to drive around in a Mini or something similar when I'd just purchased a top-of-the-range Ford. But Eric told me that to begin with I'd be driving golfer Bob Charles's car – a Ford Granada Ghia – but that this would soon be replaced with a brand-new one.

The picture was becoming clear: BCA would be sponsoring me to drive a car for them and represent and advertise them on the road.

I agreed to Eric's proposal, and within two days the Granada Ghia was parked on my drive. The wording on the boot read, 'Bob Charles drives to victory with BCA.' Of course, when the new car arrived it bore the legend, 'John Lowe drives to victory with BCA'. OK, it doesn't have quite the same meaning in this context as it does with golf, but it's still quite an appropriate phrase when you consider the many miles I was driving at the time to exhibition matches, practice sessions and the many tournaments around the UK.

As with Unicorn, my association with BCA lasted for many years. It was only when the company's chairman, David Wickens, decided to sell the company in 1983 to commercial and private security systems company ADT that our association ended, ten years and almost a million miles later.

There's one story from my BCA days that I will never forget. On one occasion in 1979 I was invited, along with golfer Nick Faldo (also sponsored by BCA), to visit Vauxhall's testing centre in Bedfordshire, where the plan was to do a photo shoot for Vauxhall and BCA on the oval track there.

After we'd finished shooting we went for lunch at the White Hart Hotel in Northampton, and I remember that outside the hotel were two brand-new Senator cars, one with Nick's name on and one bearing mine. We were standing there, having our photographs taken, when David Wickens approached me and handed me a set of registration plates marked '301 UP'. 'Put them on your car,' said David, so we fished around for some sticky tape and stuck the plates on the car.

Once the photo session was over, I took the plates off and handed them back to David. 'No, no,' he said. 'They're for you. I bought them off of a guy last week.' Nick Faldo's face was a picture: the best golfer in Europe upstaged by a darts player.

The support BCA gave to me was invaluable in my journey to the top of the darting ladder. They made travelling much less of a concern to me, helped to reduce the cost of it by at least half. In return, I gave them my loyalty. When I reached a new location, I would stop at the side of the road and Peter, my driver, would take a photograph of me standing by the sign to the city, town or village we were entering. Occasionally I'd send these pictures into David's office and he'd then call me, and we'd have a laugh at the places I'd visited.

I've had only four major representative sponsors since I began on the professional darts trail thirty years ago. Once I joined a company who had the faith in me to invite me on board, I worked very hard to make sure that their products or services were promoted well and that I didn't tarnish their good name. I like to think that I always gave as much as I received.

In 1985 I joined the Federation Brewery to undertake a series of exhibitions around their outlets. Federation is a company based in Wickham, on the outskirts of Newcastle-upon-Tyne, in the northeast of England. The brewery has been a prominent feature in the area for many years and was known as 'the Northern Clubs' Federation Brewery' for many years. They've never owned any outlets but have supplied over 5,000 pubs and clubs, including the House of Commons.

What began as a three-year association between the brewery and me grew into a fourteen-year relationship. Of course, it was the ideal partnership: the brewery wanted to sell more drink and promote their brands, while I liked drinking their drinks – especially LCL Pils – and playing in their venues. Over the fourteen-year period, I think I played in almost every outlet they supplied, including the House of Commons bar at Westminster. They paid me very well, including one little bonus: I was never expected to pay for my own drinks.

The brewery's chief executive, David Brook, who signed me to represent the company, became one of my best friends. His service with the brewery now finished, he lives in Thailand, but we continue to visit each other at least twice a year.

My fourth major sponsor lasted the shortest time – 'time' being the operative word. Watch manufacturers Citizen asked me to wear their brand name of my shirt, and I jumped at the chance to be sponsored by them. After all, they're known worldwide, their name appearing on billboards at all the most important sporting events. Although my deal with them lasted for only three years, during that time my association with them gave me credibility in world sport. Like the other sponsors I've mentioned Citizen contributed to my overall success in reaching the top and – most of all – helped me to stay there.

Being a famous and respected darts professional, knowing all the secrets to becoming a world champion, I'm constantly approached by up-and-coming darts players asking me to sponsor them. I've always politely said no, because I didn't simply walk into a sponsorship deal myself; I had to make my name and build a significant reputation and prove myself worthy before anyone would take me on board. It's a big decision for a company to sponsor an individual to represent them and their products, knowing that if he or she let themselves down then the company is also let down.

I sincerely believe that I've represented my sponsors in the manner in which they expected, and I guess a thirty-year association with my main sponsor is testimony to that. In return, all I could offer for their support was my loyalty. One goes hand in hand with the other.

CHAPTER 19

Thirty Years on The Toe Line

The year 2005 marked my thirtieth year as a professional darts player. Reflecting on those years is a very interesting exercise and one I often engage in these days.

It would be easy to just pick out the most rewarding episodes: the victories, the good guys (and girls), the friendships made, the folks who have embraced my progress. I could puff out my chest and tell folks how easy things have been, but by doing that I wouldn't be being honest with my fans or myself. With all the success comes failure: the second places, the not-so-friendly people, the bad guys and, sadly, those who cling onto the past and their own egos.

I've experienced some glaring examples of this last category. For example, In 1976 I played in a championship at a Pontins holiday camp in Prestatyn, Wales. It was dubbed 'the Pontins Open', and the event's organiser announced that, if players lost a match, they had to mark the next match. All players complied with this request, and indeed it was the normal thing to do in those days, as there tended to be more players than spectators, so it was only common sense that they would be the ones to mark the scores.

After a few years the BDO realised that most players who lost their games would leave the venue quite quickly – understandably, I suppose, as many players don't like to hang around after losing. However, rather than enforce the 'losers mark the next match' rule, the BDO introduced a new rule: the winners had to mark the next match. That rule stayed in place for many years.

Many professionals, including myself, don't like marking. When you've won a game, all you want to do then is concentrate on the next one. Marking distracted me. I couldn't concentrate on my next game until the process of marking was over, and it often took up to thirty minutes to complete a game. I couldn't prepare myself mentally for the next game during that time and often lost precious practice time, especially when I was feeling off form and needed to spend time at the dartboard, honing my game. Many of the professionals protested against the arrangements at Prestatyn, but the organisers were stubborn to the point of telling us that, unless we marked the board, we'd be eliminated from the event. Some players found a way around the rule, however, arranging for friends to mark for them or buying someone else a drink or two to mark for them.

When the PDC came onto the darts scene, we all thought there'd be a big improvement in the marking department, and to a degree we were right. However, in those days we still had to mark the board during the early stages of each event. It was only by the time the last sixteen were playing that independent markers took over.

I had a difficult situation in Blackpool at the Bobby Bourne Testimonial Championship. (Bobby was the players' marshall at all the top PDC events, and his job was to make sure that the players arrived at the stage entrance on time. Sadly, he died in 2002.) I'd lost at the top-thirty-two stage, and no one had mentioned to me that I would have to mark the next game. In fact, most of the other players who had lost had simply left the arena. I, however, had remained to watch Cliff Lazarenko play, after having progressed to the next round, and was amazed to hear the MC announce that any player who didn't mark their game would lose any world ranking points they'd gained in the event.

Well, I felt this was out of order for a number of reasons. Firstly, it shouldn't have been announced publicly like that. Secondly, the organisers were being employed by the Professional Darts Players' Association to run the event on their behalf, and the PDPA had certainly not given the organisers the right to make such decisions. And thirdly, players were already irritated by the playing conditions.

It was quite late in the afternoon by that time, and downstairs in the Winter Gardens the atmosphere was almost cellar-like. There was no air-conditioning and the temperature was over 100 degrees. As well as the heat, the players were also complaining about the £50 entry fee they'd had to pay, which should have translated into good playing facilities, which clearly wasn't the case. The fact that the organisers started the event some forty minutes late didn't go down too well, either.

I was a little unhappy with the whole set-up, and to be honest I was wondering whether any progress in the sport of darts –particularly at professional level – had, in fact, been made. It was like being back in the late 1970s in some smoke-filled building with a concrete floor that had been acquired by some promoter keen to make a few quid out of the darts players, knowing that if he could keep them there all day they'd drink the bar dry.

I refused to mark the next game, stating that they had no right to issue statements over the microphone that they weren't entitled to make. Almost immediately an apology was made, but then I was told I had to mark the board. *Had* to? Well, by this time I was well and truly past caring. Anger had replaced common sense. I was being shown up in front of people, and I didn't like it.

I pointed out that other players had left without marking, then suggested to the organisers that they bring me a copy of the rules that stated I had to mark. My lack of self-control meant that I'd placed myself in a position from which I couldn't back down. In truth, I should have just gone to the board and marked the game, and that would have been the end of it, but I didn't. I refused to mark.

Strangely, a few weeks later I read a report by Rod Harrington, the PDC representative for the running of tournaments, in which he recommended that all future players' tournaments be run by the PDC and not some contracted organisers, citing the Bobby Bourne tournament as a typical example. He didn't mention individual names, just that in his opinion the whole event from start to finish was not conducted in a manner befitting the professional sport of darts. It was as if I'd written the report myself. I'd been thirty years on the oche and was still no closer to understanding the sentence 'Players must mark their respective board.'

I noted that, in the regulations for the World Grand Prix qualifier event held in Newport in 2004, in the section titled 'Players' Obligations', the following was included: 'This tournament will be run on a 'loser marks' basis, and it is a condition of participation that the losing player of each match marks the following game.' Most of the players thought that the organisers of that event had plenty of help with marking at the later stages, but I guess some things will never change. We'll just have to get used to them. But we don't have to like them.

Over the thirty years in which I've toed the oche worldwide, one thing has always been present: alcohol. I've tried throughout this book to keep the subjects of dart-throwing and drink a fair distance from each other, but in the sport of darts it's well-nigh impossible.

I began playing darts in a bar for one plain and simple (and obvious) reason: only bars had dartboards back then. For donkeys' years, it's been a British tradition that darts matches are played between opposing teams from other taverns, inns and clubs in the immediate vicinity. There have been leagues in existence comprising sixteen teams or more for nearly 100 years, so it's an accepted part of the tradition that a pint of your choosing be taken at any time before, during and after the match. In the early days, the last leg of a match would be the gallon leg, where the losing team would buy the winners a gallon of beer between them.

Tradition is difficult to abandon, however, and most people

wouldn't condone the banning of booze. Right up until the mid-1970s, folks didn't have a problem with the association of drinking with darts. Indeed, in the early days, if your team won the local league, you'd perhaps receive a prize of perhaps just a tea service, a canteen of cutlery or a clock – no money, or at least not any considerable sum of cash.

In the 1970s, however, all that changed when coverage of the sport and what players did in their own bar was transferred to the small screen and made public to millions of viewers. The players – including me – would walk to the stage, their darts in one hand and their pint in the other. If the match went on for a while, their drink would be replenished by an official. This was all very acceptable behaviour, all part of the game, up front and honest. Even smoking wasn't an issue at this stage, which is strange when you realise that tobacco manufacturers would be banned from all sponsorship of sport before brewers.

By the 1980s, the prize money in darts had increased dramatically. Professional players made considerable earnings from the sport and drinking on camera was being frowned upon by the TV producers and the media. At around this time a sketch was broadcast on the TV comedy show *Not the Nine O'Clock News* featuring two huge archetypal darts players who appeared to be aiming at a dartboard. The commentator said something like, 'And now Fatty's going for a double, and this time ...' There was a pause, and then the viewers realised that the player wasn't holding a dart; instead of referring to a double on the dartboard he'd meant 'double vodka', and the player's hand went down to a table crammed with drinks, picked up a glass and swilled its contents down his neck. The sketch then continued in that vein – 'Treble ... treble gin. Double ... double scotch!' and so on. Its long-term damage to the sport of darts at that time was unimaginable, and became irreparable.

Soon the press began to rip the sport apart. They had a field day, publishing headlines such as 'BIG CLIFF DRINKS 25 PINTS ON HIS WAY TO THE FINAL' and 'JOCKY DOWNS 40OZ OF VODKA TO PUT HIMSELF BACK ON LINE FOR THE TITLE'. The problem was, it was all true.

In 1988 the BDO introduced a drinking ban on stage in all

tournaments, following a smoking ban eighteen months earlier. The new rule barred any player or match official from consuming or introducing alcoholic drinks on stage. Instead, a jug of iced water and glasses would be provided. If a player breached the new rule, he or she would forfeit the match.

The media couldn't believe it. Soon headlines were reading, 'DART PLAYERS TURN TO FITNESS FIRST', 'DARTS CLEANS UP ITS TAPROOM IMAGE', 'BIG CLIFF GOES DRY' and 'JOCKY STEADY ON THE OCHE'.

It was true. When we were on stage in the later stages of each televised competition, none of us took a drink. The drinking ban has been enforced right up to the present day, and I'm sure it will continue in the future. However, one thing has remained: when the tournament begins, whether it's an open tournament or a TV tournament, the bar is open for business. The old adage 'You can take the darts out of the bar but you can't take the bar out of darts' is as true today as it ever was, the only difference being that, where it was once a few pints of bitter or lager, it might now be a few bottles of designer alcohol.

It's true, however, that players look fitter. Gone is the beer-bellied darts player (well, almost), and even the media – around seventy-five per cent of them, in any case – have given the sport credibility over the last few years, recognising the skill required to play and realising that that skill would vanish if a player was full of booze.

Nevertheless, it still remains a fact that drinking and darts are practically inseparable. Many's the time I have gone around to Cliff Lazarenko's hotel room at eight o'clock in the morning and chatted with him over a few cans of Strongbow before going on to play in a tournament at ten. The time of day didn't matter; ten in the morning or ten at night, we never toed the oche without a couple of drinks inside us. The nice thing is that we'd know how far to go. We'd pace ourselves, taking a drink now and then, trying to relax while keeping the next game ever in our minds. Why did we do it? Because we'd always done so, I suppose, and so had everyone else we knew.

The sport had some notorious drinkers. I suppose Jocky Wilson was the one most written and talked about. I know he would never deny that he liked a wee dram or two, but the surprising thing about Jocky was his ability to hit almost anything on the dartboard when he was full. The downside of his drinking, however, was his temperament after the match. If he'd won, he was fine, but if he'd lost, then it was time to make yourself scarce.

It wouldn't be right for me to tell you about the habits of other players without telling you of my own experiences with regards to alcohol. In spite of my comment above about being able to pace myself, I have to admit to feeling the worse for drink on a couple of occasions during competitions. I make no excuses for doing so, however. Maybe I regret the number of times I've played for two days to reach the top eight of an event only to realise that I'd accepted far too many drinks from friendly supporters and spent far too much time chatting in their company instead of being on the practice board, away from any distractions, but I chalk up such experiences as being part of life's journey. Besides, being with your supporters and friends is part of what darts is all about. I can't think of any other major sport that allows such direct contact between stars and fans.

I'm quite pleased that I can count on two hands the number of alcohol-related mistakes I've made over thirty years of competitive play. When, as a professional, you're expected to play darts up to thirty weekends of the year, human frailty is bound to show its face, and when it does, all you can do is accept it and face the consequences. But it's more often not the alcohol that impacts on your game but little things, niggles that on occasion you can't quite deal or come to terms with. The feeling, for example, that no matter how much you've practised, it's simply not going to be your day. You instantly recognise this feeling, and at that point you have to decide that, whatever else might occur, you're simply going to just enjoy being there.

Will we ever see darts played without alcohol present? I know that there are some in the darting fraternity who would love to see a complete drinking ban introduced across the board, across all competitions and in all venues. I also know that many others have concerns about the practicalities of such a move and its impact on those who support the sport, especially existing and potential sponsors within the brewing industry, the breweries and pub-chain owners who employ professional darts players to bring people into their outlets. I've worked with many breweries over the last thirty years, and my income would have been nowhere near as high as it has been without their support. Indeed, I doubt that, without their help, I could have remained a professional darts player. Darts and the brewing trade go hand in hand.

In June 2005 darts was finally recognised by Sport England (the English Sports Council). This means that at last its organisers will be eligible to apply for Lotto cash with which to develop darts from grassroots to international level.

I always believed that darts would be recognised as a sport. Holland recognised it years ago, and, in fact, darts is now one of the leading sports in that country. The BDO campaigned long and hard, pressuring Sport England and now it's paid off. Good for them – and darts. Until Sport England and other British sports councils recognised darts as a sport, it would never have stood any chance of featuring in the Olympics. Now, with London staging the 2012 Olympics I wouldn't be surprised to see darts played at least as a demonstration sport. In that event, the association of darts with alcohol might finally be broken – well, for two weeks at least.

Finally on the subject of alcohol, as I mentioned earlier it's not classed as a performance-enhancing drug. Actually, it's known to have completely the opposite effect. Thus, apparently, it doesn't have any qualities that would influence a game of darts to the better. So why do we drink and play? Well, old traditions are very hard to break, and it would appear that darts and alcohol form one of the longest traditional partnerships in the UK. Maybe the next generation of darts players will break that tradition, but somehow I just can't see it, although there are moves afoot within the PDC to introduce random 'drug' tests to ensure that no player will be allowed on the oche if he, or she, has had a few too many drinks.

As for me, I'll play out my darting days quite happy to share the dartboard with a couple of drinks. That's how it all began and that's how it will end for me. However, there is a greater threat to traditional darts than the eventual removal of alcohol.

One development in darts that has recently seen a dramatic move into the marketplace, particularly in Europe and parts of the USA, is the use of soft-tip or electronic darts.

Here's how it works. The dartboard in a soft-tip set is part of an electronic machine, almost like a fruit machine in a pub. The machine itself is about 6ft 6in high while the darts have plastic tips (hence the name of the game), as opposed to traditional steel-tipped darts. The dartboard, meanwhile, is made of plastic and has hundreds of holes in its surface so that, when the darts are thrown, they penetrate one of the holes and the score from that segment is deducted automatically, immediately and electronically from the total score.

Gone are the days of chalking the scores. With soft-tip darts, no one has to do the mental calculation and chalk up the results; it's all done electronically. This is one of the reasons why the game has developed so quickly; players who might previously have been put off the game because of the mathematical element and were reluctant to take the chalk readily play soft tip. Of course, as with all electronic games in pubs, soft-tip darts costs money – around £1 for each best-of-three-leg game.

Soft-tip darts is a self-financing game and the units make money for whichever pub or club in which they're installed. Players feed the machine to play, the organisers and owners pay back a percentage of the takings to provide trophies and monetary prizes for the players and thus, in theory, the more people who play, the greater the rewards at both ends of the scale.

A recent survey in America recorded alarming results for steel-tip players. Apparently, no fewer than sixty-five per cent of all darts matches played in America now are played on electronic dartboards. The Soft Tip World Championships, played in Las Vegas in 2003, carried a prize fund of $600,000.

And it's not just America where the soft-tip game is expanding. In Europe, participation is growing in Germany and Spain, while in the Far East interest in the soft-tip game has exploded in Japan, so much so that Unicorn are sending their world champions, Phil Taylor, John Part, Bob Anderson and me, over there to make personal appearances at the Japanese Soft Tip Championships.

However, although soft-tip darts is flourishing and growing in popularity all over the world, there's one place where it's proving difficult to gain a foothold in the market. And that place is … you've guessed it: the UK, the home of traditional darts.

To me, the reasons for this reluctance to embrace the soft-tip game are obvious. Darts has always been an accepted part of our heritage; the English invented the modern game and, like rounders being converted into baseball, we don't like our traditional games being messed about with. Also we've never, *ever* paid to play darts (well, except to win or lose a pint, maybe) and we have no intention of starting now. Times change, though, and who knows what the future holds for darts in Britain?

It is my view that, in order to make the soft-tip game work in the UK, pub owners would have to take down their traditional boards *en bloc* and replace them with the soft-tip machines. I hear shrieks of shock horror. 'It'll never happen, John. We won't let it! And don't ever mention it again!'

OK, I know how you feel, but take a look at many of the bars in our towns and cities today. Try and find a dartboard. I suspect that, without expert local knowledge, you won't have much luck. If that trend continues and the traditional darts facilities eventually vanish from licensed premises, what's to prevent soft-tip darts from being introduced as simply another electronic game in, say, ten years' time? Some pubs already have electronic video darts games, so who's to say that, a few years from now, soft-tip darts won't be there too? Who knows?

I do. Believe me, it will happen. Top manufacturers like Unicorn are already geared up for the soft-tip revolution, their new catalogue including no fewer than six pages of soft-tip darts and accessories. I also know that the PDC are keeping a watchful eye on the game's progress.

Through the PDC, the world has become increasingly aware of the traditional game of steel-tipped darts, with the introduction of tournaments worthy of being described as professional. The prize money, too, has increased dramatically since the days of the BDO and players can now make a full-time living – in Phil Taylor's case, a cool £1 million per year. As the soft-tip game spreads throughout the world, I can clearly see the first $1 million world championship being played, maybe in America but more likely in the Land of the Rising Sun: Japan. Soft-tip darts are the darts of the future, and the PDC, I feel, will be best placed to derive benefits for professional players from the expansion of their activities into this area.

In other areas of darts, away from this revolution, some things simply stand still. The BDO Inter-County Leagues immediately spring to mind, the format of which has remained virtually the same for the last thirty years. On nine weekends a year, the top players from each registered county play a two-day match against an opposing county, the B teams on Saturday and the A teams on Sunday. Averages are kept and the top men and ladies from the leagues gain their place in their respective national sides. My point is that, while the game of darts – even darts with non-conventional points – is making an impact on the global stage, the Inter-County League, for all its value to the up-and-coming player, appears to be making no headway at all.

I first started playing county darts for Yorkshire, for the simple reason that my native county, Derbyshire, hadn't formed a team at that time. I enjoyed my time with Yorkshire County darts because we had a great team and a great team spirit. (One of my claims to fame is being the only known non-Yorkshireman to captain the county at any sport.) The support we had was fantastic; whenever we played away, we'd take two coaches full of players and supporters. I was proud to go through from Yorkshire and win my first World Masters Championship in 1976. The following season, I left the Yorkshire team and joined that of my home county, Derbyshire.

In those early days of inter-county darts, all the counties were well supported by non-playing darts enthusiasts and the gate money was good enough to cover the fees payable to the BDO. As the years went on, however, the supporters started to fall away, and today the counties are mainly made up of the players and a few hardcore supporters and their friends. The players have to pay entry fees to the venues by buying a programme, and any player travelling to an away match for a two-day match can expect no change from £80.

For all this, the Inter-County League is a good testing ground for new talent, and it gives players the chance to perform on a stage in front of an audience, preparing them well for any possible future international duty or maybe a shot at the professional championships run by the PDC. I don't suppose the inter-county game will ever make such a profitable return as it did in the 1980s, but it's important to keep it running as a stepping stone to greater heights within the sport.

My father used to say to me when he watched me take a motorcycle apart so I could tune it to gain more speed, 'Don"t mend it unless it's broken.' I have remembered those words throughout my life and have tried to be guided by them. On reflection, my father's philosophy fits the sport of darts quite well. In the past, darts has been tampered with in a number of departments – for example, the international throwing distance has been introduced, and now every country toes the oche at a distance of 7ft 9¼in from the dartboard. That was a welcome move. Different formats, too, have been introduced, with some major events being played in sets instead of legs.

Then, of course, the Quadro dartboard was introduced in some PDC competitions. This was an innovation of Harrows Darts Technology, based on a standard dartboard, with a third 'quadruple' ring added between the treble ring and the outer bull that awarded four times the points of the number of the bed. The theory was that using such a board would make the game more interesting. Well, it did – for everyone but the caller, who had a nightmare adding all the scores together, not to mention certain players who, already struggling with their finishing combinations on the orthodox board, found finishing on the quadruple board way beyond their mental capacities!

A great introduction to the sport was the concept of shooting nearest to the centre bull to determine who starts the leg. It was a welcome successor to the age-old practice of tossing a coin, which was totally down to luck.

Apart for these few changes, the game of darts has remained

the same for decades, so I guess we can say it's not broken. But what changes would I like to see?

For a start, I'd like the organisers to step confidently into the twenty-first century! Sky TV has introduced many new innovations to the sport in an attempt to make it more appealing to the viewers and spectators: the Cyclops camera, the lights down the side of the oche, the players' walk-ons to their own signature music. In my opinion, there's only one glaring part of the twentieth century still on display: two markers on either side of the board, writing the scores down on sheets of paper. How archaic is that? Unfortunately it seems that the organisers don't have the confidence to introduce electronic flat-screen panels with numeric displays. Why should that be when they've embraced the new technology in so many other ways?

I've never been given a proper explanation as to why this won't be changed. In this day and age, electronic machines are capable of so much, and subtracting a player's score from his initial total is child's play. If a mistake was made, a click of a button would recall the previous score, just as markers do now. It's time for such technology to be accepted as the norm. It's time for the chalkers to leave the stage.

I would also like to see a change in the starting number for certain tournaments – specifically, an increase from 501 to 601 or even 701. If this was adopted, the number of legs or sets could be cut slightly, which would also add a new degree of difficulty to the game. Since I achieved my nine-dart game of 501 on TV back in 1984, the same feat has been captured on at least four other occasions, and today, rather than becoming excited by the possibility of it being achieved, people are rather disappointed if a perfect nine-darter isn't hit during a major competition. If 601 or 701 was introduced as a new discipline, this would offer a new challenge and a new perfect game of darts: eleven darts in the case of 601 (180–180–180–61) and twelve in the case of 701 (180–180–180–161). The odds would increase because of the higher level of difficulty. We'd still be playing the same numbers game, but we'd have moved the finishing post.

When someone clears the bar in a high-jump tournament, the

bar goes higher. I'm suggesting something similar for the sport of darts. The 'world record' perfect game of 501 in darts has been achieved and equalled, not once but many times, so it's time the bar was raised.

It's time for darts to move on to a new challenge.

CHAPTER 20

Where Do I Go
From Here?

The question is, should John Lowe also move on to another challenge? Where do I go from here? Now sixty years of age, I have to consider this question with more sincerity than at any other time in the past.

In terms of life experience, I've probably lived for over 100 years. I've been around the world more than forty times, I've driven over a million miles and the 2004/2005 season was my twenty-seventh year without missing one world championship. I have over 1,000 international darts titles to my name, including twenty-two that carry the term 'world'.

As well as this, I captained my country for seven years, during which time the team didn't lose. I played over 100 times for England, and if my international career hadn't been cut short by the BDO's ban of the sixteen 'rebel' players I would have undoubtedly gone on to add probably another 100 caps to my tally. I've enjoyed a truly remarkable career, throwing those precision-made Unicorn 21g golden darts.

But could I have been better? Could I have achieved more?

It's often said that you shouldn't think of 'what ifs', but yes, I could have done more. I've probably sacrificed pure quality for a career of longevity. I have purposely cut down on practice time over the last five years. To have carried on in the selfish, single-minded, almost blinded lifestyle that's needed in order to remain at the very top all the time would have destroyed me. Instead I've consciously made an effort before each tournament I've entered and built up my confidence sufficiently for me to perform at an acceptable level on each occasion.

I've had to find the balance between being just a professional dart player and a professional dart player who has time for not only his own life but also the lives of others who are part of his life. I believe that I've now found that balance. I no longer need to travel the world in search of those damned ranking points, the ones so many other players are still having to purchase rather than win in order to keep their ranking status. In February 2004, I made a conscious decision that I would simply let things happen for and to me from that time on.

Peter Sharma, a great author of life's lessons, once wrote, 'Don't wait until you're on your deathbed to realise the meaning of life and the precious role you have to play within it. All too often, people attempt to live their lives backwards; they spend their days striving to get the things that will make them happy rather than having the wisdom to realise that happiness is not a place you reach but a state you create. Happiness and a life of deep fulfilment come when you commit yourself, from the very core of your soul, to spending your highest human talents on a purpose that makes a difference in others lives. When all the clutter is stripped away from your life, its true meaning will become clear: to live for something more than yourself.' Or, put more simply, the purpose of life is a life of purpose.

I have no doubt that I can carry on playing darts and competing with the very best for the foreseeable future, while I enjoy being in good health and having particularly good eyesight – and, indeed, that's what I intend to do. I still find my exhibition work enjoyable, although I don't bill them as 'fun' exhibitions; I bill them as a challenge – the punters' challenge against me, John Lowe, three times winner of the Embassy World Professional Darts Championship. I find that people like to accept that challenge and go about it with the respect the challenge commands. Young players in their teens toe the oche against me and know that their age will be of no advantage to them: they still have to outscore me and double out first. Rest assured, Old Stoneface won't give them an inch.

When I entered the world of darts, I did so with a competitive will to win. I still carry that same will today. At the moment of writing, I am ranked twentieth in the PDC world rankings. I may well slip down that ranking table over the next twelve months, as I don't intend to enter every event that has points on offer, just those that are viable and those I know I'll enjoy.

The new foundation of darts in the twenty-first century comprises the eight British Open qualifying events, each played at a different venue around the UK over a two-day weekend period and each carrying valuable points and a £20,000 prize, plus the Professional Dart Players' Association's five events, which carry the same ranking status and prize fund. These events will, without doubt, bring about the demise of the BDO inter-county weekends. You don't need to be a rocket scientist to be able to work out that playing for your county over a two-day weekend can cost a lot of money in coach travel, two nights' hotel accommodation, entrance to the venue, plus food and drink. All told, a weekend trip can set a player back about £100 or more.

The entry fee for the PDC and PDPA weekend events is currently set at £50, and each player must win at his or her allocated venue on the Saturday in order to be placed in the last sixteen. Those matches are played on the Sunday at one venue, so there's no need to book a hotel. If you qualify, all it takes is a phone call to a local Travel Inn.

The beauty of these events is the fact that you have to win only a couple of matches to receive a refund of your entry fee. More and more of the inter-county players made their debuts in these competitions in 2005, and I feel sure that they'll influence many more players to take up the challenge of serious darts. After all, if you never try, you'll never know.

The BDO has been a big influence on my career as an amateur and professional darts player. The organisation didn't only give me the chance to play the sport; it also gave me the option to play at a better level. I accepted that offer, and from 1974 through to 1994 I enjoyed twenty years of highly competitive darts, becoming a household name in the process.

I didn't leave the BDO; they, in their wisdom, banned me from taking part in any more of their tournaments. The door was slammed in my face – in sixteen faces, in fact – and thus, as a professional player – and a successful one, at that – I had to find an alternative route forward, so I put my heart and soul into the WDC and the PDC. It wasn't a case of 'Where else can I go?'; it was a case of believing in what those organisations were trying to achieve: an open playing field for all darts players, with the ultimate goal of placing the sport of darts on a level with other professional sports.

Call it fate if you like, but remember that all I had to do was sign the BDO's inter-county registration form, that form of allegiance to the BDO, and I would have become their most prized possession and England captain for the foreseeable future. I would have been the Embassy touring roadshow darts player, the voice and the shop window for the British Darts Organisation. Instead I decided to stay with my fellow professional players who had made a stand for the future of the sport.

We made a few people very happy by taking that stance. Bobby George, for example, became the front man for the BDO and the darts pundit for the BBC. Tony Green also took on a role of BDO letter-writer, finding an incredible way of completely dismissing the banned players from his vocabulary for the next seven years. Martin Adams, meanwhile, grabbed the England captaincy like a beggar accepting a five-pound note, and although his England performances might suggest he should be replaced, he has nevertheless proved eager to wear the England colours at every possible event, keeping him firmly within the BDO camp of admirers. Martin tried the professional circuit and the PDC for a year but, no fool, quickly ran back to the safety of the amateur ranks; with the PDC boys, he had to be at his best all of the time, not just some of the time.

I'm now happy with my darts and the PDC events in which I take part. The last ten years have been a hard slog, not just for me but for the organisers of the PDC, too, people like Tommy Cox and Dick Allix, who have stood by their convictions and backed up their words with actions. I'm sure that without them the BDO would now reign supreme and today professional darts players would be still playing for peanuts – in which case I probably would have returned to the joinery trade.

The most significant factor in the success of the PDC in recent years has been the emergence of Barry Hearn and his willingness to be elevated to the position of chairman of the PDC, plus his expertise at negotiating and securing television rights and sponsorship for the years to come. I remember someone at a players' meeting with Barry asking him once where all the money he spoke about was going to come from. Barry's reply was, 'Don't worry about money. I have sheds full of the stuff.' What a lovely way to reply! I applauded him then and I do so today.

So my decision to let my life take its own course within the darting world has been made. I wouldn't mind if I received a call from Buckingham Palace in the near future, should they choose to recognise my thirty years in the sport, three world titles, over 1,000 titles earned across the globe (including six World Cup and seven Europe Cup wins) and a lifetime spent promoting this most British of all sports worldwide. That would surely be a better recommendation than being a substitute in a World Cup win. However, I think the withdrawal of Phil Taylor's MBE has now affected my chances.

I'm going to continue on the rollercoaster ride that is professional darts, enjoying competing and doing exhibitions. An attitude of 'lucky come, lucky go' might be a little dangerous for my fellow competitors, as my will to win remains ever strong, but any disappointment I suffer at losing a major darts match at the age of sixty will hardly be life-threatening. However, I'll stay competitive at the very highest level. Can I win another World Championship? Can I beat Phil Taylor? Of course I can. Why not? I never play to lose, and I certainly know how to win. While I keep qualifying for major events, there's always the chance I will lift the trophy at the end of play.

While I continue to be involved with darts, my private life will never be truly private. Personally, I don't mind sharing my life with the autograph hunters, the photographers and the girls offering their assets for me to sign. (I used to oblige those girls, but Karen politely asked me to refrain, unless I could do the signing without holding the part to be signed steady with my other hand.) Whenever I'm asked to sign autographs or have my photograph taken, I know I'm still a part of the sport, not just for today but forever.

When I met Karen, I changed dramatically. Before Karen came into my life I was becoming depressed, almost to the degree of being manic. I would go to the pub and never know what time to come home. Now I'm quite willing, and even look forward to, staying in and watching the telly. I even watch *Coronation Street* and *EastEnders* and, what's more, I tell people I watch them. I just love to see the look on the faces of some of the macho guys who can't wait to avow their abstention from watching these shows. 'I never watch that rubbish,' they say. Nowadays, I reply, 'Neither did I, and that's the reason I thought they were rubbish.'

I've learned that life is more than just being John Lowe, the darts player. I remember attending a christening in 2004 and remarking to Karen, 'I can't see anyone I don't like here.' I must have changed a lot!

I could have filled this book twice over with stories from around the world, but instead I've tried to fill the pages with true, meaningful stories and events from my life, that of the little kid born at Holly Hurst, New Tupton, Derbyshire, on 21 July 1945, the son of Frederick and Phyllis Lowe. I sincerely hope you've enjoyed reading it.

CHAPTER 21

The Legend – The Stats

No autobiography of any sportsman would be complete without a record of the greatest achievements of that sportsman.

John estimates that during his career as a professional darts player, which spans four decades, he has won well in excess of 1,000 titles worldwide. Thus it would be impossible – and impractical – to include them all here.

What follows, then, are the major titles John has won during his amazing darts career. The list is in alphabetical order, and where John has won the competition on two or more occasions the number of wins is shown in brackets.

SINGLES CHAMPIONSHIP TITLES
American Champion of Champions (3)
American Lucky Lights (3)
American Open (2)
Australian Open
British Gold Cup (3)
British Matchplay (2)
British Open (2)
British Pentathlon (10)
Canadian Open (3)

Danish Open (5)
Dartshathlon (3)
Embassy LVA
Embassy World Professional Championship (3)
European Singles Championship (3)
Finland Open
Golden Gate Classic
Irish Masters
London Elkadart Classic
National Singles
News of the World Individual Darts Championship
Pacific Masters
Phuket Open
Swedish Open
Swedish Pewter Tankard (2)
Scottish Masters
Sydney Open
Thailand Open
WINMAU World Masters (2)
World Cup Singles (2)
World Matchplay (2)

PAIRS TITLES
American Open, including mixed pairs (8)
Australian Open
British Open
Canadian Open (2)
Danish Open (2)
Europe Cup (4)
Finnish Open
Guinness Gold Dart
Sydney Open
Thailand Open
World Cup (5)

ENGLAND INTERNATIONAL WINS
Europe Cup, pairs (3)

Europe Cup, singles (3)
Europe Cup, team (5)
Home International (9)
Nations Cup (8)
World Cup, pairs (5)
World Cup, singles (2)
World Cup, team (6)
World Triples (3)

In addition, John ...

- has played over 100 times for England;
- holds the record for the most wins in the North American Open;
- holds the record for the most World Open wins;
- holds the record for the most centre bulls (1,320) recorded in ten hours while retrieving his own darts, achieved on 27 October 1994; and
- captained the England darts team for seven years, during which time they never lost a match.

And, of course, on 13 October 1984 John became the first player ever to achieve a televised perfect nine-dart game of 501, in the process winning £102,000. The following day, he won the MFI Matchplay title and the prize for the highest out-shot of the tournament, making his winnings a total of £115,000. At the time of writing, this remains the biggest pay day ever for a professional darts player.

But it doesn't end here. John continues to play against the best established and up-and-coming dart players at home and abroad, and will undoubtedly pick up even more silverware along the way. He has no intention of hanging up his darts just yet.

CHAPTER 22

Tribute to Barry Twomlow, 'The Man Who Taught The World to Play Darts'

Before finally closing this chapter of my life and looking to the future, I must pay special tribute to someone who is no longer able to walk the path with me. Sadly, one of my closest friends, Barry Twomlow, passed away during the writing of this book. Barry was important to my development as a professional darts player, and indeed it's possible – no, probable – that I wouldn't have got as far in the darting world as I have without his friendship, help and guidance.

Saturday, 29 May 2004 was one of the saddest days of my life, as it was the day Barry passed away, and yet it was also one of the proudest. On that day, Joe Mooney – another close friend of Barry's – rang to tell me that, while Barry had been travelling with his wife, Margaret, to see friends in Scarborough, he'd been taken ill and died *en route*. I was truly saddened, and for a few hours my mind was muddled and confused, thinking of all the many hours Barry and I had spent together over the last forty years, all the great times we'd enjoyed, all brought about by one common denominator: darts. My sadness turned into pride, though, when I remembered the Barry Twomlow I'd grown to like, listen to and, more than anything else, respect.

The friends who knew Barry – and there are many of them –

will all have their own way of remembering him, but the one thing they'll all remember is his catchphrase, which he said at the end of any meeting: 'Just one more for the road.' Boy, have I shared a few for the road with the big guy!

I well remember having a couple of drinks with Barry and my driver, Peter Lippiatt, one evening in the Bridge Inn on Hollis Lane, Chesterfield. As usual, we were talking about some trip we'd shared abroad for Unicorn. A couple of drinks turned into three, maybe four, and we didn't leave until well past midnight. The night was warm, the door of the pub was open and at about 12:45am two policemen walked into the bar. They looked at Barry and me, both with full pints, and said, 'Hello.' We returned their welcome and carried on talking and drinking, oblivious to the time. The two policemen then asked the landlord to step outside, which he did, returning after a few minutes with a big smile on his face.

'What's wrong?' asked Barry.

The landlord replied that it appeared the two policemen had come to ask about the man who lived next door, whose car had been stolen.

'Oh, nothing to bother about, then,' said Peter.

'Well, the inspector did mention it was 12:45 and that Barry Twomlow and John Lowe were still drinking at the bar almost two hours after closing time, but it's OK,' said the landlord. 'They didn't mind you having a drink. They just thought you should have made an attempt to hide it or put it down.'

Barry looked at me and I knew what was coming. He smiled and said, 'John Lowe, you've kept me out late again. We'll just have one more for the road.'

I could tell stories about Barry for hours on end but would prefer to tell you instead of my thoughts about the Barry Twomlow I knew. In 1969, Barry came to a crossroads in his life when he won the *News of the World* Individual Darts Championship in that year. He found he had a choice: either to join Unicorn Products and take up darts as a full-time occupation or work with his brother-in-law, Billy Newton, as a salesman in Billy's business, which supplied office furniture. Barry chose

Unicorn, and for the next thirty years he tirelessly preached the Unicorn darts gospel worldwide. It didn't matter whether he was on official Unicorn business or not; the conversation would always contain the word 'Unicorn'.

Barry was proud to be associated with Unicorn, and he genuinely believed and meant every single word he used to promote their fine products. He was just as dedicated to promoting darts to the masses, from the townships in South Africa to Poolsbrook in Derbyshire. Indeed, he was a never-ending supporter of Derbyshire darts, and at the end of his competitive playing years he became the county team's president. He believed in promoting darts at all levels.

In his darting life, Barry was connected with many organising bodies, including the National Darts Association of Great Britain, the British Darts Organisation, the World Darts Federation and the Professional Darts Corporation. He would discuss the merits of each organisation for hours, but never once did he put one above the other. To Barry, each was contributing to the promotion and expansion of the sport of darts. Needless to say, we didn't always agree, but that's what friendship is all about – to be able to disagree and still remain the best of friends.

Barry Twomlow was the man who discovered John Lowe. We both played in local leagues and would meet up occasionally in knockout cups and the like. He kept a watchful eye on my progress and eventually asked if I'd like to be a member of Team Unicorn, later becoming my mentor as well as my friend. The people who knew Barry knew he was capable of playing and beating anyone on the planet – his darting skills were quite brilliant – but he was always willing to come out and practise with me before a big competition, telling me he was trying to improve his game. I knew different. He was trying to boost my confidence. And he liked nothing better than to see me win, especially on television.

At eleven o'clock on the morning of 9 June 2004, the Derbyshire town of Staveley stopped to say farewell to Barry. A packed Methodist church listened in silence as one of Barry's old school pals gave a moving tribute. Stanley Lowy (MBE), the retired chairman of Unicorn Products, also gave a glowing tribute to the work Barry did and the time he gave, not only to his company but also to darts players worldwide. It was a tearful, smiling, sad and happy hour of memories, a celebration of the life of a very dear friend. I knew I was representing many friends of Barry's from around the world, and I told him so.

After the service, a gathering of around 150 people met at the Chesterfield Hotel for refreshments and to pay tribute to Barry by signing his remembrance book and reading through the memorabilia his wife Margaret had laid out there.

Barry, the man who always had one more story to tell, managed to surprise us right to the end. The day he died, he won a spot-the-ball competition in the local newspaper. For those who are unfamiliar with this, I'll explain. The newspaper prints a shot taken during a football match from which the ball has been erased. The player then marks a cross where he or she thinks the ball is. Barry's cross had hit the spot dead on, winning him £25,000, so Barry ended up providing for his family both while he was on this Earth and when he left it.

I could fill an entire book with memories of the life and times of Barry Twomlow but will settle for this memorial to him. At the time of his death, I received hundreds of messages from people around the world wishing to express their sadness at Barry's demise. I've selected just one of those messages, one that I think summarises very simply the feelings of everyone who knew and loved this great man. BJ Clark, an American friend who now lives in Thailand with his family, wrote:

Barry will be missed by everyone in darts, but most of all by those who considered him to be their friend.

I know you're listening, Barry, so, on behalf of your many thousands of friends, I thank you for your friendship, hospitality and honesty and, perhaps above all, your passion for the sport of darts. I ask everyone to raise their glasses and have 'just one more for the road'.

Goodbye, great friend.

John

The Leighton Rees Interview

This is the text of John's interview with Leighton Rees that appeared on his website during 2002. It was the last extensive interview that Leighton ever gave.

JL: Leighton you began playing darts in the toughest school of all: the money school. Was this the reason you were able to handle pressure with seeming ease?

LR: Yes, because the pub that I began playing darts in, the Bridge Hotel in Pontypridd, required a wager before beginning a game of darts, either money or alcohol. From that early point in my darts career, I became money-orientated.

JL: Did you believe this was as good as darts would ever get?

LR: Yes, I did. At that time, the only other things you could take part in were the *News of the World*, the National Darts Association of Great Britain and the CIU [Club and Institute Union] tournaments.

JL: When the Super League and Internationals came along, you were right there at the top of your game. Did it come as a surprise when the organisers decided to move the oche from 7ft 6in to 7ft 9¼in?

LR: The oche move was no surprise. My only surprise was that darts players weren't allowed to play from 7ft 6in or further back, the choice being that of the players. The 7ft 6in rule had been in place since I began playing, in 1958. The only time the oche distance changed for me was when the Area Finals of the *News of the World* took place. I then played from 8ft.

JL: Did it affect your game in any way?

LR: Yes, it did. When I played from 7ft 6in, it was a known fact that not everyone toed the oche at that distance. Some players would try to edge up an inch or two when there was no raised oche, myself included. So, John, as my wife, Debbie, said when we married, an extra three or four inches could make a hell of a difference. Know what I mean?

JL: Your throwing style has always been recognised as special to watch, a repeated action and stance that could last forever. Did you work on your style or did it come naturally?

LR: My throwing style was an adaptation of different players' styles which I watched before I became famous.

JL: The names Evans and Rees became household names. You were the first really famous named player from the sport to reach the high street. Were you constantly recognised? Did you ever expect this? And how did you handle this new-found adulation?

LR: I found that the adulation was a bonus rather than a chore. The time to begin worrying is when you don't get recognised.

JL: Leighton, you were the favourite to land the *News of the World* title in 1976. When you reached the final, TV decided to take a long break. Subsequently you lost to Billy Lennard when transmission resumed. Did that break cost you the title you so much wanted to win?

LR: No, I don't think it made a difference. Billy handled the situation better than I did. It was a very warm day there and I was exhausted from the heat and the drink.

JL: It would be no good asking if you were disappointed. I watched on my TV set and I felt the atmosphere generated by the Welsh supporters when Billy's final double went in. Did you feel you could come back one day and win this great event?

LR: It was always my ambition to win the *News of the World*, but after 1976 it became harder to qualify due to work commitments. I realised that 1976 was my best chance as I was playing in the final. I never lost hope.

JL: Did it ever bother you when people used to regard Alan Evans as being 'the Prince of Wales' and the Welsh number one when you were playing the better darts on most occasions?

LR: It never caused me any great concern as I thought too much of Alan as a friend. As far as I'm concerned, Alan probably was 'the Prince of Wales' and responsible for my career beginning.

JL: In the great money match days between 1970 and 1977, you played in some memorable matches. This was my own introduction to the sport at the highest level. I remember playing a bit part on the Evans/Rees challenge at Stockport. I played one game of 1,001 against Blackpool's Jack Kellard. Can you tell us about this?

LR: Alan and I began playing for money, as this taught us that, if you could do this and win, you were prepared for any stage. I was involved in many memorable singles matches – to name a few, Nobby Clarke and Charlie Pitches from Lancashire, Brian

Langworth and Tony Lockwood from Yorkshire, Eric Bristow, Tony Bell, Willie Etherington, Tommy O'Regan, Peter Chapman, Alan Glazier from London and the great John Lowe. May I add that, of all those games, I only lost one against you know who!

JL: 1978 saw the inaugural world championship run by the BDO and sponsored by Embassy. Mike Watterson was the promoter and he had secured BBC TV to cover the event. What was your reaction to this great news: that darts was to take the next step up the ladder?

LR: I was very excited about the news and even more excited that I was invited into the tournament. I'd previously met Mike at an event in Shropshire, along with yourself, and I was very impressed with his plans for the game of darts.

JL: You were playing at your very best at this time. Were you quietly confident you could win the title? After breezing through the early rounds, you came up against your friend and playing partner, Alan Evans. Was it tough to play a close friend? You won the match and scored the best ever game of 501 ever seen on TV: ten darts, just one away from the perfect nine-dart game. I remember Alan took his defeat badly. What did he say to you after the match?

LR: Yes, Alan was very disappointed. He congratulated me and wished me all the best in the final.

JL: Your opponent in the final was a player from Derbyshire – myself. I can tell you, I was up for the final and looking forward to playing Mr Rees, a person and a player I greatly admired and respected. What were your thoughts on that match?

LR: I was excited at playing in the final of the first Embassy World Championship, and it was on television. I think that it was a good match; no one went more than two legs in front at any time. I was extremely relieved at hitting the winning double.

JL: What was the reaction when you returned home to your beloved Wales the world darts champion?

LR: That's something I'll never forget. I was coming up the main street of my village on the Monday after the event and there were streamers and banners across the streets. When I reached my house, it was then that I felt like royalty. Half of the village had come out to welcome me home.

JL: Darts had never had a world champion before. What was the next twelve months like for you?

LR: The busiest of my life. I was out practically every day, doing exhibitions and personal appearances. I also travelled to Australia, New Zealand, Canada, Barbados and Bermuda, doing exhibitions.

JL: The second Embassy World Championships had a new venue, Jollees nightclub at Hanley, Stoke-on-Trent, and the format had also changed from straight legs to sets. The venue was a vast improvement and record ticket sales came with it. After one week of battle on the oche, the seedings of rounds one and two were to meet in the final over the best of nine sets. Lo and behold, there was a rematch of the previous year: Lowe v Rees. What are your memories of that final?

LR: My memories are that I was well beaten on the day by five sets to nil. Not sour grapes, but our playing time was brought forward as Alan Evans was caught sick and didn't make an appearance. The earlier time slot didn't suit me as it meant I didn't have enough time to get pissed!

JL: A few years on and one thing was noticeable: prize money in the sport wasn't keeping pace with Embassy's other TV world championship, snooker. Did this concern you? The BDO had removed the promoter, Mike Watterson [according to Mike they 'stabbed him in the back'] after seeing no need to pay him a substantial commission. Unfortunately, they didn't negotiate in the same level as Mike, who was still the main man in snooker, and the gap between the two sports widened to the extremity. Do you think Mike should have been retained as an independent negotiator? After all, without him there would probably have never been an Embassy World Championship at all.

LR: I totally agree with your comments. It's not the first time the BDO stabbed somebody in the back. They got rid of the National Darts Association [of Great Britain] by making darts players choose which way they would go, either playing BDO or NDA[GB] tournaments. In my opinion, if Mike Watterson or a similar promoter could have been retained, darts would not have had the problems it's had over the last few years.

JL: In the 1980s, darts events began to disappear from our TV screens, TV bosses claiming there were too many, that they'd all become so similar that the public didn't know which event they were watching. Change was needed. The players became disgruntled and demanded they be heard by the BDO, so a players' association was formed. You attended many [of the organisation's] meetings and offered a lot of advice. Why do you think the BDO wouldn't listen to the players through the association? Was it a threat to their control of the sport?

LR: In my opinion, like the NDA, Mike Watterson and the Professional Darts Players' Association, anyone that Mr Croft and company thought would become a threat to their domination would be crushed.

JL: We all wanted the BDO to carry on as the overall organisers of the sport. We just wanted a say – a say in the formats, the prize funding and the presentation. Could we have done anything differently?

LR: Again, John, we went through the proper channels. While the BDO had achieved a good job in getting darts to its present position, it was time to move on and allow different promoters with different ideas to move the game forward for the good of professionals and amateurs alike.

JL: Times changed for Leighton Rees. After a while darts no longer became your main source of income and you decided to go into the licensed trade, becoming a landlord. Did you find this suited you, being a professional darts player, and, more so, one who was a local hero?

LR: Yes, extremely well. It's something I'd always wanted to do. It was quite an experience to be the other side of the bar for a change. Debbie had a full time job but found time to help me in the pub as well. After four years, though, I found myself with health problems and was forced to leave. A very sad day for all.

JL: I know things weren't going well for you at this time [with your heart problem]. What were your thoughts? Can you tell us about your hospitalisation?

LR: My thoughts were that, after all these years and all the good times I've had, I was now restricted with my mobility. My heart wasn't in good condition – too much drinking and smoking. I was discharged with a daily dose of fourteen tablets and an angina spray.

JL: Your luck didn't improve and you were involved in a driving accident. What happened that day?

LR: I remember that day well. I began by making sandwiches for Debbie for work. The next thing I remember is that I'd collapsed while still holding the knife I was spreading the butter with. I put it down to a one-off and continued to drive Debbie to work. After doing this, I continued to my GP in Ynysybwl, where I was examined and sent home. On the way home I had another dizzy spell, at which time I rolled the car over and ended upside-down. I had the seat belt choking me and my loving dog barking in my ears. The fire brigade had to cut me out of the car. My dog was all right and collected by my son Ryan, but I went straight to hospital, where they fitted a pacemaker.

JL: Inter-county and international matches can drain a player's bank account. I remember the World Cup in Brisbane, Australia. We travelled to the other side of the world and were given only £110 in expenses, plus our hotel and breakfast. This worked out at £18 per day. When I returned home I received a letter from the Inland Revenue enquiring why my earnings from the World Cup weren't disclosed in my annual return. I subsequently went through an investigation by the Inland Revenue, who didn't believe me when I said it cost me money to play for my country. What are your thoughts on this, having played for your country over 100 times?

LR: Compared to other sports, I thought that darts players were treated like second-class citizens. We didn't receive the same acclaim as other sporting personalities from the media. I, too, have audits from the IRS. I thought the amount of revenues raised by us professionals, playing for our respective countries, against daily expenses given to us was inadequate.

JL: When you look back at your life in darts, especially in Wales, where your success was recognised by the naming of a road after you, would you have changed anything?

LR: The road is named Leighton Rees Close, and I was very embarrassed by this. However, I would never change a thing. I would certainly have looked after my health and money differently. If only I had a crystal ball at the time.

JL: Leighton, I've shared many a friendly drink with you after many international matches. I have great memories I will always treasure, like the time you waited over five hours to pick me up at Los Angeles Airport when my plane was delayed, and the time we played in North Wales and kept the landlords and ladies in the town up so late. There wasn't a pub open the next day before one o'clock.

LR: OK, Mr Lowe. Remember Oakengates in Shropshire? They have very large shop doorways, much to my surprise. Gotcha!

JL: OK, it would be unfair to leave such stories untold. I remember Oakengates very well. We'd just won the tournament, a four-man team event, and after the finals I became friendly with a lady and we decided to take a stroll down the street. As you say, the doorways in the town are quite large. We stopped off in one to talk about 501 – of course! – and then, lo and behold, a voice came from the next doorway: 'And how is Mr Lowe tonight?' Leighton Rees was also discussing 501!

JL: Leighton, on the lighter side of life, you married an American lady, Debbie, and she moved from America to live in Wales. I know you lived with your parents for a while. What did they think of their son's new wife, who spoke differently and had a wicked sense of humour?

LR: The reception Debbie and her son, Ryan, had was good from the majority of my family. Unfortunately, my mother and eldest sister saw things in a different light and made that known to her. The time my mother asked both of us if we'd like a joint for Sunday dinner seemed an ice-breaker to Debbie. She thought her luck was in and that Ynysybwl wasn't so bad after all.

John Lowe Signature Darts

**These darts are the John Lowe signature darts.
Made of Tungsten and Titanium and available in
a range of weights:**

21 23 25 27 gram

**I have used these darts to win over 1000 titles
world wide. They are available to you at:**

jloweprodart@aol.com

**Mail: Darts, 17 Greenways, Walton,
Chesterfield, Derbyshire, S40 3HF**